How (and Why) to
Get Students
TALKING

78 Ready-to-Use Group Discussions About Anxiety, Self-Esteem, Relationships, and More (Grades 6–12)

Updated Edition

Jean Sunde Peterson, Ph.D.

free spirit
PUBLISHING®

Library of Congress Cataloging-in-Publication Data
Names: Peterson, Jean Sunde, 1941– author.
Title: How (and why) to get students talking : 78 ready-to-use group discussions about anxiety, self-esteem, relationships, and more, (grades 6–12) / Jean Sunde Peterson, Ph.D.
Other titles: Talk with teens about what matters to them
Description: Updated edition. | Minneapolis, MN : Free Spirit Publishing, [2019] | Updated edition of: Talk with teens about what matters to them : ready-to-use discussions on stress, identity, feelings, relationships, family, and the future / Jean Sunde Peterson. c2011. | Includes bibliographical references and index.
Identifiers: LCCN 2018045290 (print) | LCCN 2018052047 (ebook) | ISBN 9781631984075 (Web PDF) | ISBN 9781631984082 (ePub) | ISBN 9781631984068 (pbk.) | ISBN 1631984063 (pbk.)
Subjects: LCSH: Counseling in secondary education—United States. | Discussion—United States. | Group guidance in education—United States. | Teacher participation in educational counseling—United States.
Classification: LCC LB1620.5 (ebook) | LCC LB1620.5 .P43 2019 (print) | DDC 373.14—dc23
LC record available at https://lccn.loc.gov/2018045290

2011008926

Edited by Catherine Broberg
Cover design by Emily Dyer
Interior design by Lois Stanfield and Emily Dyer

10 9 8 7 6 5 4 3 2 1
Printed in the United States of America

Free Spirit Publishing Inc.
6325 Sandburg Road, Suite 100
Minneapolis, MN 55427-3674
(612) 338-2068
help4kids@freespirit.com
www.freespirit.com

Dedication

· ·

To those who taught me about adolescent development—students and clients in many places, my siblings, and my children, Sonia and Nathan

Acknowledgments

· ·

This is a book about process—the process of development. The discussions within are primarily intended to help students make sense of their experiences during adolescence, certainly a complex life stage. However, development continues across the lifespan, and I have found that the topics in this book usually also resonate with adults, since many of the themes continue to be important.

I recognize that experiences and people continue to influence my own development. I have been educated by a multitude of individuals in my life. By example, my mother taught me that teaching is a worthy profession, and my father showed me that meaningful work may not feel like "work." Both demonstrated that community service is important for both self-development and progress and that process, not product, is where the fun is. A liberal arts education, a long and varied teaching career, and a multifaceted life have instructed me further. Nicholas Colangelo, Volker Thomas, and John Littrell steered me in important professional directions along the way, and I am grateful for the wisdom of longtime friends. My husband, Reuben, continues to provide unwavering and crucial support for projects like this one as we continue to develop together.

Important in eventually directing me toward counseling and group work with adolescents were school administrators who gave me autonomy and helpful guidance. They supported experimentation with teaching methods and content and encouraged my professional growth. I worked with several fine principals along the way, but I am particularly grateful for Jack Lauer and Fred Stephens in the Sioux Falls, South Dakota, area.

As I became acquainted with students, I grew more and more interested in adolescent development and, eventually, in counseling. My enduring friendship with college roommate Norma McLane Haan, who has had a long career as a therapist, has had a consulting dimension. I appreciated her guidance as I dealt with complex issues in the discussion groups that were an important part of a program I directed. She inspired me to pursue graduate work in counseling, which moved me into a new career.

Early in my teaching career, I began to regularly attend workshops, conferences, and in-service sessions dealing with social and emotional development. I took notes, added my thoughts to filed materials, consulted with mental health professionals, and read books. As an English teacher, I brought in community experts to help students understand context and themes in literature. When I coordinated a program for gifted students, I organized an ongoing weekly lecture series featuring medical, business, and mental health experts, as well as college and university speakers. Therefore, when I began to facilitate discussion groups, which eventually led to my first books, I had much to draw from. The background information for many of the sessions in this volume is based as much on the information, materials, and thoughts I accumulated during these experiences as on formal coursework and training.

Contents

Focus: Family 233

Focus: The Future 243

Final Session   275

List of Reproducible Pages

(Downloadable PDFs are available online. See page 289 for downloading instructions.)

Preface

It has been many years since much of the material in this book was originally published in two volumes called *Talk with Teens About Self and Stress* and *Talk with Teens About Feelings, Family, Relationships, and the Future*. During this time, dramatic societal changes have occurred, yet the basic needs and concerns of teens remain. It has been said that adolescents express the pain of society, and I have seen evidence of that. All students are likely to experience confusion, pressures, and distractions, but many also lack a nurturing environment at home. Employment insecurity and low wage levels continue to affect families, family structures continue to change, and a mobile society means relocations and loss of support from extended family and trusted peers. If parental control depends on heavy-handed, harsh, or unpredictable discipline, adolescents may feel a low level of personal agency and be uncomfortable and fearful when around adults in authority. They may act out their tension in ways that preclude comfortable connection with significant adults in their lives. Currently, probably more than ever, adolescents need to be able to set healthy personal boundaries, and they need to develop skills in conflict resolution, including the ability to perceive others' intent accurately. They need to be able to communicate discreetly, directly, tactfully, and effectively. They need to consider the perspectives and well-being of peers. They need to self-reflect. Online social media and complex electronics have greatly changed the social landscape, as well as vulnerabilities related to them. This updated edition addresses many of these realities.

Facilitating more than 1,600 small-group sessions with adolescents has convinced me that all young people can benefit greatly from small-group discussion about growing up. All adolescents need opportunities to interact with peers in the presence of a nonjudgmental adult, to make connections, and to be known as unique, interesting individuals with special strengths. Adolescents at all ability levels, at all socioeconomic levels, and in all cultural and ethnic groups are challenged by universal developmental tasks. They experience these tasks in the context of cultural norms, economic and educational levels, and family structures. They all are probably more resilient than adults might think, but they need information, a safe place to ask basic or awkward questions, vocabulary and skills related to oral expression, and opportunities to develop social skills.

How (and Why) to Get Students Talking is an updated version of *Talk with Teens About What Matters to Them*, which was a combination and restructuring of three earlier volumes. Throughout these revisions and updates, new topics reflecting current issues have been added, and the sessions have been made easier to use. The content has remained appropriate for all adolescents, but more sessions have been geared toward middle school students and students at risk for poor educational outcomes. These changes are the result of my own continuing direct and indirect work with students. I included more suggestions for hands-on activities, but learned that physical activity sometimes detracts from developing oral skills and can exacerbate hyperactivity. Therefore, I have retained the emphasis on oral-expressive skills—skills important for future relationships and not attended to adequately in schools. Currently, ubiquitous electronics appear, too often, to have replaced nuanced face-to-face conversation with peers and family regardless of context, making an emphasis on oral communication even more important.

The base I drew from, and continue to draw from, is my own and my graduate students' experiences in schools with adolescents. This updated volume continues to focus on semistructured, development-oriented, prevention-oriented small-group work. Such groups can be facilitated by degreed counselors as well as by laypersons who have studied the introductory material and conscientiously adhere to the "semistructured, development-oriented, prevention-oriented" aspects of this approach. The introduction continues to offer rare guidance for this kind of group work.

Research studies attest to the effectiveness of this approach (see page 283). Michelle Lorimer and I studied the implementation of a small-group curriculum in a private middle school. Students and teacher-facilitators both gained confidence about discussing social and emotional concerns, and both believed the groups had a positive effect on the school. In a 2017 study of using this approach with culturally and internationally diverse middle and high school students in a residential summer program, young-adult counselors observed gains in their own confidence as facilitators, and 93 percent of the 101 campers interviewed spoke positively of their experience and reported gains in self-confidence and expressive language, more openness with peers, deep cross-cultural communication, social contact extending beyond group sessions, and insights about the universality of developmental challenges. Finally, the Peterson Proactive Developmental Attention Model, of which the approach detailed in this book is the most common application, was formally introduced in scholarly literature in 2018.

If the guidelines and admonitions explained in the thorough introduction are followed conscientiously, you are likely to see the benefits.

I remain open to suggestions for new topics and for new ways to address "old" topics. You can email me at help4kids@freespirit.com.

Jean Sunde Peterson

Introduction

About This Book

Description and Benefits

How (and Why) to Get Students Talking helps adolescents to "just talk"—to share feelings and concerns with supportive peers and an attentive adult. These guided discussions have evolved over many years of working with students and listening to them.

I have facilitated hundreds of small-group sessions with adolescents, with many of the discussion series lasting a semester or full school term. Most have been in various kinds of schools, such as public and private schools for the general population, alternative schools for students at risk for poor personal and educational outcomes, and schools for high-ability students. However, some single-session and short-term groups have been in residential and outpatient treatment facilities, community centers, YMCAs and YWCAs, and faith-based settings. The suggestions, activities, and written exercises in this book, as well as the semistructured-but-flexible format, have been thoroughly tested. You can use these materials with confidence.

I have witnessed the benefits of guided discussions for individuals of many ages, ability levels, cultural backgrounds, and family circumstances. Such groups can accomplish the following:

- produce inspiring outcomes in both well-adjusted students and those with significant risk factors, including when these students are mixed in groups

- help students lower stress levels, normalize "weird" thoughts, and sort out personal conflict

- give students who are cynical and negative about school an experience that makes it "not so bad"

- help group members learn to anticipate problems and find support for problem-solving

- help them become comfortable with others and allow their "real selves" to show and be validated

- serve a preventive function by improving self-esteem and social ease

- allow educators and counselors to make the most of their time, since the sessions give them an opportunity to interact about social and emotional development with several students at the same time

- allow helping professionals to facilitate interaction about social deficits and disadvantages that, arguably, are at the root of many of the concerns that come to the attention of counselors—such as depression, bullying, and other social aggression—or that drive school violence

A Note from the Author About This Update

For this updated and retitled edition, I have refreshed the content to better support you in your work with groups of adolescents. The updated introduction offers best practices for group leaders, and new sessions address issues of adolescents in today's world. Updated sessions reflect current language and information and include more specific recommendations for noncounseling professionals leading discussion groups.

Genesis

For twenty-five years, I was a teacher in public schools. For nineteen of those years, I taught English literature, language, and writing to middle and high school students in Iowa, Minnesota, South Dakota, and Germany. My years in the classroom tuned me in to the social and emotional worlds of adolescents. When they wrote essays, interacted with me during yearbook meetings, worked with me in club activities, and lingered after class, they taught me about adolescent development.

I learned that they had common concerns, but with idiosyncratic dimensions and complexities. I also saw that my students wanted to *be known*—to be recognized for their individual worth and for their uniqueness. They readily accepted my invitation to respond in writing to the literature we were reading. In fact, we did not discuss literature much orally; instead they wrote in journals about what they were reading, and I responded in the margins. We used class time for acquiring vocabulary and background information so students could understand the contexts of what they were reading.

There were many reasons for this teaching approach, and some of them relate to the discussion groups I later developed. Namely, students need information, and they need to develop skills. I wanted my students to learn to express themselves on paper and to become self-reflective, independent thinkers. I wanted to hear from everyone equally, not just from the highly verbal and assertive. I used an interactive approach to foster immersion in learning, employing hands-on classroom activities, media and community resources, vocabulary-in-context exercises, and classroom dialogue. We learned together, and the students became more and more comfortable with complexity and ambiguity. Some of these strategies are similar to those I recommend for the development-oriented discussion groups that are the focus here.

Some students stayed after class to talk about difficult personal matters. Experiences like these are not uncommon for teachers. Adolescents are hungry for acknowledgment and nonjudgmental listening. Through these interactions, I learned that there were many important things students did not discuss with their peers, and some students likewise did not have a comfortable enough relationship with a parent to ask tough questions or express concerns or anxiety.

My students were typical. They fought with siblings, had "crushes" and breakups, and were scared about the future. Some struggled with the hypocrisy of the adults around them and the sad state of the world as they saw it. They responded to these and other issues with sadness, problematic behaviors, frustration, irritability, lack of motivation for schoolwork, and sometimes depression. They had difficulty managing their complex, fragmented lives. Sometimes they felt like exploding from tension. They needed someone to talk with. They needed affirmation. They needed to have their feelings and experiences validated.

Eventually, in another high school, I considered creating an extensive small-group program for students. Group work had never been done there. I thought back to the adolescents in my classes who had let me know them. I certainly had seen a need for support and attentive listening.

The discussion groups did not catch on immediately, but by midyear, after more than one carefully crafted invitation, I had three groups, with eight to ten students each. The following year there were six groups, and then ten the next, with two groups per day during a two-period lunch schedule. Usually once each year I invited an administrator, a student teacher, or someone from another district to observe the groups—in order to acquaint others with this proactive approach to working with teens. Group members were eager to demonstrate their group. I was careful to choose a topic for those sessions that would not require a great level of trust and would not compromise privacy (for example, "What do you wish teachers and administrators understood about teens these days?"). Almost invariably, observers commented that they had never suspected that students had so much to deal with.

The students faithfully attended the group meetings, even though attendance was voluntary. Group members bonded through steady, undramatic weekly contact, and when there was a personal or institutional crisis, the groups were a ready support system. The students taught me, they taught each other, and they learned about themselves. The topics were not particularly heavy, but they resonated. The students responded. They relaxed and "just talked." This book includes many of the session topics I used with those groups.

In other locations, I continued to form middle and high school groups with various populations. Concurrently, I finished degrees in counseling and counselor education, became a licensed mental health counselor, began university-level teaching and research, and worked part-time in one or more venues, including private practice, school counseling, a mental health agency, alternative teen facilities, and substance abuse treatment centers. For several years, I directed a program in which my graduate students and I facilitated as many as twenty weekly groups in various kinds of schools, with students in grades five to twelve, most of whom were in challenging circumstances at home or at school. In addition, the interns I supervised were regularly involved in group work. These direct and indirect experiences all informed me about group work—and about adolescents.

Purpose

The purpose of the guided discussions in this book is to support the social and emotional development of adolescents. Whether in small- or large-group discussion, students become increasingly self-aware, and that in turn helps them make better choices, be better problem-solvers, and deal more effectively with their various relationships. They learn to self-affirm their complexity and make sense of their emotions and behavior, and they feel more in control of their lives.

This support is a result of encouraging group members to express themselves. Most students need practice putting concerns and feelings into words. As much as some of them talk socially, they may not be skilled at communicating feelings clearly, genuinely, and effectively. That skills gap is not new, but electronic communication may currently be further limiting oral, face-to-face expression. Learning to talk about what is important to them and to listen attentively to others can enhance students' current and future relationships. Adolescence is a good time to learn these skills. Small groups, if trust and comfort develop, offer three important opportunities that may be lacking elsewhere:

- a noncompetitive environment where no grades are given

- a social context where everyone is fairly equal, since there is a relative absence of hierarchy when the focus is on social and emotional development

- a safe place to talk with peers about the experience of adolescence

According to the feedback groups and trainees have given me, the topics included in this book are often not otherwise discussed with peers, siblings, or parents. In end-of-year written assessments, students told me that they were grateful for guidance in important areas of their lives and for having a safe, supportive environment in which to talk about concerns. Many indicated that their group helped them feel connected to others, deal with stressors, and realize they were not alone in dealing with the challenges of growing up.

Fundamentally, group members gain social skills through group interaction. Often, social discomfort contributes to, and is exacerbated by, poor functioning in school. In terms of school accountability, small-group work may be viewed as a strategy for improving student learning. When considering aggression and violence against school peers, students' learning what they and others have in common, learning to listen, gaining experience in initiating and responding respectfully within conversation, and becoming aware of peers' concerns can improve social ease, self-esteem, and perceptions of others. Becoming acquainted with even just six to eight peers in a small group can help students feel more connected and comfortable in school, thereby avoiding negative academic and personal outcomes.

The format of this book is not designed to teach specific group skills or to acquaint adolescents with the vocabulary of group process. However, many such skills and some aspects of group dynamics will likely develop and become familiar. With guided group discussion, process is more important than product, and one goal is to enhance the skill of articulating social and emotional concerns. The focus, objectives, and suggestions for content and closure contained in each session provide a framework for good, solid, invigorating group experiences.

It is important to understand that the purpose of these discussions is not to "fix" group members. Even though the questions are designed to provoke reflection and introspection, the emphasis is always on articulating feelings and thoughts in the presence of others who listen and care. These groups are not meant to be therapy groups. Yes, group work in any form has potential therapeutic value, and some noticeable changes in attitude and behavior often occur in the kinds of groups promoted here. However, even when it appears that these changes occur because of the response and support of a group, other factors, such as changes at home, the healing effect of time, or developmental leaps, may also have contributed. Nevertheless, a group might be crucial in helping a student navigate a difficult year. It is important to note here that mental health professionals can use many of these sessions and activity sheets in group and family work to foster communication and personal growth.

As is the case whenever adults stand firmly and supportively beside adolescents, establish trust, and participate in students' complex lives, you will serve your group best by listening actively, with the focus fully on them, and offering your nonjudgmental presence as they find their own direction.

Meeting ASCA Standards

The national standards for school counseling programs, developed by the American School Counselor Association, focus on academic, career, and social-emotional development. The focused discussions outlined in *How (and Why) to Get Students Talking* address standards in each of these three areas, with particular attention to specific elements.

In relation to academic development, various foci help students develop positive attitudes toward school, toward teachers and administrators, and toward learning. Group members become more aware of their learning preferences. Topics related to postsecondary options help students think about the future, and group activities help them connect school to the world of work and to life in community with others.

Related to career development, almost all discussion topics are intended to enhance self-awareness, including of personal strengths and interests. A basic premise of the book is that bringing teens together in small groups helps them make comfortable interpersonal connections—through listening and responding, supporting and being supported, and appropriately expressing feelings and opinions. They break down cultural and socioeconomic stereotypes and learn about the perspectives of others. Interpersonal skills and sensitivity to others will enhance working relationships in the future. In addition, several sessions focus on the world of work and postsecondary education. Group members reflect on the work attitudes modeled by significant adults in their lives and are encouraged to imagine themselves in future work contexts. They also learn about postsecondary educational settings and are able to ask questions and receive important information. Group facilitators are provided suggestions for organizing career-oriented experiences outside of school as well.

Most important, this book focuses on social-emotional development—on simply "growing up." Session topics encourage self-reflection about identity, feelings, and peer, family, and community relationships. Members develop skills in a social microcosm, interacting with peers and with a nonjudgmental adult, potentially enhancing their lives in the present and after the school years. In addition, group members learn about emotional and physical vulnerabilities related to technology, high-risk social situations, relationships, and stress, and they consider ways to be social without putting themselves at risk.

Assumptions

The format and content of *How (and Why) to Get Students Talking* reflect the following assumptions, which you may want to keep in mind as you lead your own group.

1. All adolescents have a desire to be heard, listened to, taken seriously, and respected.

2. Some who are quiet, shy, easily intimidated, or untrusting often do not spontaneously offer comments, but they, too, want to be recognized and understood as unique individuals.

3. All adolescents need support, no matter how strong and successful they seem.

4. All feel stressed at times. Some feel stressed most or even all of the time.

5. All are sensitive to family tension. Some are trying hard to keep their families afloat or intact, perhaps even using problematic behavior to keep their parents focused, involved, and together.

6. All adolescents feel angry at times.

7. All feel socially inept and uncomfortable at times.

8. All worry about the future at times.

9. All, no matter how smooth and self-confident they appear, need practice talking about feelings.

10. Everyone wears a facade at times.

The Nuts and Bolts of Group Work

Group Members

The guided discussion sessions in *How (and Why) to Get Students Talking* are appropriate for the entire age range of adolescents, including a number of special populations (for example, students new to school, at risk for poor personal and educational outcomes, diagnosed with mental health disorders, or lacking appropriate social skills) and students with a wide range of ability levels, including high ability. However, especially when groups include preteens, topics should be selected according to students' developmental level. Adjustments in vocabulary, session length, and content can be made as needed. A few topics might be best suited for older teens, but being selective with the suggestions in these discussions may make them appropriate for younger teens as well. Behavioral concerns and parental cautions vary from community to community and should guide topic selection. Because it is important that older adolescents not feel "talked down to," the language used in the suggested questions and activity sheets is generally and intentionally "up."

Ideally, group membership does not change after the group begins. Each time someone is added, a group must focus again on developing trust. Group dynamics also change, of course, when a member leaves. Group organizers need to consider school attendance patterns for the target population when determining group size, since only two regular attendees, for example, in a group of five is not optimal.

Group Settings

The session structure of *How (and Why) to Get Students Talking* is appropriate for both small-group and whole-classroom or other large-group discussion. Groups with a developmental emphasis can be formed in a wide variety of settings:

- school counseling and advisory groups
- regular classrooms
- athletic and academic teams
- music groups
- school clubs
- youth service organizations
- leadership programs
- faith-based settings and youth groups
- peer counseling groups
- family therapy groups
- treatment facilities
- retreats

- at-home discussions involving parents and adolescents
- homeschool events or series

Because the topics are developmental in emphasis and often applicable throughout the lifespan, some sessions are appropriate for women's groups, men's groups, and adult support groups. I have often used them in teacher workshops focused on listening and responding skills, with personal benefits apparent beyond the skills training. In addition, because drug use can arrest social and emotional development, and because addiction does not preclude a need to connect with others, most sessions can be useful in centers focusing on substance abuse.

Length of Meetings

Ideal meeting length varies depending on group members' ability level and behavior. Students who are hyperactive and distractible, who do not enjoy verbal activity, or who have low cognitive ability may do well with thirty-minute meetings in grades six and seven. However, if hands-on activities are included, having adequate time is essential. Eighth graders and high school students usually appreciate a full class period, although thirty minutes also can suffice. Short meeting times work best for groups with only three or four members. I recommend that "lunch-bunch" groups be allowed to leave class a few minutes early, so that they can get their food before classes are dismissed and maximize the time available for discussion.

Small Groups

Group Size

For small-group work, ideal group size varies according to age level. For middle school students, a group size of five to seven seems to work best, given the usual length of class periods and students' ability to articulate thoughts, attain depth, and feel heard adequately. (If fifth grade is included in a middle school, I recommend four or five students per group.) I do not recommend more than eight, regardless of students' age or ability. These are general guidelines. My counseling students and I have experienced successful small-group discussion with as few as three students, who bonded well and developed trust after other members moved away. I have also had success with groups of ten high-functioning and articulate students in full-hour meetings, but that number can preclude close connections and adequate time for each member to feel heard and understood. The level of personal concerns might also be a factor when considering group size. Feeling heard is always important. When working with high-risk teens, I sometimes limit a group to six to ensure adequate time for individuals to talk and respond to others.

Meeting Location

For small-group work, I recommend a small room (instead of a classroom), especially for group members who have problems with attention or hyperactivity. Such a space is also more likely to be private and uninterrupted, have fewer visual distractions than a classroom, and promote a sense of intimacy and safety. I also prefer to have a table to sit around, not only to contribute to comfort but also since many of the sessions involve brief writing.

Large Groups

How (and Why) to Get Students Talking can be useful in large-group settings as well, such as the regular classroom, community youth groups, and teams. Weekly discussions, or a daily series of discussions limited to a week or two, can be part of the curriculum in health, family and consumer sciences, life skills, social science, or language arts, among several possibilities. Discussion is particularly meaningful for adolescents when it deals with the self. Homeroom or advisory periods or community time, when designed to foster positive interaction in a school, can use an activity sheet or other discussion catalyst effectively if the time allowed is adequate (at least twenty minutes).

Group dynamics differ, of course, depending on whether a large group has thirty members or ten, but the focus and most of the strategies work with both sizes of groups. Since a discussion of an activity sheet can easily take an hour with a group of eight verbal students, adjustments must be made when activity sheets are used with larger groups. Classes can be divided into small groups (three to five members) for sharing, for example, with supervision and appropriate directions.

Group Composition

I have found that the best groups are often those where members do not know each other well outside of the group. Members seem to feel free to share, and they do not have to preface all comments with "Well, someone in here has heard me say this before, but . . ." On the other hand, I have had effective groups where most members knew each other well—and learned to know each other better. Even best friends may not typically discuss topics like those in this book.

Depending on the size of the student population you draw from, you may not have much choice about whom to group together. If some or all members of your group know each other well, it is important to move the group beyond the natural division of friends and nonfriends. Having a focus, with specific activities and written exercises, helps to ensure that students who are friends do not dominate or irritate the others with "inside humor." Encouraging members to change seating each time also can be helpful, although it is important to make this a group norm at the outset, since groups—especially middle school groups—may be resistant to it later.

Groups can break down barriers. In broad-population discussion groups, I prefer a balance between achievers and underachievers, members at risk and not at risk for poor outcomes, members highly involved and not-so-involved in other activities, and students of varied ethnic and socioeconomic backgrounds. The mix indirectly challenges stereotypical thinking as group members discover common ground.

If, as a counselor, you form a group because members share a common concern or to have a specific purpose and agenda, you can still use these guided discussions with confidence, since they deal with common adolescent challenges. I offer two cautionary guidelines, however. Homogeneous grouping of students who struggle with depression, hyperactivity, substance abuse, disordered eating, or severe behavior problems, for example, potentially creates groups with too many "problems" and no positive peer models. Especially in schools, I believe it is unethical to group by pathology, since privacy (regarding having the "problem") is inherently compromised. Nonetheless, anyone can benefit from connection, support, and learning about self and others. *Discussion does not need to focus on the common major problem.* Struggling teens can benefit from the developmental emphasis and a chance to connect to peers.

If several groups are being formed at one time, distribution can be accomplished by initially compiling a list of all students who accept the invitation to participate and then sorting the list. Of course, recruitment needs to target those least likely to feel welcome. In some cases, the highest-functioning students may be the most reluctant to join, fearing that the groups are geared only to "problems" and that participation will somehow stigmatize them. However, underachieving students and those with other risk factors may think they are the only ones with stressors, vulnerabilities, fears, and problematic performance or attitudes. They can benefit from realizing that everyone has developmental concerns. All social groups have a great deal to learn from each other, and the group setting is an ideal environment for mutual learning.

Mixing genders is also good, even though it is not always possible and might not be advantageous or appropriate for certain topics. However, it is important for students with differing gender identities to learn about each other in a safe and nonjudgmental environment, outside of the regular classroom and apart from usual social settings. It is also important for all students to learn how to communicate with, and in the presence of, each other. Granted, students representing various gender identities may differ greatly in physical, social, and emotional maturity, particularly in middle school. Still, a late-maturing boy, for example, can gain from hearing about the concerns of the early-maturing girls he is around daily, and vice versa.

A discussion group can provide a chance to have contact with the other gender and with peers who do not identify exclusively with either gender. Regardless of whether teens are shy or highly social, a group can raise awareness of gender and gender-identity issues and enhance students' ability to function effectively in complex social relationships now and in the future, including in marriage and other partner relationships, in employment, and in corporate leadership.

On the other hand, same-gender grouping also has advantages and is particularly appropriate when the issues are gender-specific, especially troublesome and gender-related, or perceived by students to be unsafe for discussion with more than one gender identity represented in the group. Same-gender groups can sometimes empower members in ways that mixed groups cannot. Gender homogeneity may be desirable in an addictions-recovery or sexual-trauma-recovery group in a treatment center, for example. Obviously, decisions about grouping depend on the goals and purpose of the group. I have had good success with same-gender groups in middle schools. The all-male small groups talked just as much and just as openly about social and emotional concerns as the all-female groups did. I also have had mixed results, possibly related to purpose, special population, or grade level, with mixed-gender small groups in middle schools. With high school groups, I routinely mix genders.

Because the sessions are geared to social and emotional development, not to cognitive or academic concerns, having group members of approximately the same age is optimal. Sixth graders are developmentally different from and have different concerns than eighth graders, for instance, and even seventh and eighth graders may have difficulty connecting with each other about social and emotional concerns. Tenth-grade issues are usually different from eleventh-grade issues. Seniors are usually looking ahead in ways that younger students are not. Relationship issues differ along the age continuum, from grade level to grade level, and it is beneficial when students can communicate with others in their own age group about these concerns—even though group members' social experience and physical development might differ.

It is your responsibility, as a group facilitator, to ensure the physical and psychological safety of each group member. Behavior management may be a particular concern in some groups, as well as teasing and name-calling. When forming a group, I suggest some basic screening, since individuals who have great difficulty in all or most social situations (because of an emotional or behavioral disorder, for instance) may be not only disruptive, but also psychologically harmful to other group members.

Treatment centers for behavioral disorders are likely to use group work as part of a treatment plan for addressing severe problems. In schools, by contrast, even though ideally all students should have an opportunity to discuss development with peers, group leaders should keep in mind that severe behavioral problems are difficult to deal with in groups. Group goals may be difficult to achieve when a great amount of time is focused on behavior management and when impulsive, negative behavior and harshly critical statements are intended to harm either the group or individual members. However, I don't consider a group member's initially being unwilling to talk, or even being unwilling to sit within the group space, as being critical of others or as being severe negative behavior. Someone who is untrusting and uneasy with talking about development may need a few, or even several, meetings before interacting verbally. I typically use this nonjudgmental approach: "It's okay if you want to wait. When you're ready, just join in—even if it's a few weeks from now." Eventually, such situations are often resolved quietly.

I recommend providing teachers with a rationale for the group experience and a checklist and encouraging them to take social functioning in the classroom into consideration when recommending students. If group members cannot function at somewhat the same level, have significant problems controlling negative impulses, or are rude and disruptive, the group may not experience the benefits associated with depth of discussion about developmental concerns. Similarly, students who detest each other, or who have significant personality conflicts, should probably not be put into the same small group. A treatment center might be able to use group work to break down such barriers, but putting those students into a new and potentially intense situation like a small group in a school is not as defensible. If attendance is voluntary, other members may even choose not to attend.

Disruptive students deserve attention to developmental challenges, but if it takes nine or ten sessions to move beyond persistent disruptions, all other group members have then lost out on potential gains from an extremely rare opportunity. One suggestion is that if a group member has not settled down by the third or fourth meeting, perhaps that individual should not participate further. Facilitator and student should talk, one-on-one, about that possibility after the second meeting and then again if the decision has been made not to allow participation. Group members should have an opportunity to discuss their feelings about this loss at the next meeting, since they may have mixed feelings, including guilt.

Inviting Students to Join a Group

In a school, the best way to encourage students to join your group, if membership is voluntary, is to invite them personally. In any event, I recommend that you not call it a "counseling" group when describing it to prospective group members—even if you are indeed a counselor, but especially if you are not—since then there are extra liability concerns. In addition, some students are automatically turned off and turned away by the counseling label. Later on, if someone asks if it is a counseling group, explain that "counseling" basically means "talking and listening" with someone trained in that process. In that regard, if you are a trained counselor, your group could be called a counseling group. However, for recruitment purposes, "discussion group" is both accurate (because of the purpose) and appealing, without potentially negative stigma attached.

"Support group" is appropriate when there is a common, specific agenda or a shared problem area. However, if the group is largely preventive, with self-awareness and personal growth as goals, then "support" is probably too problem-oriented for many students. "Discussion group" is my preference.

In schools, I have contacted students individually to explain a proposed group, and I have gathered together a few students or full-size discussion groups to hear the plan.

In either case, you need to assure students that joining the group involves low risk, with potentially big benefits. The advantage of calling in the group as a whole is that students can see who else will be attending. On the other hand, some might decide against joining for that very reason, without giving the group a chance. When meeting with students individually, you might give them the names of a few prospective members—but *only if they ask* and only if it is possible to share names in advance. If a student wants to ensure that friends will be in a group, I prefer to say, simply, "I encourage you to come and be surprised. It's good to get to know new people, and sometimes it's even best *not* to know anyone else well at the outset. If you decide later that you are not comfortable with the group, you have the option of not continuing." If you decide to meet with all prospective members together, be prepared to do at least a typical, brief activity from the book (perhaps the "Warm-Up" on pages 21–22) to demonstrate what the group will be like.

Be sure to emphasize both the social and the emotional purposes of the group. Students respond well to the idea of meeting new people and getting to know current acquaintances and friends in new ways. They also can relate to the idea of talking about adolescent stress. In fact, I routinely mention stress as an example of the discussion topics. You can explain that, beyond pursuing general goals, the group will determine its own unique atmosphere. That much of an explanation usually suffices. If students want to know more, show them the table of contents for this book. The session titles are varied, and students usually find them interesting—and unexpected.

If you use this book with high school students, it helps to tell them that once you get to know them better through the group experience, you will be able to write more complete and accurate job, college, or scholarship recommendations for them. Explain that you also will be a better and more informed advocate for them if they ever need assistance.

How to Approach Students Who Have Significant Risk Factors

As a school counselor, you may wish to form a support group to serve students with a common concern. When a particular phenomenon, such as one of those listed below, is affecting several students concurrently, a counselor can utilize development-oriented sessions in this book, without necessarily addressing the common problem directly, to help those students stay connected to school and to supportive peers, a worthy purpose in itself. The problem may come up spontaneously, of course, and then the facilitator's professional expertise is crucial. Otherwise, staying focused on selected developmental topics can generally be beneficial.

- family disruption
- parental or student substance abuse
- school tragedy affecting several families
- family tragedy

- pregnancy
- sexual or other kinds of abuse
- victimization by bullies
- bereavement
- terminal illness in a family member
- potential for dropping out of school
- frequent family moves
- poverty
- parental military deployment
- being new in school

Bringing teens together to "talk about growing up" can offer support and connection during a difficult time without labeling the group. An informed layperson who carefully follows the topic-oriented, development-related discussion format of the sessions in this book can facilitate that kind of discussion. However, *only degreed counselors or other degreed helping professionals should facilitate groups focused on any of the first nine situations in the previous list* because of the need for special expertise and because of risk, including risk of retraumatizing. In addition, as mentioned earlier (see "Group Composition"), privacy is inherently compromised when the facilitator names the serious common concern as the reason for organizing the group. Privacy is a concern during any major life challenge, and school and mental health counselors, counseling and clinical psychologists, and social workers are guided by and trained with ethical codes related to privacy.

Students may not be eager to join a group. If attendance is voluntary, I recommend that you first meet with the high-risk students individually. Explain that you will be leading a discussion group for students who are dealing with stress and you are inviting them to participate. If a student has difficulty with authority, is underachieving with high ability, or has been suspended from school more than once, for example, you don't need to mention those concerns. Instead, simply say that you are looking for interesting, complex students who can help to make a good group. Say that you are looking specifically for students who express their abilities in unusual ways, because you do not want a group that is afraid to challenge and think and you do not want students who always do only what is expected of them. Reframing characteristics usually considered troublesome in this positive way may surprise students and encourage them to participate.

However, no matter what a particular student's behavior might be, always present the group's purpose honestly: to provide an opportunity for students to talk about concerns that are important to adolescents. Be sincere, accepting, and supportive in your invitation. With students in distress, as with all prospective group members, take care not to frighten them away by sounding (or being) invasive or too personal. Give them time to warm up to the idea of interacting with others about growing up. Even traumatized teens can benefit from *non*-therapy-oriented discussion groups that are not focused on "fixing." Many life situations are not "fixable," and uncomfortable feelings can be purposeful and associated with the long process of healing.

Sessions for Special Populations

How (and Why) to Get Students Talking is appropriate for primary prevention, in the form of focused, development-oriented discussion meant to prevent problems and enhance adolescent development. It is also appropriate for secondary prevention, for use by counselors when there appears to be potential for problems. For the latter, the sessions are appropriate and potentially beneficial for a variety of special populations in either homogeneous or heterogeneous groups:

- students at risk for poor academic outcomes
- students with behavior problems (including students on probation)
- students experiencing difficult family situations or transitions
- students having difficulty with adult authority
- teenage parents
- underachievers
- students labeled "gifted" who are at risk for stress-related disorders, severe underachievement, disordered eating, self-medication with substances, or depression
- students returning from treatment for substance abuse or an eating disorder
- students with poor social skills
- students new to a school
- students who have learning difficulties

Underachievers and students who have behavior problems, difficulty with authority, or poor social skills often are best served when group membership is mixed (that is, perhaps half of group members have at least average skills, behavior, or achievement).

Although the sessions are arranged in a purposeful progression for long-term series, they may certainly be rearranged to create a short-term program or to have a particular focus. Feel free to choose sessions that are most appropriate for your group.

Following are sessions that would be especially helpful for some special populations.

Individuals experiencing major family transitions can benefit from any session in the Stress section. They may also find affirmation and be able to express uncomfortable feelings in some sessions in the Identity section (for example, "Giving Ourselves Permission," "In Control, Out of Control"). Some of the family-oriented sessions in the Relationships section (for example, "With Parents, Guardians, and Other Caregivers," "Gifts from People

Who Matter") may also be helpful, as well as some in the Feelings section (for example, "Disappointment," "Anger," "Fear, Worry, and Anxiety," "Coping with Change, Loss, and Transition," "When Parents Divorce," "Dealing with Holidays and Family Gatherings") and the Future section (for example, "When and If I'm a Parent").

Teens at risk for poor personal or educational outcomes might benefit from these sessions:

- "Stuck!"
- "Does the Stereotype Fit?"
- "Learning Styles"
- "What Defines Us?"
- "Risk-Taking"
- "In Control, Out of Control"
- "A Prisoner of Image"
- "Feeling Free"
- "Coping with Change, Loss, and Transition"
- "Sadness, Depression, and Dark Thoughts"
- "Encouragers and Discouragers"
- "Influencers"
- "Responding to Authority"
- "Getting Our Needs Met"

Group members who are feeling sad or depressed often find some of the sessions on stress to be helpful in addition to these:

- "Three Selves"
- "In Control, Out of Control"
- "Having Fun"
- "Being Alone versus Being Lonely"
- "It's Complicated"
- "Getting Our Needs Met"

Students returning from or currently in treatment for substance abuse or an eating disorder may also find these sessions helpful.

Leading the Sessions

Facilitators

Since these sessions are designed to be used in a variety of settings, group facilitators may be the following:

- school counselors
- teachers (including those who work with specific populations)
- leaders of youth groups or summer-camp activities
- counselors in community agencies, treatment centers, or private practice
- social workers

- probation officers and others involved with corrections
- coaches

Parents might use sessions for weekly family discussions, and homeschool organizations and groups can use them as catalysts for social interaction.

Are You Ready to Lead a Discussion Group?

Especially if you are not accustomed to dealing with group discussions in an informal setting, and even if you are, you may find the following suggestions and perspectives helpful:

- For teachers, the social-emotional dimension involves more personal risk-taking than the academic. Discussion related to social and emotional areas is much less "controllable" than academic, philosophical, intellectual, or debate-like discussion.

- Significant adults in students' lives might have focused more on behavior than on feelings, more on academics than on social-emotional needs, or more on performance than on personal development. Some adolescents are eager and immediately grateful for the emphasis on the social and emotional. Some might be uncomfortable with the developmental focus at first; some might even be frightened by it, especially those whose families guard privacy at extreme levels, or where emotional expression is discouraged. Regardless of response, your concentrated attention on social and emotional concerns will probably be a new experience for them. Discomfort may even generate problematic behavior initially.

- If you are careful to focus on social and emotional issues, there will be little opportunity for group members to play competitive, "one-up" verbal games. Social and emotional concerns are not likely to be debatable.

- Be prepared for a wide range of verbal ability, learning preferences, personalities, and behaviors in small groups. Consider the format for each session carefully in that regard.

You may also want to consider your own motives for establishing groups for students, as well as your sense of security around various personalities and behaviors. Consider these questions:

- Can you view adolescents as simply (and complexly) "developing"?
- Are your self-esteem and self-confidence strong enough to stay on firm footing in the midst of negative behavior?
- Can you stay poised and focused on the social and emotional, no matter what comes up?

- Can you deal with students simply as human beings with frailties, insecurities, sensitivities, and vulnerabilities, regardless of their behavior and/or school performance?
- Can you avoid needing to "put them in their place"?
- Can you accept their defenses, including bravado, and give them time to let themselves be socially and emotionally vulnerable?
- Can you recognize that they may not take risks socially, academically, and/or emotionally, and that they might benefit from encouragement to take appropriate risks in these areas?
- Can you look honestly at some of your own stereotypes or negative feelings that might interfere in your work with various student populations, and can you put them aside for the duration of the group experience?
- Can you let group members teach you about themselves without judging them?
- Can you avoid being too interested in ferreting out details about students' families and personal lives?
- If you are a teacher, can you move from an evaluative to a supportive role?
- Can you move out of an adult-expert position and accept that teens know themselves and their world better than you do—and that *you* need to learn from *them*?
- Can you enter their world respectfully?

If you can answer all or most of these questions in the affirmative, don't worry. You're ready to take on a roomful or small group of adolescents. If your answers were mostly negative or unsure, perhaps you should consider other ways to work with students or should (if you are not a counselor) consider co-facilitating a group with a counselor, at least initially. Such co-facilitation may help you develop listening and responding skills and move toward a nonjudgmental posture.

General Guidelines for Group Facilitators

The following general guidelines are designed to help you lead successful and meaningful discussion groups. You may want to review them from time to time over the life of a group.

1. Be prepared to learn how to lead a group by doing it. Let the group know that this is your attitude. If you are a trained counselor, you may need to become comfortable with *focused, semistructured* discussion intended to facilitate connection, not to "do therapy." In addition, even if you lead groups regularly, reviewing basic tenets of group work can be beneficial. If you are *not* a trained counselor and are not able to co-facilitate a group with a counselor,

you might ask a counselor for information about group process and about listening and responding. However, if you study this introductory material, keep the guidelines in mind, and use the questions provided, you will likely behave appropriately.

2. Don't think you have to be an expert on every topic. Tell the group at the outset that you want to learn with them and from them, and that you want them to learn from each other. Most of the content will come from them. It is usually better to be "one-down" (unknowing) than "one-up" (expert) in relationships with adolescents. They will respond to that approach. For most sessions, having information is not the key to success. Trust your adult wisdom, since that is one thing you have that group members do not. It will serve you well. But recognize that your job is largely to facilitate discussion, not to teach and not to "fix" or change kids.

3. Monitor group interaction and work toward contribution from all members without making it an issue. Remember that quiet individuals can gain a great deal just by listening and observing. You can encourage everyone to participate, yet not insist on that. Sharing about written exercises and activity sheets provides quiet group members a comfortable opening. Even uttering a simple phrase from a sheet can feel huge for a shy person and may represent significant risk-taking.

4. Keep the session focus in mind, but be flexible about direction. Your group may lead you in new directions that are as worthwhile as the stated focus and suggestions. However, if they veer too far off track, especially with only one or two students dominating, use the focus as an excuse to rein in the group.

5. It is probably best to go into each session with two related sessions in mind, since the one you have planned might not generate as much response as expected. You can always unobtrusively guide the group into the second direction. However, try several of the suggestions before dropping a topic. It might simply require some "baking time." Ask questions confidently, leaning slightly forward, with your face expectant.

6. Be willing to model how to do an activity, *even though that is usually not necessary.* The activity sheets are fairly self-explanatory, but on rare occasions you may need to demonstrate a response. If you are not willing to self-disclose, your group may wonder why they should be expected to reveal their thoughts and feelings. However, your doing only one small, discreet, carefully selected self-disclosure early in the life of a group may suffice for an entire series of meetings. Your modeling should be only to clarify something in an unfamiliar activity. Too much from you, too often, can actually inhibit group response.

Attention should be focused on group members, not on you. The group is for students' benefit, not yours.

7. Every now and then, especially after the group has established a rhythm (perhaps after five or six meetings), ask group members how they are feeling about the group. Is there anything they would like to do differently or change? Are they comfortable sharing their feelings and concerns? What has been helpful? Have they noticed any problems that need addressing, such as discussions being dominated by a few members, not enough flexibility in direction, a personality conflict within the group, or too much leader direction? Processing group dynamics provides an important opportunity for members to practice tact in addressing group issues.

Incorporate members' suggestions that fit the overall purpose of the group. If you do not yet feel comfortable as a facilitator, and if students are being negatively critical, tell them you are still learning about groups, and they are as well. Be aware that some students may press for "no focus" for a long time. You may want to review the rationale for focus outlined on page 13 prior to your first request for feedback. *Depending on group composition, you may also choose to delay questions about format until the benefits have become fairly clear.* Or simply be prepared to explain the purpose of the format while emphasizing that the format is flexible. Support the group and give guidance as they make progress in overcoming group challenges. Above all, try to be secure in using the focus. If you seem unsure and ask too frequently about the format, you may experience mutiny, especially if there has not been sufficient time for the group to bond and appreciate the benefits of some structure. I often ask for feedback midway and also late in the life of a group, otherwise relying on students' level of cooperation to inform me sufficiently about how the group is functioning. If lack of cooperation is a problem, I process that (see #9 below).

8. If group energy consistently or increasingly lags, discuss that in the group. Let the members help you figure out how to energize the discussions and/or deal with group inhibitions. However, *do not readily reject the idea of maintaining a focus for each session.* Perhaps you need to alter your questioning style (see page 16) or more deftly follow some directions that come up spontaneously. Or perhaps you need to be more selective when choosing your topics. The written exercises and activity sheets often encourage sharing. Being creative, especially in incorporating physical movement into the activities, might help to engage some group members. Matching activities to your group's preferred learning style and personalities can improve interaction.

9. Anything can be processed in the group—crying, interrupting, disclosing something unexpected,

being rude, being sad, belching, challenging the facilitator. That is, group members can discuss what just happened—in the present. A facilitator can say, "What was it like for you to challenge me just now?" or "How did the rest of you feel when she challenged me?" or "How are you feeling right now, after he disclosed that?" or "That comment was a surprise. How is it affecting us?" *Then wait for a response*. Processing what happens in a group gives members a chance to reflect on their own feelings and on the group's interaction and to learn skills in expressing emotions.

Making Adaptations for Your Group

Group facilitators often do not adapt the format to their particular groups as much as they should—and as much as I would expect. I encourage you to approach the topics creatively, responding to each unique group. At the very least, time constraints may mean that some written exercises need to be shortened. Depending on the group's level of cognitive development, context, and purposes, some vocabulary might need to be changed. In addition, some of the suggestions provided for each session might not fit your setting or your group's level of ability. In that case, ignore those or devise your own approach to the topic. You will need to examine the individual sessions to determine which ones might be most helpful, enjoyable, and appropriate for your group's developmental level. However, beware of underestimating group members' awareness of the world or need for information based on their age or ability. In addition, be aware of, and respect, community sensitivities. For example, parents and other members of the community might object to discussions related to sexual orientation, sexuality and sexual behavior, gender roles, gender identity, and family roles. Even discussions about depression, disordered eating, or cutting might not be deemed appropriate.

Ethical Behavior

Your ethical behavior as group leader is extremely important. Sharing confidential group information in the teachers' or agency lounge, with parents, or in the community is not only potentially hurtful, but may also ultimately destroy the possibility of any small-group activity in your school or other place of employment. Trust is quickly lost, and it is difficult and sometimes even impossible to reestablish.

If you plan to conduct groups in a school setting, but are not a counselor and are unfamiliar with ethical guidelines for counselors (including those specifically related to group work), get a copy of such guidelines from your school counselor or through the website of the American Counseling Association (www.counseling.org) or the American School Counselor Association (www.schoolcounselor.org) and read the guidelines carefully. Be aware that counselor training may have an entire course focused on ethics and professionalism. Be especially aware of your responsibilities

regarding confidentiality. Familiarize yourself with situations in which confidentiality must be breached, such as when abuse or neglect is suspected or when someone is in danger or may be a danger to others. The "informed consent" aspect should be addressed by discussing purpose, format, content, confidentiality, and your responsibilities at the first meeting.

Confidentiality cannot be guaranteed in a group. You can explain to your group the actions you will take to protect confidentiality, but you should emphasize that you can guarantee the behavior only of yourself, not of group members. The ethics of confidentiality and privacy apply regardless of whether a leader is a degreed counselor. However, since trust is so essential for comfortable group discussion, you should strongly encourage students not to share, outside of the group, what is said in the group. Tell group members that not keeping comments "inside the group" can destroy the group and even prevent *any* groups from existing in the school or organization in the future due to of lack of trust. Avoid the word *secrets*, however, since it may raise unwarranted concerns and because it may be frightening to students whose families remind them often about not sharing personal information. Any discussion about confidentiality should be matter of fact, not threatening and not overblown. You might remind a group, now and then, about respecting member and family privacy (for example, "How are we doing with respecting privacy after we leave this room each time?").

You may wish to address these issues in a letter to parents asking their permission for their children to attend the group. For a sample letter, which you may modify, see page 19. Please note that this letter is appropriate for groups not designed to address a specific problem area. Feel free to adapt it when necessary.

Group Members Who Are Quiet or Shy

Earnest (but nonstrident) efforts to ask students who are quiet or shy for at least one or two comments during each meeting can help them to feel included and gradually increase their willingness to talk. Although listening can be as valuable as speaking in finding commonalities and gaining self-awareness, it is important for reticent individuals to be heard by their peers, even if only at modest levels. The value of communicating with peers during meetings, in contrast to communicating with you, the facilitator, should not be underestimated. Group members' feedback has indicated, to me, that quiet members gain as much as, or more than, assertive members.

Groups can actually help to validate and support quiet personal styles through discussing personality differences in general and by overtly recognizing quiet members' listening and observation skills, which gregarious members may not have. Even small talk between a leader and a shy student while everyone is arriving may contribute to comfort and ease, which eventually might generate spontaneous comments. In addition, using the activity sheets gives everyone, including shy members, a chance to have low-risk attention in the group and be heard.

Group Members Who Dominate

One strategy for dealing with verbal dominators is to revisit the group guidelines (page 20) as a group, with no one the target. Processing group discussions after the fact can also be used to raise awareness (for example, "How does it feel to be in the group at this point? How are we doing in making sure everyone gets a chance to talk and no one dominates?"). If you notice someone rolling eyes when a dominant group member talks, call attention to that (for example, "I was just noticing something nonverbal in the group—an expression on someone's face. [Name], would you be willing to share with the group what's on your mind? It might help us be a better group.").

Counseling Individual Group Members

I have found that when trust has been established among members and between members and facilitator, individuals with pressing needs sometimes, understandably and appropriately, seek consultation outside of the group if the facilitator is accessible. A trusted facilitator, sought out during a crisis, may indeed play a crucial role in ensuring the well-being of a group member.

If you will not be on the premises every day, it is important to tell the group, at least at the outset of the group series, about when you will be available. I do not recommend giving out your phone number or email, since it is easy for particularly dependent students, and those with poor boundaries, to abuse such access. On the other hand, it may be possible (though not easy) for you to model boundary-setting if the email or phone calls become invasive. Anyone can usually find contact information on the internet if persistent enough, of course—another reason for not giving it out to the group. I don't recommend that you participate with group members on social media, not only because oral communication is a focus of the discussion groups, but also because modeling good social and emotional boundaries is important. Keeping track of what is said, and by whom, becomes even more complex when social media are involved, and group members may be less discreet when not face to face. A small group can be a rare setting for getting acquainted in new ways. Moderation, good boundaries, and appropriate caution are all important here.

It is important to note that too much emphasis at group sessions on outside conferencing can turn off members who do not want to connect the groups to "counseling" and might also encourage some to steer their communication away from the group inappropriately in order to have a special relationship with the facilitator. Facilitators should certainly not refer to outside conversations in group meetings. In addition, if members complain about the group to the facilitator between sessions, they should be encouraged to bring their concerns to the group, putting responsibility

on the group member and giving the group an opportunity to gain skills in resolving conflict.

Handling "Bombs"

Most students, including those in early middle school, are appropriately discreet in what they share in small- and large-group meetings, especially when the facilitator does not pry for private information. However, you can probably expect a few highly charged moments to occur along the way, such as when someone suddenly drops a "bomb" after deciding that the group is trustworthy.

What happens when something shocking is revealed, when someone cries, or when intense conflict erupts within the group? No one can predict these events, of course, since every group has unique dynamics, and groups are generally full of surprises. However, with some basic admonitions in mind, you will learn to trust your instincts. With time and experience, you will be able to anticipate—and perhaps avert—most crisis situations. If they occur, you can be prepared.

Have tissues handy for the student who cries, and simply convey a silent request to a group member to pass the box to the person who needs it. It is important that you affirm the emotion with a compassionate facial expression and perhaps a slight head nod and accept the tears with poise. In fact, your empathetic composure will model for group members that it is all right to cry and express emotions genuinely, that others do not have to rush in to "fix" the situation, and that it is important not to be hyperreactive to others' discomfort, since objectivity and the ability to help may then be lost. When appropriate, ask the individual what, if anything, is needed from the group. Overt support? Just listening? Nothing at the moment? It may be helpful to process an outburst after the fact, asking questions like, "How did it feel to have someone express emotion through crying?" or "Is there anything you would like to say to (name of student who cried)?" and perhaps then (to the student who cried), "What was it like for you to hear that?"

If a student makes a dramatic revelation, immediately put your hand out at arm's length, palm forward, and remind the group about the importance of confidentiality. You might say, "Let's pause a moment. It probably took courage for (name of student) to share that. She/he trusted you as a group. Remember, what was said should stay in the group. If you are tempted to share this information with someone outside of the group, bite your tongue. That's very important. We want to protect our group." Beware of exaggerated responses, both nonverbal and verbal, which can reinforce the idea that a particular revelation is "too much to handle." The sharer might, in fact, have been testing that belief.

If you work in a school and are not a counselor, you should consult with a school counselor or administrator to learn what to do in specific situations. For example, if a student makes a comment (or even just hints) about abuse or suicidal thoughts, you should know how to follow up (see the session "Sadness, Depression, and Dark Thoughts," page 153, for some guidelines). Your school or organization likely has guidelines specific to these issues, and it is best to know them ahead of time. If students contact you independently about a personal concern, remind them that you are not a counselor, but you will certainly listen, and you may subsequently want to encourage them to see a school counselor, depending on what the concern is. If you are a counselor, it is of course important to follow a revelation about abuse or neglect with a one-on-one meeting with the student to determine if the revelation was made seriously and genuinely, to validate the experience through supportive comments, and then, if appropriate, to call the appropriate child protection agency. Regardless of your professional status, you can quietly ask the group member to hang back as the group disperses so that you can meet for a few minutes to help you decide what to do.

Groups are ideal settings for practicing conflict resolution. You can help those in disagreement to listen carefully to each other. Group members can offer supportive thoughts and guidance. You might also pursue helpful material on conflict resolution in your school library. If you are not a counselor, ask a school counselor for strategies your group might use to deal with disagreements or ask the counselor to conduct mediation. Be aware that you yourself might have some resistance to dealing with conflict. Your own fears, discomfort, or emotionality about conflict may actually prevent group members from handling the situation in a healthy manner.

Announcing the Session Topic

If your group is voluntary and a session topic is announced in advance, some individuals may decide not to come if the topic does not sound interesting or relevant to them. You want group attendance to be consistent; it is distracting and can prevent trust from developing when all eight students show up one week and only two the next. Therefore, I recommend that you use a "trust me" response when students ask about the next session's topic. Suggest that they show up and be surprised. Remind them that one can never anticipate the interesting directions a particular topic might take. Besides, many topics are more complex than they first appear.

Journal-Writing

Journal-writing can add a dimension to a group experience. When adolescents have an opportunity to put their thoughts into writing, they can articulate, clarify, expand on, and sort ideas and issues that are important to them. They might then remember ideas and issues they want to bring up in their group and may feel more confident about expressing them. However, since an important goal of the group experience is learning to articulate thoughts and feelings orally in order to enhance relationships, especially important when social media are often the default modes, I strongly advise keeping the focus of groups on oral communication.

In general, I prefer to use the entire group time for open, semistructured discussion, since time available for middle and high school advisor-advisee or homeroom meetings, for instance, is already probably less than optimal for group discussion. Adding discussion related to journals diverts time and attention away from the new focus, as journal entries are likely to relate to preceding, not present, topics. In addition, some schools use this book as a guidance or advisee curriculum and encourage multiple classroom facilitators to deal with sessions at the same time and in the same sequence. If journaling is indeed done, it is important to consider if and how it will be attended to in group sessions, including how much time will be available for each new focus, and how much time will be required for you to read and respond meaningfully to journal entries. *Fundamentally, it is important to remember that the emphasis in this approach to group work is on building skills through oral expression, with present and future relationships in mind.*

About the Sessions

The Focus

Why have a focus for each session? Development is the common denominator for the sessions—not a particular issue, behavior, need, or goal, as may be common in group work in treatment centers or agencies. Nevertheless, working with an explicit focus or theme is worthwhile, since it provides a starting point for discussion and an excuse to curb negative and unproductive group behaviors. It also insists on addressing important, developmentally appropriate topics that might be somewhat uncomfortable to talk about. In addition, all adolescents are not as flexible as they may appear, and product-oriented members may quickly tire of "not really doing anything." Others need structure to contain their anxiety and impulsivity. On the other hand, some are quite flexible and, especially if they are verbal and spontaneous, may prefer a loose format. In fact, they might say, "Just let us come in here and talk about whatever we want to talk about."

The structure that is recommended here can benefit a wide range of personalities and meet many needs. Even individuals who resist structure often find the variety of semistructured approaches interesting and worthwhile. It will be important that you consider carefully how much structure is warranted. Complaints may initially reflect only apprehension about addressing developmental concerns and exploring emotions. In addition, be reminded that the recommended format helps to keep discussion oriented to prevention, development, and connection, which are appropriate territory not just for laypersons as facilitators, but for degreed counseling professionals as well, regardless of setting.

Individuals who like order and structure and who are uncomfortable when there is no "map" or clear purpose usually want group time to be worthwhile in specific terms. If there is no "felt focus," and if group membership is voluntary, students may choose not to attend when something else seems preferable—like finishing homework or eating with friends. They may also object when assertive members set the pace and direction each time. Group members with new and dramatic needs each week can quickly dominate, and others may then defer and listen, or they might leave, frustrated that their own issues are not addressed. Discussion groups should not be just for "natural talkers."

On the other hand, group discussions need not be rigidly programmed. Although *How (and Why) to Get Students Talking* proposes a focus for each session, sometimes with several sessions building on a theme, there is great potential for nimbly changing direction during discussion. A flexible facilitator can accommodate strands that emerge, yet still gently steer the group to closure, overtly acknowledging that the focus inspired unexpected directions. Especially with topics that members view as intimidating and difficult, the focus is an excuse to persist with tough questions and deal with issues and problems, not just gripes and frustrations, gossip, and banter.

Also important is the reality that a focus helps group facilitators in schools communicate with administrators, parents, and teachers about groups, which need advocacy and protection in today's educational climate. Those adults might assume that discussion groups are for teacher-bashing, airing family secrets, or simply "hanging out." Being able to say, "We've been dealing with stress for the past four weeks," or "We're focusing on self-awareness this semester," or more specifically, "We've been talking about bullying" helps to lessen anxiety and suspicion. Listing even a few topics underscores that these groups deal with significant issues and are worth the energy required to resolve daunting logistical challenges associated with group work in schools.

I have found that focusing on "self-esteem," "motivation," or "friendship," per se, for a full meeting is often not productive in small-group work. That is not to say that enhancing these is not a worthy goal. However, meaningful discussion, connections with peers, new social skills, and information about development can all potentially enhance how teens view themselves, peers, and schoolwork. Self-esteem and motivation can be affected by developmental challenges, and friendship skills can be improved through making connections *about* development during small-group discussion. Therefore, focusing on development-related topics makes sense if general goals include improved sense of self, motivation, and peer relationships. (The one session focused entirely on self-esteem, for example, looks at that concept from several angles, including developmental.) I also believe that focusing on strengths (a hallmark of counseling), rather than on limitations, deficits, or pathology, is key to helping teens stay on, or move to, solid ground during adolescence—including socially and academically.

Background Information

At the beginning of most sessions, a few paragraphs of background information are provided. These are designed to help you prepare for the session and think broadly about the topic at hand, to provide basic information that might be useful during the session, to inspire further reading, to anticipate student concerns, and to assist you in determining a possible direction for the discussion, according to the needs of your group. *Usually, it is not appropriate to read this information to the group;* in only a few sessions are you directed to do that. A section at the end of the book provides trusted resources for additional background on some topics as well as some resources that are appropriate to recommend to students who request additional information.

Objectives and Suggestions

The objectives listed for each session tell you what to work toward and what to expect if the general suggestions are followed. They may also help you communicate purpose and content to administrators, parents, and teachers who wonder what your group is doing. You may want to prepare a list of objectives for parent conferences, for example. However, *the objectives are not meant to be read to group members.*

The suggestions are just that—suggestions. Use all, some, or none of them, and adapt those you use to address the needs of your group. Time limits, ability level, and group temperament are among many factors to consider when selecting suggestions and activities. The suggested questions provided are generally open-ended and likely to generate conversation.

Activity Sheets

Several of the sessions include activity sheets that may be reproduced for group use. They are also included in the digital content for this book (see page 289 for downloading instructions). In my experience, these written exercises do not make discussions too structured, and most adolescents do not resist them. However, receptivity depends on how the sheets are used.

Especially when activity sheets are not used too often, groups have told me they appreciate the handouts as an opportunity to think quietly and focus at the outset of a meeting and to write, objectify, and edit their thoughts. The sheets also give everyone a chance to be heard. Quiet or shy members can share, in turn, without having to compete with assertive peers. Discussion can involve only a few or all items on a sheet. Activities using paper, pencils, markers, index cards, masking tape, string, or other items provide opportunities to consider thoughts and may even help teens express strong feelings and opinions without the pressure of eye contact. However, with some teens, those items easily become paper airplanes, something to "rattle," and a distraction. If group members can curb impulses to throw them, soft balls, bendable plastic sticks, and small stuffed animals can give students something to fiddle with and may provide safe distraction when topics evoke uncomfortable emotions—especially early in the life of a group, before members develop trust and establish a rhythm.

Group members who have learning disabilities (affecting reading and writing abilities and general comfort in the classroom), have physical disabilities (affecting writing), or are hyperactive may have a more difficult time than others with settling in. Discomfort and anxiety can be expressed through disruptive behavior. You may need an extra layer of patience and perseverance as these students learn to relax and enjoy the group experience. I recommend responding calmly and quietly to disruptions, not taking negative behavior personally, and not immediately assuming that the discussion format is inappropriate. With that said, however, more creative and quietly kinesthetic approaches to the topics may be helpful. Students with classroom difficulties (in learning and/or in behavior) often believe that "teachers don't like them." Your holistic, nonjudgmental interest in them and your focus on strengths and "normal development" may be new and welcome. If you have organized a small group, being able to work with smaller numbers is your advantage.

You may want to keep a file folder for each student in the group and, for the sessions utilizing activity sheets, have group members put the sheets into their folders at the close of each session. You can then return the folders to a secure place, ensuring that personal information will not end up on the classroom floor or circulating through the halls through carelessness. You might also gather the sheets (with names) at the end of a session and file them in students' folders yourself. I recommend that group members look over the accumulated stash during the final group meeting and then shred the sheets themselves during that meeting. At the time they were filled out, the sheets provoked self-reflection and were private. Personal "editing" could occur even when information was shared with the group, with some information withheld if considered too private to share. *Looking the sheets over, at the end, reinforces that the group experience was broad and complex.* As always, the *process* of glancing over the sheets, rather than the content, is the key—and is sufficient. Shredding the sheets reinforces the right to privacy, affirms the developmental challenge of establishing a separate identity, and confirms the respect of the group leader for both of these elements. Another option is for you to simply dispose of the set of sheets at the end of each session by shredding them.

Under no circumstances should the sheets be shown to any school personnel. However, because you have been clear at the outset that abuse, neglect, and danger to self and others must be reported (see page 11), group members who share that kind of information on the sheets will be aware of your responsibility. Meet individually with students who indicate a threat to safety, remind them of your responsibility, check out the seriousness of the situation, encourage contact with an available counselor (if you are not one) or accompany them to the counselor's office, and follow through, if appropriate, with a report to child protective services. In the case of suicidal ideation, make sure you or a counselor contacts the student's parents and provides appropriate guidance or, if parents are unavailable, ensures the safety of the individual.

Session Closure and Series Ending

Each session includes a suggestion for closure. It is always a good idea to end a session with a summary, whether you provide it yourself or solicit it from the group. Inherent in closure is the reminder that the discussions are purposeful, that members have common concerns, and that members have been heard. Even if an important new thought is introduced in the closing minutes, it is still good to have some kind of deliberate closure, perhaps also suggesting that the group continue with the new idea next time. However, I normally recommend that session topics not be continued into the next session. Each is meant to stand alone or be combined with another topic for one session. The purpose is to learn through process, not to cover content. It is fine to conclude discussion on a topic before it feels "done." You will have provoked thought and provided an opportunity for discussion and skill-building in that session, and that is the value.

If you complete the session and the closure and time remains, you might use it to begin the next writing activity, ask questions designed to encourage thinking about the next session or focus, or just chat with the group.

Getting Started

How to Begin

Begin the first meeting by letting students know how pleased you are that they will be part of the group. Remind them that the purpose of the group is to "just talk" about various topics related to growing up. Their contribution will be to share feelings and concerns and to support each other.

Explain your role in the group. If you are a teacher or other professional without counselor training, tell the students that during group meetings you will not be a "teacher" in the usual sense of that word. Instead, you will be a discussion leader or facilitator, and the focus will be on them. It will be *their* group, developing uniquely. You will be their guide, listening carefully, sharing insights when appropriate, and helping them to connect with each other. Emphasize that you will all learn from each other. If you are a counselor, explain that the group is not a typical counseling group with a focus on a particular problem. The purpose of the group is the same no matter the facilitator: making connections through talking about growing up.

Move next to introductions and a generative get-acquainted activity, such as the "Warm-Up" (pages 21–22), that sets the tone for the group experience. Tell the group to read through all the sentence beginnings silently and slowly, writing responses to complete the thought. Then invite them to read their responses—either to one sentence at a time across the group or with each member, in turn, reading the entire sheet all at once. Or, if you prefer, go directly to another session you have chosen to start the group. During your first meeting, since it is important that group members experience what "being in a group" will be like, avoid becoming bogged down with rule-setting and warnings. Instead, conduct an activity that generates interaction and gives them an idea of who is in the group. Then explain that at each meeting the group will similarly talk and do things together. Thank them for getting the group off to a good start.

At some point during your first or second meeting, you might choose to hand out copies of the "Group Guidelines" (page 20). Go over the guidelines one at a time, with volunteers reading them. Ask if anyone has questions or if there is anything they do not understand. Tell the group that everyone—including you—is expected to follow these guidelines for as long as the group exists. Explain that although they may not know how to do all of these things and behave in all of these ways right now, they will be learning and practicing these skills over the life of the group. Stay positive and optimistic, indicating that the guidelines are simply common sense.

Be aware that optimal group behavior can become established by complimenting members when it occurs. Adding a comment like, "That kind of behavior helps make a good group," can also help to "norm" group functioning positively.

How to Proceed

First-year groups, particularly at younger ages, often need more structure than more experienced groups. It also takes a while to establish ease and fluidity in discussion, even when members are well acquainted outside of the group. Groups of older students are usually able to deal with abstract and personal topics with little introduction, and they are also likely to be more patient and tolerant regarding experimentation with format. Groups of older adolescents usually attain depth more quickly than younger groups, although the presence of even one or two spontaneous, forthright middle schoolers can move a young group quickly into significant interaction.

Follow the suggestions in each session for introducing the topic, generating discussion, and managing the activities. There are usually more suggestions than you will need for a session. Teachers and counselors who have used earlier versions of this book have told me they appreciate having several suggestions to choose from; therefore, I have continued to include multiple options here.

You may find it difficult to follow the printed text while leading the discussions. Rather than reading anything word for word to your group, it's best to familiarize yourself thoroughly with the content of a session before your meeting. Then you'll have a general direction in mind and some ideas for pursuing various directions, while keeping an eye on the session materials, if necessary.

Sometimes your group may generate a good discussion for the entire session on only the first suggestion. This is not unusual or "wrong." The more flexible you are, the better. Never think you need to finish everything suggested. In fact, as mentioned earlier, move to a new session focus at the next meeting, regardless of whether you have applied all suggestions.

Be aware that even when students in a school enjoy a group, they can forget to come to meetings that are not part of the regular classroom schedule. If your group is voluntary, you may need to remind them for several weeks about meeting times and places. Eventually attendance may become a habit for most. However, I have found it worthwhile and beneficial to groups to send a reminder to everyone (a "pass" sent to a homeroom or a group email or text) about every meeting. If paper passes are used, students can simply fill them out for the next week at the outset of a meeting, including the name of the teacher who will distribute the passes.

Tips to Keep in Mind

1. Remind the group, now and then and as needed, that anything said in the group stays in the group. Confidentiality is especially important when sensitive information is shared.

2. Ask open-ended questions, not yes-or-no questions, to generate discussion. Questions beginning with *how, what, when, where,* and *what kind* are preferable to closed questions beginning with variations of *is/are/were, does/do/did,* and *has/have/had,* since the former require more than a yes-or-no response. However, for reluctant contributors, closed questions such as, "Was it a sad time?" offer low risk, and such questions are also appropriate in conjunction with open-ended questions when a point of information is needed. In general, however, discussions can be facilitated entirely without using questions. Statements often can be more facilitative than questions (for example, in response to a group member's comments, "Middle school can be challenging," "You've had a rough week," "I can hear that it was very upsetting.")

3. When a member offers a comment that begs for more detail, respond with, "Tell us more about . . . ," "Put words on that feeling . . . ," "Help us understand . . . ," "Can you give an example of . . . ?" or "What do you mean by . . . ?"

4. Always allow group members to pass if they prefer not to speak. This guideline applies to any group activity, including activity sheets, checklists, and group discussions. Make it clear from the beginning that nobody has to speak, even though you hope you can get to know all of them and that they can become acquainted with each other.

5. Don't preach. Students probably hear enough of that already. This experience should be different.

6. Don't judge. Let your group "just talk," and accept what they say. Feel free to say, "Wow," or "That's an interesting view," or "Pretty risky, huh?" if they share experiences related to unwise decisions or behaviors or make comments that are not smooth or are potentially inflammatory. In responding calmly, *without judgment*, you are establishing a climate where students can explore developmental challenges with an adult present.

7. Take them seriously and validate their feelings. For some group members, this might be a rare or entirely new experience. Paraphrasing ("You felt she didn't understand," or "You had a long, difficult day"), checking ("Did I hear you correctly? This happened a week ago?"), asking for more information ("I don't think I quite understand; tell us more about that"), acknowledging feelings ("I can hear how frustrated you were," or "It makes sense that you felt angry"), or simply offering an "Mmmmm" in response to a comment shows that you are listening and thinking about what was said.

8. Relax and let the group be more about process than product. It may not always be apparent that something specific has been accomplished, but as long as members keep talking thoughtfully, you're probably on the right track.

9. Beware of sharing your own personal experiences too often and in too much detail. Always remember that the group is about *them*, not about you, and that every time you self-disclose, you take attention away from them. Group members will feel that shift and may quickly tire of your talking about your family or adolescence. Your personal experiences are also likely not as helpful or pertinent to their situations as you think. I rarely fill out the activity sheets myself, and therefore I do not participate in a "go-around" with the sheets. Having a policy of limited self-disclosure from the outset establishes an appropriate facilitator posture. If someone asks you a personal question, consider saying something like this: "This group is for you, not for me. Discussions in groups like this should be among peers. I'm just the leader. I want to be careful to do my part well."

10. Be alert to moments when it is wise to protect members from each other and themselves. For example, if a group member begins with something like, "I've never said this to anybody—it's about something pretty bad that happened to me," you may want to encourage a pause before continuing. To do that, reach out one hand toward the speaker, palm away, and ask, "Are you comfortable sharing this with the group?" Then ask the group, "Are you ready to be trusted? Remember what we said about

confidentiality." Then go back to the speaker: "Do you still want to share this with the group?" In doing this, you give the student time to reconsider (especially if the student has too quickly assumed trustworthiness), and you also have reminded the group about their responsibilities. After the speaker finishes, you might process the telling with the group: "How did that feel to be trusted with that information?" The focus remains on feelings and support.

11. In situations where members of the group verbally attack each other, another kind of protection is needed: facilitator intervention. In addition, the group can process what has happened by sharing their feelings about the conflict. In fact, processing the experience can, in itself, defuse conflict. When there is conflict, ask, "What is/was that like for us to have conflict in the group?" This is an excellent time to talk genuinely about strong feelings and experience conflict resolution.

12. If a student reacts emotionally with momentary discomfort or tears, offer verbal support, a tissue (which should be handy), or touch (a pat on the arm, perhaps, if in proximity). Group members may follow your lead. However, be aware that some may not want to be touched. In fact, beware of assuming that a hug is "best." A hug may meet facilitator needs more than student needs. Touch, for some, understandably means danger and discomfort— or is simply not common culturally.

13. Listen carefully to the student who is speaking, but also be sure to monitor nonverbal behavior in the entire group. Be alert to those who are not speaking. Are they showing discomfort (averted eyes, moving back, facial tics), frustration (agitation, head-shaking, mumbled negatives), or anxiety (uneasy eyes, unsteady hands, tense face)? Depending on the situation and the student, you may want to ask sensitively about what you are noticing.

14. Be sincere in your comments and compliments. Watch for and act on opportunities to compliment group members ("You put words on a very complex feeling," or "You explained that very well"). Avoid insincere, noncredible comments about members' strengths, but be on the lookout for demonstrations or descriptions of courage, compassion, kindness, wisdom, common sense, responsibility, and problem-solving abilities, for example. All adolescents are hungry for positive strokes, and whatever genuine positive support you give them will be taken seriously.

Endings

How to end a series of group meetings should be carefully considered, since members might have become quite attached to the group. It is wise to wind down purposefully. "An Informal Assessment" (page 275) can be used to conclude a series of meetings.

Most important in the final session, or sometime during the last few sessions, is to invite members to talk about what they have experienced in the group. I have found that asking them to write a few simple sentences or paragraphs during a final session is helpful. Sometimes, when group attendance was voluntary, I have asked, "Why did you keep coming to the group?" At other times, I have simply invited members to talk about what they have gained in personal insights, what they have learned about adolescence in general, what common ground they have discovered, and if and how they have changed over the period of time the group has met.

All groups, regardless of size and duration, need to prepare for the time when the group will no longer meet. Most participants will miss the group when it is done and feel a sense of loss. Especially if they have become dependent on the group for support, they may feel anxious about facing the future without the group. If they have become well acquainted through the group, and if they have made friends, they may wonder if they will lose touch once the group disbands.

A few sessions prior to ending a series, mention casually that there are only a few meetings remaining. Continue to do that until the next-to-last session. At that time, mention what you have in mind for the final session, or ask the group for suggestions. You might plan a party, have food brought in, and/or take a group photo. Be aware, though, that changing the "mode" of the group may create discomfort at a time already stressful because of the ending. After all, the focus until then has been on discussion. Even the addition of food or music changes group dynamics. Everyone must interact socially in a new way, with no "topic" and little time to become comfortable with it. With that said, however, use your own judgment. You know your group.

Be sure to leave time at the final session for them and you to say good-bye. If it is possible that they will not have much future contact with each other, provide a way for them to share home and email addresses and phone numbers and to wish each other well. Be aware that you will be modeling strategies for ending what has likely been a profound experience. For many people—adults and students—that is a difficult process.

Evaluation

It is not always easy to "read" a group and know whether it is moving in a positive direction. Individuals who readily and frequently give feedback cannot speak for everyone. Quiet members may be gaining insights that they are simply not sharing. A session that seemed to generate an indifferent or poor response might, in fact, have made an impact, but the effects may not be apparent. Groups are complex, and members' needs and what they respond to differ. Therefore, it is wise (in a long-term group) periodically to

have group members fill out an evaluation. An evaluation is particularly important at the end of a group experience.

On page 278, you will find a "Discussion Group Evaluation" form to copy and use. Or you might choose to create your own form, tailored to your group and to what you hope to learn. Feedback provided on such evaluations can be invaluable when assessing past groups and planning for future groups. To administrators, teachers, or funders, evaluations can also help to defend group work as part of a general school curriculum, as part of a school counseling program, or as a program at some other facility.

A Note for Parents

How (and Why) to Get Students Talking can be a valuable tool for parents in getting to know their children. It can help parents access what their children are thinking and feeling, the issues that are important to them, and their problems, hopes, and thoughts about the future.

Parents and adolescents often have difficulty sustaining conversations. Both middle schoolers and high schoolers may become increasingly reticent and private at home. Sometimes it is hard for parents to know what to talk about besides schoolwork, family members, video games, chores, and food. They often do not know which subjects are "safe" and which are taboo with their children. Sometimes all subjects seem to be off limits. *How (and Why) to Get Students Talking* provides a potentially intriguing way (to both students and parents) to break down barriers.

By scanning the background information and suggestions, parents can find possible topics and conversation starters. They can also discover insights into developmental issues that they and their children may be wrestling with. It is easy to forget what adolescence felt like, and the background information can help parents understand the complexities of adolescent life today.

Most of the sessions—especially those in the Identity, Relationships, and Family sections—can help to generate family discussion. Some students I've worked with have asked to take the activity sheets home for their parents to fill out. Many personal issues persist into adulthood and are good to discuss even with young adolescents, who are beginning to be aware that these are their issues too. Such sharing can be helpful to adolescents as they forge their own separate identities and prepare to be launched into the next developmental stage.

Several of the sessions in the Stress section are also worth discussing as a family. Expectations, coping strategies, procrastination, and sources of stress are particularly good subjects for family sharing. We are never "done" with such concerns in our lives, and it is good to admit our humanness to growing children. Such nonauthoritarian "realness" can help create dialogue, especially if adults do not dominate the conversation and if they communicate genuine interest (without judgment) in students and their world.

Permission for Student Participation

Dear Parent/Guardian/Caregiver,

I have invited your son or daughter to participate in a discussion or group. The purpose of the group is to provide an opportunity to talk about growing up and to improve skills in talking and listening. Such skills are important to students now in relationships with peers, teachers, and parents—and later with spouses, partners, coworkers, and children. In general, the groups offer support to teens as they deal with the challenges of adolescence and prepare for the future.

Adolescence can be a stressful time in even the best of situations. Not only are there physical changes, but there are also new emotions and new expectations. There are new activities to be involved in, academic choices to be made, and the future to think about. Social relationships are probably also changing.

Our discussion group will focus on such concerns. Even though we may discuss academic concerns now and then, the group will be different from the often competitive school world. Students will relax with each other and find out what they have in common, including the challenges of adolescence. They will learn how to support each other. They will become acquainted with classmates—for the first time or simply better than before.

If your child participates, you may soon notice positive changes both at school and at home. Communication may improve. Talking about stress, developing strategies for problem-solving, gaining a clearer sense of self, feeling the support of trusted peers—all of these group experiences may improve self-esteem and satisfaction.

The group will begin very soon. If you give your permission for your child to be involved, and if your child decides to participate, please sign below and return the form to me as soon as possible. If you have any questions, please contact me at _____ .

(email and phone)

_____
(Signature of facilitator)

_____ has my permission to participate in the discussion group.
(Name of student)

_____   _____
(Parent signature)   (Date)

Group Guidelines

The purpose of this group is to "just talk"—to share thoughts, feelings, and concerns with each other in an atmosphere of trust, respect, caring, and understanding. To make this group successful and meaningful, we agree to the following terms and guidelines.

1. Anything that is said in the group stays in the group. We agree to keep things confidential. This means we don't share information outside of the group. We agree to do our part, individually and together, to make this group a safe place to talk.

2. We respect what other group members say. We agree not to use put-downs of any kind, including words or actions. Body language, facial expressions, and sighs can all be put-downs, and we agree to control our own behavior so that everyone feels valued and accepted.

3. We respect everyone's need to be heard. We agree that no one will dominate the group. We also understand that just because someone is quiet or shy doesn't mean the person has nothing to say. We also know that listening and keen observation are valuable skills.

4. We listen to each other. When someone is speaking, we look at the speaker and pay attention. We use supportive and encouraging body language and facial expressions.

5. We realize that feelings are not "bad" or "good." They just are. They make sense, under the circumstances. Therefore, we don't say things like, "You shouldn't feel that way."

6. We are willing to take risks, explore new ideas, and explain our feelings as well as we can. However, we agree that someone who doesn't want to talk doesn't have to talk. We don't force people to share when they don't feel comfortable sharing.

7. We are willing to let others know us. We agree that talking and listening are ways for people to get to know each other.

8. We realize that sometimes people feel misunderstood, or they feel that someone has hurt them accidentally or on purpose. We agree that the best way to handle those times is by talking and listening—to the group and to the people involved. We encourage assertiveness.

9. We agree to be sincere and to do our best to speak from the heart.

10. We don't talk about group members who aren't present. We especially don't criticize group members who aren't here to defend themselves.

11. When we do need to talk about other people, such as teachers and peers, we don't refer to them by name. For example, we may want to ask the group to help us solve a problem we are having with a particular person, but the person will remain anonymous.

12. We agree to attend group meetings regularly. We don't want to miss information that might be referred to later. Most of all, we know that we are important to the group. If for some reason we can't attend a meeting, we will try to let our leader know ahead of time.

Warm-Up

Name: _____

Complete these sentences:

1. I've heard that groups like this are _____

   _____

2. I hope the group will _____

   _____

3. Probably the most interesting thing about me is _____

   _____

4. Something I have that is very special to me is _____

   _____

5. I'm good at _____

   _____

6. I've never been able to _____

   _____

7. A really dramatic moment in my life was when _____

   _____

8. I'm proud that I _____

   _____

9. Probably the biggest accomplishment in my life is _____

   _____

   (continued)

10. I like people who _____

_____

11. I'm probably most myself when I _____

_____

12. You probably wouldn't believe that I _____

_____

13. The time of day I feel best is _____

_____

14. I'm looking forward to _____

_____

15. I can imagine myself someday _____

_____

FOCUS
···
Stress

FOCUS Stress

....

Mention the word *stress* to a teen, and you will have begun a serious conversation. Starting at an early age, most young people become well acquainted with the stress of living in an increasingly complex world. Parents bring home the stress of the workplace, or they suffer job loss, both having a ripple effect on the family. Ours is a mobile society, and dislocations and relocations contribute to stress. There are pressures at school, with some children coping well and some not so well with the demands of the classroom and activities and the inherent social challenges. Illness, accidents, or other life events can have dramatic physical and emotional repercussions for months or years. Having a learning difference or physical disability can contribute to stress. Being taller, shorter, heavier, or thinner than most peers may be a stressor— or having interests that differ from those of peers. Facing difficult classes and assignments can stress both young and older adolescents. Being in a cultural minority may be stressful as well.

Stress is part of life—growing up, growing old, facing change, being ill, working, and caring for family members. Pessimism, multiple responsibilities, trying to respond to everyone's needs, and isolation all can heighten stress levels. Being tensely and intensely connected through social networking, with little quiet and unengaged time to step back and contemplate feelings and perceptions, may also contribute to stress.

Consciously or unconsciously, families teach children coping skills. Some adolescents have learned healthy and effective ways to cope with life's stressors. They talk about the stress they are experiencing, step back and gain perspective on stressful situations, and apply problem-solving techniques. They release tension through a healthy level of exercise, socializing, relaxation, diversion, or a deliberate change of pace and pattern. Others learn unhealthy ways to cope with stress, trying to escape or deny stress through alcohol and other drugs, overeating or other unhealthful eating behaviors, workaholism, moving to a new location (the "geographic cure"), sleeping, daydreaming, or watching too much television. Some resort to tantrums or abusing those around them. Others cope by blaming, scapegoating, punishing, or accepting a victim posture. Some experience depression. More and more have anxiety.

The sessions in this section of *How (and Why) to Get Students Talking* give students a chance to think about their stressors and to begin sorting them into two basic categories: those they can do something about and those that probably cannot be changed. Within the safe, supportive environment of the group, they can discuss their coping styles and perhaps begin to deal with stressful situations more effectively.

Simply having a chance to talk about stress can be valuable. Your primary responsibility as group facilitator is to listen carefully, hear what group members are saying, communicate that you have heard them, and commend them for their openness, genuineness, and willingness to articulate complex issues and feelings.

General Objectives

- Group members learn about stress.
- They learn to talk about stress and stressors and to sort out stressful situations.
- They consider various ways to cope with stress.

FOCUS Stress

What Is Stress?

Objectives

- Group members increase their understanding of stress.

- They discover similarities within the group regarding stress and stressors.

- They find out that people respond differently to similar stressors, depending on their personality, how they interpret various situations, and what kinds of coping strategies they have learned.

Important

All of the other sessions in this section depend on group members having some understanding of stress and stressors. Be sure to present this session before any of the other sessions on stress.

Suggestions

1. Introduce the topic by asking the group to define the term *stress*. If necessary, provide a few synonyms: *anxiety, pressure, tension, worry.* Then ask volunteers to tell what they know about stress. Afterward, introduce information from the following that has not been brought up in the group discussion.

   ~ Stress can be good and helpful. It can lead to high productivity, a good level of competitiveness and performances, and high alertness. Some people even seek out stress, loving the adrenaline rush and performing better when the pressure is on.

   ~ Excessive stress can cause problems if people do not cope with it effectively.

   ~ Physical responses to stress can include accelerated heartbeat (as the body prepares for fight or flight), cold extremities (as the capillaries constrict to make more blood available at the center of the body to protect the major organs), tight muscles, tense shoulders, a pressure headache, dry mouth, clammy hands, and/or stomach or intestinal discomfort, among several possibilities.

   ~ Prolonged periods of stress can lead to significant physical problems. Medical professionals see many illnesses that may have origins in stress. When they see patients with pain and distress for no apparent physical reasons, they might conclude that the symptoms are related to stress.

~ Emotionally, stress can affect concentration, sleep, safety, and appetite. It can cause irritability, extreme reactions to normal problems, self-blame, tearfulness, anxiety, depression, panic attacks, and debilitating perfectionism. Sometimes it can lead to addictions.

~ Most people react to excessive stress in a particular way. They may develop colds, diarrhea, stomachaches, headaches, skin problems, or tense neck and shoulders, for instance.

~ Stress can result from having to do something new or do something differently from before—for example, move to a different home, change schools, adjust to a divorce or a new family, deal with a physical problem, adjust to a new baby in the home, use new and complex technology, start new kinds of school assignments, or adjust to a loss.

2. Encourage group members to describe their own physical and emotional responses to stress. Ask, "What tells you that you are under stress? How do you behave? How do you feel? How does your body react?" (You might consider copying an outline of a human form and inviting members to color, with crayons or markers, where they typically feel stress physically.)

3. Ask group members to tell about stressful situations in their lives. Every so often, as a way of supporting those who are sharing, ask the group, "Does this sound familiar? Has anyone else experienced something like this?" Depending on the situation, respond with something like "That does sound stressful" or "Wow, that's tough" or "That's certainly a huge change for you."

4. Ask, "What kinds of things in your life are stressful? Raise your hand if you feel stress in connection to

~ competition in a talent area, including sports

~ getting along with others your age

~ doing well in your classes

~ feeling uncomfortable in school

~ having to work faster than you'd like to

~ trying to please everyone."

5. Consider inviting an expert to speak with your group as a follow-up session. This might be someone from a stress clinic or an expert on biofeedback, meditation/relaxation, or yoga.

6. Consider making "stress balls" as a group, carefully considering whether your group is likely to react favorably or unfavorably to a hands-on activity, whether hyperactive members would be engaged or overly stimulated, whether the group would have difficulty settling down afterward, whether they would expect physical activity at every meeting thereafter, and how much spilled sand might be a problem. Materials

needed include a tray of fine sand, a funnel, something to pour sand into a funnel with, and two balloons per member. Directions to the group, broken up into partners, follow here:

~ One partner stretches the neck of the balloon while the other partner uses a funnel (or spoon) to pour in an amount of sand equal to what could comfortably be gently squeezed in the hand.

~ Someone ties a knot in the stretched balloon neck.

~ Someone clips off the end of a second balloon. One partner stretches the neck of, and rolls down, the second balloon while the other partner eases the filled balloon into it, with the tied neck in first. The outside balloon is then rolled out around the filled balloon (pantyhose-style).

The students are to take the stress balls home to use while watching television, doing homework, feeling stressed, or settling down after vigorous activity—as a stress reliever. They should not throw them or otherwise cause commotion with them at school.

7. Ask group members if there is a specific stressor they need help coping with. For the various stressors mentioned, ask the group for suggestions.

8. For closure, invite volunteers to summarize what they have learned, felt, or thought about during this session.

FOCUS Stress

Sorting Out the Stressors

Objectives

- Group members learn that it can feel good to talk about the stressors in their lives and related feelings.

- They hear about the stressors of other group members, which helps to put their stress into perspective and also helps them to feel less alone in their struggles.

- They evaluate various stressors and determine which ones are short-term and which are long-term, as well as which can be remedied and which cannot.

- They learn that focusing on the present, as opposed to looking anxiously to the future—or vice versa, if present circumstances feel overwhelming—can alleviate some stress.

- They explore whether making adjustments in their lives might enable them to concentrate on themselves in healthy ways and relieve some stress.

Suggestions

1. Introduce the topic with references to the preceding session, "What Is Stress?" Be sure that session precedes this one. Briefly share any other relevant information you have learned about stress and stressors, perhaps from recent newspaper or magazine articles. You might say that businesses and educational institutions often offer stress-reduction programs to their employees because stress potentially affects performance, production, absenteeism, health, and ultimately medical insurance rates.

2. Hand out the "Stress Boxes" activity sheet (page 32). Instruct the group to write the name or description of a specific stressor in each of the boxes on the left. (Examples: "School" is not specific; "third period math class" is. "Family" is not specific; "my little sister invading my privacy" is. "Noise" is not specific; "dogs barking when I'm trying to sleep" is.)

   When all group members have finished, ask them to draw a squiggle on the line connecting each stress box to its paired box. The density of the squiggle should indicate how much stress they associate with that particular stressor. (The more stress, the more dense the squiggle.) Then, in each empty box on the right, direct them to write a large "X" if the box is connected to a short-term stressor (one which probably will not be a concern after a few weeks or months), an "O" if the box is connected to a long-term stressor, which might be with them for many years, or a "+" in each box paired with a stressor they could do something about tomorrow if they chose to.

During this activity, be alert for group members who seem unable to discriminate among their stressors, or who have drawn dense squiggles for all of them, since they may be feeling overwhelmed by many significant stressors. Rather than calling attention to high-stress individuals in the group in this regard, make a general suggestion at the end like, "If you had a hard time sorting out your stressors, since they all feel huge right now, I encourage you to talk with a caring and trusted adult, including the school counselor (if you are in a school), to sort through them and get a handle on them." If you sense that a particular student is highly distressed, seek him or her out privately at your first opportunity and ask, "Should I be worried about you?" If the answer is yes, ask if the student would like you to call a parent and / or if he or she would be comfortable talking with the school counselor. If you are the school counselor, extend the conversation to determine the seriousness of the situation.

3. Encourage students to share their stress boxes. One way they can do this is to list stressors in order of intensity, and then explain which ones they could do something about if they chose to, which one are short term, and which ones (if any) might be long-term.

4. The first three suggestions often take up an entire session. The process of naming and describing stressors, and sorting them out, can be a powerful and valuable exercise in itself. While I do not encourage moving into problem-solving for this session, if time allows and group members express an interest, the discussion might shift to how the stressed students have tried to resolve situations that were described as potentially resolvable. Then, if appropriate, you might also ask the group for suggestions for coping and resolution. Here are some sample stressors and suggestions from adolescent groups:

~ Short-term stressor: Too much makeup homework. Suggestions: Try harder not to miss school; complete assignments on time; work on organization (use an assignment notebook) to remember assignments.

~ Short-term stressor: Can't find anything in my room. Suggestion: Clean the room and get some storage boxes.

~ Short-term stressor: A big project that's due soon. Suggestions: Start working on it today. Break it down into smaller steps and finish one today, continuing with small steps.

~ Short-term stressor: Single parent is recovering at home from surgery and cannot do any housework. Suggestions: Focus on what you need to do at home to survive, including being organized about homework and chores. Check in with the school counselor. Take a walk or exercise in another way.

~ Long-term stressor: Working on a joint project with a peer who doesn't do his or her share. Suggestions: Be more assertive. Set limits. Talk to him or her directly about the problem.

~ Long-term stressor: No privacy at home. Suggestions: Set limits. Be assertive about asking for what you need. Hide the diary.

~ Long-term stressor: Constant family fights. Suggestions: Ask parents to set up a family meeting to discuss problem-solving. See if the family will agree to a "count-to-ten-before-you-yell" rule. Break the pattern by not responding in your usual way.

~ Long-term stressor: Worries about the future—starting high school, graduating, and leaving home, in particular. Suggestions: Talk to a school counselor. Talk to someone who is currently in high school or who attends the type of school you are considering for after high school or who works in the field you would like to work in.

To conclude this part of the discussion, you might say something like this: "We can't (and wouldn't want to) eliminate all stressors from our lives, since stress can be beneficial, but we can learn to cope with those that bother us, and we can alter the way we respond to them. We can also make sure that we take care of our health, so that during negatively stressful times we can cope well and be less likely to feel overwhelmed."

5. Some teens would probably benefit from focusing more on the future. However, some could deal with stress more effectively by living more in the present, particularly those who seem intensely absorbed in what comes next (a habit which can become lifelong). You might encourage students who are stressed about the future to try not to be preoccupied with it, even though there are decisions to make and goals to set. If they mention stress related to others' expectations, turn the discussion to the importance of paying attention to their own needs as well. That doesn't mean they should ignore the values or wishes of their parents and others, but they also need to reflect on what they are comfortable with and what their dreams are.

6. For closure, ask the group to comment on what the experience of this session was like. As they leave, remind them to keep sorting through their stressors. Doing that may help them to feel more in control of them. Dispose of the activity sheets or add them to the group folders.

Stress Boxes

Name _____

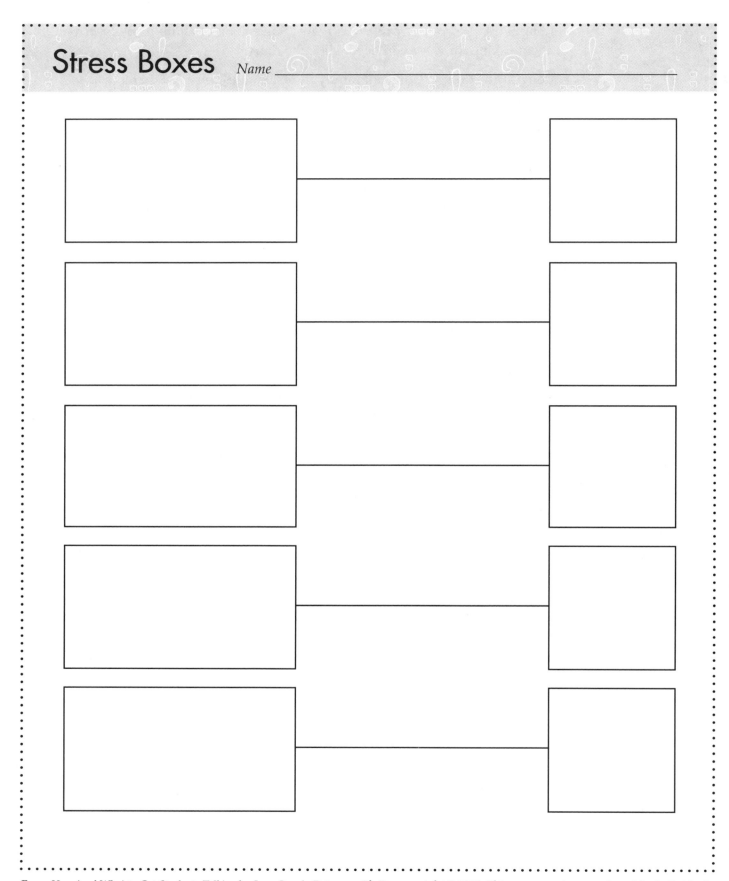

FOCUS **Stress**

Role Models and Strategies for Coping with Stress

Background

This session focuses on adult role models for coping with stress. As students consider how they have learned to cope, it might be helpful to offer the following thoughts about learning to cope effectively with stress:

- We are capable of managing stress and making situations less threatening.

- We cannot avoid all stressful situations, but we can learn to respond to stress in more healthful and effective ways.

- Learning to recognize our reactions to stress is one key to coping well.

- We can pause before reacting to stressful situations and think about our options and the consequences of what we might do.

- We can respond creatively and learn to see stressful situations as chances to learn about stress, ourselves, and our responses to stress—and grow personally.

- We can remember that fears about "catastrophes" are usually unfounded— they don't prove to be true.

- Instead of avoiding stressful situations, we can figure out ways to handle the challenges of life effectively and become more and more resilient.

- We can talk to our family, friends, teachers, coaches, or coworkers about stress and how we cope with it. A good listener can help us sort out our stress. We can even tell our listeners that we do not want advice. We just need someone to listen while we try to make sense of a situation.

- We can learn to relax, take time to rest, exercise, eat healthfully, and avoid caffeine. We can learn to cope without using eating, drinking, stimulants, or sleep aids as a coping strategy. When we feel good physically, we can cope with stress better.

Objectives

- Group members recognize that responses to stress and coping strategies are often learned from adult role models.

- They discover that it is possible to learn new responses to stress and unlearn responses that have become bad habits.

Suggestions
....

1. Introduce the idea that we learn how to cope with stress from important people in our lives who model coping behaviors. Some are better models for us than others. Ask the group to list on paper the significant adults in their lives and then briefly describe how each deals with stressful situations. Explain that these should be not only adults they like and respect, but *any* adult who plays an important role in their lives. Encourage the group to share their lists and descriptions.

2. Ask students to list three ways they can tell that they are stressed (for example, feelings, physical changes, behaviors). Invite them to share these.

3. Invite comparisons between their coping styles and those of the adults in their lives. Ask questions like the following:

   ~ How do your typical responses compare with the adults' responses?

   ~ How does your coping style compare to the style of the adult you know best?

   ~ How well do the adults' coping strategies work? How well do yours work for you? Are they effective?

   ~ Has your way of reacting to stress ever made a situation worse?

4. Turn the focus to some specifics of how group members respond to stress. Ask questions like the following:

   ~ How do you express anger or frustration or other strong emotions? How good are you at talking about anger or frustration or sadness? (Encourage them to see feelings as "making sense," given the circumstances. We can learn through experience how to express feelings so that they do not make situations worse or hurt ourselves or others.)

   ~ How much do you feel you must always stay in control, be rational, and stay even-tempered? If control and calmness are your ideal, how does it feel when you are stressed?

   ~ How many of you have someone to talk with about stress? Would any of you be willing to tell us who that is? (Then perhaps tally the number who mentioned friends, parents, a counselor, sibling, or other confidants.) How often are you able to do that? What is that like to talk about stress?

   ~ If your way of coping isn't working well, what different ways could you try for relieving stress? What might happen if you responded to stress in that new way?

5. Invite the group to share successful coping strategies. Ask, "When you find yourself in a stressful situation, how do you help yourself to feel okay? What do you do to stay clear-headed? How long do you usually stay upset?"

6. Invite members to tell how they respond when others around them are stressed. You might remark that people who are upset usually do not want to be "fixed"; they just want to be listened to. Listening to people can help their stress to dissipate.

7. Demonstrate how stress can build by shaking a can of soda. Ask the group what would happen if you opened the can now (Warning: Don't open it!). Invite students to comment about that metaphor for coping with stress. Ask them to raise a hand if that metaphor applies to them—that is, if they tend to let their stress build up to dangerous levels. Then ask how they can avoid an "explosion." (Talking about stress and sorting it out are some ways that can help.)

8. Lead the group in a simple relaxation exercise, or invite someone in the school or community to visit your group for this purpose. (Be aware that some parents might object to your doing that, so it would be wise to ask parental permission, explaining what the process will be.)

9. For closure, ask one or more volunteers to summarize what has been helpful in the session. If appropriate, commend the group for their honesty and thoughtfulness. Wish them "good coping" over the next several days, and encourage them to observe their own and others' responses to stress.

FOCUS **Stress**

Is It Harder to Be an Adolescent Today?

Background

Is it true, as some say, that many of today's children and teens are spoiled by a "soft life" and have a sense of entitlement? Perhaps—but consider the enormous numbers who live in poverty, in blighted urban or rural areas, in abusive and dysfunctional families. Consider, too, the changes related to family structure, geographic mobility and shallow roots, not living near extended family, danger- and fear-saturated news, advertising on prime-time television related to alcohol and prescription drugs and television shows and movies depicting drug use, insecure economic circumstances, military deployment, online dangers, societal and family violence, addiction, the impact of media on behavior, and the continual bombardment of information from many sources. Consider also how quickly change happens. It is possible that adolescents today are stronger and more resilient than any preceding generation because of all they must deal with and adapt to.

This session gives adolescents a chance to explore the validity of that claim of strength and resilience. Do they have more to deal with than their parents or grandparents did when they were young? Can preceding generations even begin to imagine what it is like to be a middle school or high school student today? Can teens apply the same strategies their parents used to survive their adolescence, or are these strategies no longer appropriate or effective? A discussion generated by these questions can be empowering for adolescents.

This session is not meant to promote a "poor us" attitude in a group. It can, however, be another opportunity for group members to gain skills in articulating feelings and concerns and to shed new light on how young people are faring today, whether or not circumstances are worse than they were in the past. Seeing themselves as strong for what they are accomplishing in stressful times might help students to feel confident and positive. There will be no "right" or "wrong" in this discussion, and as the facilitator, you should try to avoid a "yes, but . . ." attitude.

Objectives

- Group members are reminded that growing up today is different from growing up in their parents' or grandparents' generations.
- They learn to articulate the stresses in their lives and consider them in the context of this decade.

Suggestions

1. Introduce the topic by asking, "Have you ever been accused of being lazy, being spoiled, taking things for granted, or having an easy life compared to your parents or grandparents when they were your age? Has any adult told you that your adolescent life is more difficult than theirs was?" Then brainstorm ways this decade is different from preceding decades, in regard to being an adolescent. List responses on the board or a large sheet of paper. Ask, "What makes life today easier? more difficult? just different?"

2. Ask, "What are your parents' hopes for you?" After members report, encourage the group to consider whether each generation's adults look to their children to achieve what they did not in school, relationships, marriage, and career.

3. If your group includes individuals who do not have economic or other advantages, ask questions like those below the note. These questions are appropriate for others as well.

   NOTE: If the group has not developed sufficient trust, you might choose to read the third section below as a series of statements rather than questions (altering the beginning to "Several of you might be . . ."). This approach will affirm group members collectively as hard-working and responsible. Then invite students to comment on the list.

   ~ How has your life been affected by recent changes in our society? (Mention some ideas from the background information if they aren't mentioned spontaneously.)

   ~ How do you feel you compare with your parents' generation in personal strength? wisdom? the ability to deal with stress?

   ~ How many of you are working hard at jobs outside of school? caring for brothers or sisters? cooking for the family? doing family laundry and other housework? walking a long way to school? lacking private space? distracted from schoolwork by circumstances at home? contributing to family income? being a "parent" to someone in your family (or to your own children, if already a parent)? paying for all or most of your own personal expenses? dealing with your own or someone else's chronic illness, physical disability, or learning difficulty?

4. Invite the group to consider the social stresses of today's teens. Ask, "How are things different socially today from ten to twenty years ago?"

   In exploring this issue, it does not matter whether the group assesses preceding generations accurately. There is value simply in expressing their feelings about their lives. Avoid defending past generations or questioning group members' perceptions. The group may do that themselves. Remember that "process" (participating openly in a discussion) is more important than "product" (such as an accurate assessment, a conclusion, or agreement).

5. For closure, ask, "What thoughts and feelings did you have during this discussion?"

FOCUS Stress

Taking a Load Off

Background

This session gives group members a chance to talk about the safe havens in their lives—places and moments where they feel they can be themselves and be accepted unconditionally; where they do not feel judged or criticized; where they feel in control, comfortable, and peaceful; and where they can "take a load off." This is a low-resistance topic, and even the most cynical probably will feel free to comment.

Sharing a no-sharp-edges self, with no stiff defenses, in a supportive group atmosphere can contribute to an improved outlook on life. There may be individuals who do not feel they have a place to relax and be themselves. Perhaps they can feel appreciated unconditionally in your group. Your unconditional adult acceptance of them will be important.

One part of the suggested format for this session involves members' sharing places or circumstances where they feel "dumb" and where they feel "smart"—or "bad" and "good." Discovering what they have in common is likely to help them feel connected to others and comfortable with them.

Objectives

- Group members articulate positive feelings associated with places and circumstances where they feel especially comfortable.

- They let down their defenses and pay attention to their own and others' feelings, needs, and experiences.

- They learn that everyone feels "dumb" in some environments and "smart" in others.

Suggestions

NOTE: Depending on your group, it may be preferable to begin with suggestion #3 and then move to #1 and #2.

1. Ask students to think of a place where they feel peaceful, comfortable, and good—or of a person who helps them feel that they can unload their burdens and relax. Group members may enjoy drawing this place or person—continuing to add to the picture as the discussion goes along. Encourage them to share their thoughts or drawings, describing the environment or person in enough detail that the other group members can understand the importance of the person or place. They might talk about home, their room, a place in nature, school, their place of worship, teachers in general, one teacher in particular, one or both parents, a friend or friends, one or

more siblings, a special relative, a youth group leader, or even a pet, to name several possibilities. Invite those with pictures to show them to the group if that would be comfortable for them.

2. If some can think of no such place or person, ask them to describe an ideal, hoped-for, supercomfortable situation. You might also ask, "How have you learned to cope with not having such a place or person in your life?"

   If someone takes this opportunity to describe a chaotic, debilitating, or otherwise nonsupportive home environment, listen with receptive body language. You might softly respond with something like, "That's certainly a tough situation. I admire your strength and courage in dealing with it as well as you have." Your role is not to offer suggestions for improving the situation, since that is probably not in your power, but to acknowledge it genuinely and affirm strengths. Thank the student for sharing. You might say, "We appreciate knowing that you are dealing with difficult circumstances. We will remember that and think kind thoughts about you." At subsequent meetings, as the group gathers, ask how that student is doing.

3. Ask students to list on paper those situations or places where they feel "dumb" or inept. Encourage them to share by reading their lists. Next, ask them to list on paper those situations or places where they feel "smart" or confident, and encourage them to share these as well.

   It is assumed that even students who do not do well in school feel smart in other situations—perhaps with their friends, at home, or when involved in their areas of interest. If someone has trouble thinking of a strength, ask, "What kind of things do you do well?" (If needed, suggest video games, managing a website, reading and understanding directions for new technology, playing an instrument, babysitting, blogging, fishing, motocross, sports, skateboarding, cooking, mechanics, singing, farming, card playing, etc.) It may be comforting to hear that everyone experiences "feeling dumb" in some situations and that some who appear highly confident are, in fact, not always at ease.

4. For closure, ask one or more volunteers to summarize the session. What kinds of places or people did many in the group mention as comfortable? uncomfortable? What thoughts did they have as group members talked? How did it feel to talk about this topic?

Procrastination

Background

Procrastination! Parents and teachers of adolescents know what a problem it is. Adolescents themselves probably find it equally frustrating.

Many students have learned that they can delay and delay and then finish a project or paper at the eleventh hour. The results may or may not be favorable, since some students might not be able to deliver in the end. For some group members, procrastination in schoolwork may have more to do with being drained from other activities or responsibilities. It might also reflect perfectionism—the inability to begin something that may not be perfect, concern over not having the perfect idea to pursue, or fear of failure.

Most teens procrastinate at something—cleaning their room, doing homework, calling Grandma, sending a thank-you note, applying for a job, turning in next year's registration form, taking out the garbage. Perhaps it makes little difference most of the time, but procrastination can become a dangerous and self-destructive habit. It can cause stress and tension during the final, intense effort. It can also cause concern and frustration for those who worry about the procrastinator.

What can students do about procrastination? They can begin by talking about it in a caring, supportive, understanding group that probably contains a number of procrastinators. Even if students have not experienced any negative effects from procrastinating, talking about it with peers can provide insight and may even be enjoyable.

Objectives

• Group members look objectively at procrastination and how it affects them personally.

• They consider what might contribute to their procrastination and ways to do something about it—if it is a problem for them.

Suggestions

1. Introduce the topic by having the group say the word *procrastination* and then asking for a definition. (Possibility: Putting off or delaying until later, doing something that could/should be done at that time.) Then ask, "Are there any procrastinators in this group?" After possibly some joking denial, some—or all—group members will probably admit to procrastinating occasionally or often. Then ask, "What kinds of

things do you procrastinate about?" List their responses on the board or a large sheet of paper.

2. Ask the group, "How much does procrastination cause problems for you? (You might make this a scaling question: 'On a scale of 1 to 10 . . .') for other people in your life? what kinds of problems? How much should parents and teachers be concerned about it?" (As an option, provide the group with a simple sketch of a "procrastometer," with a dial containing the numbers 1 to 10. Hand out sheets of paper and invite students to draw a needle to the appropriate level of procrastination they feel they have. Underneath the "meter" they can list the kinds of things they procrastinate about—perhaps in rank order and perhaps in a box.)

3. Encourage the group to delve deeper into their procrastination. If they need help, ask questions like the following:

~ What kind of payoff is there for procrastination?

~ What do you do in other areas while procrastinating in one area (if anything)?

~ How efficient or inefficient are you when you do things at the last minute? (Be prepared for a wide range of answers here.)

~ How effective are you at these times?

~ What feelings do you have when procrastinating?

~ On a scale of 1 to 10, how well are you able to concentrate on what you need to do when you get down to action?

~ How has your procrastination changed in recent years—if at all?

4. Help the group to identify areas where they tend to procrastinate. Ask polling questions like the following:

~ How many of you procrastinate only in schoolwork? only with household chores? only with tasks that involve planning for the future, such as choosing classes, setting up summer activities, or filling out job or other applications? only when you need to ask for something? only when you need to talk with someone about something?

~ How many of you procrastinate in almost every area of your life?

~ How many of you procrastinate, but with no bad effects from it for anyone?

~ Which of you thinks you are the "best" procrastinator (procrastinates with everything) in this group? (Invite those who raise their hands to "make an argument" to convince the rest. Or, based on what they have heard in the discussion so far, have them line up along a wall in the order they think they should be in—from the "best" procrastinator to the "worst"—and justify their positions.)

5. Use questions like the following to help the group explore possible connections between procrastination and other issues. It is important here to recognize that levels of procrastination vary considerably, from mild to severe, from harmless to debilitating. Skip these questions if procrastination is not a significant problem for your group.

   ~ How much do other people worry about—and remind you of—the things you have to do? (If a lot, acknowledge that the others' worrying and reminding can also be habits.) Here again, you might make this a scaling question from 1 to 10.

   ~ Does anyone nag you about procrastination "all the time"? (If so:) How does this affect your relationship with that person, if at all?

   ~ Consider this thought: Procrastinators hold a certain power over others or situations—or they *want* such power. What do you think about this?

   ~ Do you think that procrastination is connected to stress? Do nonprocrastinators have more stress than procrastinators—or less? (Don't imply that there is a correct answer here.)

   This suggestion and #6 might be done while the group stands in rank order (see suggestion #4).

6. Ask the group to consider what would happen if they suddenly stopped procrastinating and did everything early—or at least without a last-minute rush. Invite them to explore this idea by asking questions like the following:

   ~ Who would be affected? Who would notice first?

   ~ How would your life change?

   ~ What would you lose?

   ~ What would you gain?

   ~ How would you feel?

7. For closure, ask the group to comment on what they heard and felt during this session.

FOCUS Stress

Substance Abuse

....

Background

Most adolescents probably know something about substance abuse; it may have been a topic in health classes and/or school assemblies, or they may have knowledge of the issue through personal life experiences. However, they may not have had the opportunity to discuss this vital subject in a group of peers led by a stable, caring, nonjudgmental adult. This session gives them a safe place to express their feelings and thoughts about substance abuse and to hear what others have to say.

Important

Prior to this session, be sure to familiarize yourself with the topic through research and consultation (such as talking with police about local trends in use of specific substances among youth and trends regarding drug use in general; talking with the school counselor about school issues related to substance use or about children of substance abusers). Contact organizations that deal regularly with those issues, and check out the resource section (page 279). You will need a reasonably good understanding of various substances and their effects in order to feel confident talking in depth about this topic and to avoid providing erroneous information. However, it is best if you do not present yourself as an expert (even if you are). Let group members teach you—first. Students will likely have a lively discussion if you avoid teaching or preaching. Even if you hear obvious misinformation (not unusual, unfortunately), delay correcting it until students ask for information. At the end of the discussion, you can gently ask if they'd be interested in hearing (or reading) pertinent information. If they do not show interest in such information, volunteer to bring in some resources "in the next few weeks" (being careful not to act as if they don't know anything). I have never had a group, regardless of individual circumstances, resist this, even though they might not express much interest outwardly. Most have been eager for information—including those already using illegal substances heavily.

As with all topics in this book, the fundamental goal is discussion—for example, making connections, learning how to communicate effectively, gaining confidence, becoming more self-aware. The value lies in process, not product—the discussion itself, not any particular content. This session may justifiably and effectively avoid being informational.

If your group has been created to deal specifically with substance abuse problems, most or all of the sessions in this book are appropriate, since the challenges of adolescence are closely linked with substance use, and developmental support may actually be the key to prevention or reduction of substance use. Therefore, do not assume that having a group of users/abusers means that you must talk about substances much or at all. With that said, however, for this session you may want to gather specific information about substance abuse to distribute and to be prepared for a detailed discussion.

Also consider inviting a counselor or administrator from a local substance abuse treatment center to visit your group. Suggest that he or she explain what treatment involves (it usually includes dealing with family issues and personal problems), how addiction affects adolescents, and current drug trends. Do not assume that students are well informed on this topic.

Objectives

- Group members learn how some of their peers feel about substance use and abuse.

- They articulate their feelings about substance use and abuse occurring in their age group.

Suggestions

1. Begin by taking a one-down (in contrast to an expert-teacher one-up) posture and asking the group to *teach you* about substance use and abuse in their age group. What can they tell you about available substances, numbers of peers and substances involved, parties, behavior (especially dangerous behavior), frequency of use, types of groups involved, and parental attitudes about alcohol, tobacco and e-cigarettes, and other drug use? What do they know about particular substances currently popular among teens? Expect some bravado and claims of (and actual) expertise during this part of the discussion, but also expect that some group members may have very little knowledge in any of these areas. Remember that any evaluative comment moves you away from the one-down position.

   Remind the group of the need for confidentiality; some individuals may share information that could be damaging if shared outside of the group. Encourage them not to name names in the discussion.

2. Ask the group some process questions: "How does it feel to talk about this very serious topic here? How do you feel about the information you have just shared or heard?" After hearing their feelings, continue the discussion with questions like the following:

   ~ How much pressure to use alcohol or other drugs is there in your social group? (Perhaps on a scale of 1 to 10, with 10 representing great pressure.)

   ~ If there is pressure, and you are not using, how do you feel about not using alcohol or other drugs? (Perhaps on a scale of 1 to 10 , with 10 being "good," 5 being "mixed feelings," and 1 being "very uncomfortable.")

~ Without naming names (here and in the next two questions), do you know peers whose substance abuse is interfering with schoolwork and other aspects of their lives? (Raising hands might suffice here and for the next two questions as well.)

~ Do you know of anyone who has died, or almost died, from alcohol or other drug abuse?

~ Do you know anyone who has been in treatment for substance abuse?

~ Do all adolescents have the potential to become involved with alcohol and other drugs? to become addicted?

~ What motivates someone to use alcohol or other drugs? (Rebellion and the pressure to fit in will likely be mentioned. Be aware that people often "self-medicate" with drugs to deal with problems such as depression, even though alcohol is a depressant. Suggest that the reasons for drug use may be complex—including, for example, insecurities, feeling overwhelmed, having substances available, role models, and lack of adult presence at home or at parties.)

3. Instruct the group to consider how their families view the use of alcohol and other drugs. Remind them of confidentiality guidelines. Ask questions like the following:

~ How does your family feel about alcohol use? other drug use? (If parent and teen attitudes differ, ask, "How do you feel about that?") How much do you talk with your parents about drug use? (Perhaps on a scale of 1 to 10, with 10 being "very often.")

~ What do you know about alcoholism? addiction? particular drugs of abuse? misuse of prescription medicine? (Ask students what they know about other drug- or substance-related concerns, including about nicotine and caffeine.)

~ What kinds of addictions, other than to substances, are there? (Examples: eating, not eating, exercising, smoking, chewing tobacco, using inhalants, drinking coffee or caffeinated soft drinks, video games, self-injury/self-mutilation, gambling, shopping, pornography, sex.) How vulnerable, in personality and/or genetic makeup, to becoming addicted (to *anything*) do you think you might be? (Perhaps on a scale of 1 to 10, with 10 being "very vulnerable.")

4. Ask about their personal "rules" regarding alcohol, nicotine, and other drugs. Do they make a distinction between alcohol and other drugs? Should they? Should society?

5. When would you be concerned that you might be addicted to alcohol or other drugs? (Examples: Using/drinking more than planned; no memory of the use later; preoccupation with finding, planning, and paying for substance use; family or friends being concerned; using alone; being worried about addiction having a negative effect on work, school, relationships, health.)

6. For closure, ask a volunteer to summarize the discussion, with special emphasis on the information shared in suggestion #1. Express your hope that group members will make wise choices with regard to substance use.

Stress

Stuck!

When working with students individually and in small groups, the notion of "developmental stuckness" usually resonates across age and ability levels. I use the word *stuck* when I hear that someone is unable to move forward—with looking for a summer job, trying to make a decision, applying to colleges, making an overdue life change, letting go of anger or a grudge, apologizing for hurting someone's feelings, stopping a harmful behavior, or asking directly for help at home or at school. "Stuckness" can refer, in terms of development, to not knowing who we are, where we're going, how to be more self-reliant, or how to progress toward increasingly more mature relationships.

Peers may not view students who are successful in school as struggling with anything—and certainly not as struggling with developmental hurdles. However, "successful" students may have no other identity than "performer" or "winner." They may be frustrated with not having clear career direction in spite of academic success, may regret a decision they made based on family expectations or simply because they wanted to be done with deciding, may be upset with themselves for not taking time to relax and be social, or may wish they weren't so overscheduled with school activities. They may feel vague sadness, weariness, "stuckness," and stress about any of these.

Students who are not as successful in school, and who may struggle even to come to school every day, may also feel stuck—in behaviors they wish they could stop, in relationships they don't feel good about, in bad feelings about personal losses or adults who let them down, or in a lack of direction. They may feel overwhelmed by situations and contexts beyond their control or tensely resistant to what others tell them they should be or do. They, too, might be experiencing developmental impasse. Who are they? Where are they making progress? in social relationships? in becoming increasingly independent? They may feel misunderstood, unsupported, isolated—and stuck.

Regardless of the ability levels, personalities, and school and home contexts of your group members, students may unexpectedly find common ground around the concept of "stuckness." Even if they appear to be fairly similar, they may discover that they feel stuck differently.

- Group members articulate where they feel impasse.
- They find common ground as they explore and explain feelings of "stuckness."
- They consider what is probably in their control and not in their control regarding their own "stuckness."
- They acknowledge that feeling stuck can be stressful.

Suggestions

1. Invite group members to describe areas they associate with feeling stuck, with wishing they could make a change of some kind, with wishing they could move ahead, or with wishing things could be different. If examples are not forthcoming, perhaps ask the group to consider life in general, school classes or activities, jobs, social relationships, procrastination, projects, what they are practicing or learning to do, teachers, parents, siblings, peers, sadness, needs, maturity, skills, or performance.

   After each speaks, you might say, quietly, "I can hear your 'stuck' feeling," or "I can hear your frustration (or sadness, pessimism, loneliness, disappointment)," or "That sounds frustrating," or "Can anyone relate to what was just described?"

   Ask students what themes they heard about "stuckness":

   ~ Were any examples mentioned by more than one person in the group?

   ~ What feelings did you have when others spoke about their "stuckness"?

   ~ Based on what you've heard here, what would you say if an adult asked you to explain teen "stuckness"?

   Ask each group member, "What do you wish someone would say to you if you were to mention that you feel stuck?" (Instead of advice, they might want validation: "It sounds as if you've got a big hurdle in front of you.") You might say, "We probably don't want or expect to get advice, but we want someone to listen and 'get' what we're feeling."

   Ask each member, "When do you expect to put your stuckness behind you?" If all or most express doubt that they will ever be "unstuck," you might say, "Feeling stuck probably seems like it'll last forever, but rest assured, nothing stays exactly the same, and I expect that you'll be able to unstick yourself eventually—or even soon. I can hear that you feel pessimistic about that today."

2. Ask, "What might you offer to someone who feels stuck in some area of life?" Here, suggestions become important communication—and may reflect empathy. Group members' simply offering supportive statements may be more valuable than advice. ("That probably feels like a big hurdle," or "Maybe that goes with being our age— something we just have to get through," or "Maybe we'll all finally figure out what to do.") Some might simply listen quietly and nod. Ask if they can remember a supportive comment someone said to them lately or in the past.

3. Ask the group these questions:

~ Where do you feel you're making good progress with growing up (for example, in knowing who you are, in having some sense of what you might be doing as an adult someday, in having good relationships or a special relationship, in being fairly independent even if living at home)?

~ How independent are most kids your age? How independent are the peers you know well?

~ How clear do you think most kids your age are about where they'd like to be in the future—or what they'd like to be doing? What do you see for yourself in the future?

~ In what areas of life do you wish you were further ahead right now?

~ What do you wish adults understood about you? people your age? your struggles? What do you wish your peers understood about you?

~ What do you think *most* kids your age struggle with?

4. Then go around the group, asking each student these questions:

~ What is one thing that is in your power to change that can help you feel less stuck?

~ What would be a small step in that direction?

~ When could you take the first step? How might you feel after taking this step?

~ Who would probably notice first if you took that step toward change?

~ How do you think this person would react?

5. For closure, ask what the group felt during this discussion. Ask what the average level of "stuckness" seems to be for their group, based on the discussion. What do they have in common? What are the biggest differences among them? Ask for a volunteer to define "stuckness" now that the discussion is done.

FOCUS

···

Identity

FOCUS Identity

General Background

"I don't know who I am." Spoken aloud or left unsaid, this is a common thought among people of all ages, especially adolescents. Developing a personal identity is an important part of adolescence.

Teens learn who they are through hearing what others say about them, identifying what they feel and value, and thinking about themselves in relationship with others. However, they often get mixed messages—from parents, peers, teachers, and others. Sometimes they receive mostly negative messages and let these define them. Adults who model for them how to relate to others may not be good models, and the adolescents in turn may behave in ways that prevent their getting positive messages about themselves. Depending on who their friends are, their gender, and their family experiences, teens may have little opportunity to talk about their doubts, fears, and hopes. They also might be unable to articulate such thoughts and feelings, not having had much practice with either family or friends.

Confusion and doubt about themselves can lead to tension, inappropriate behavior, and acting out. Frustration about an unwanted social identity or lack of clear identity can cause trouble in relationships, another adolescent challenge. Not knowing the self can interfere with finding career direction, a developmental hurdle.

Group discussions give teens an opportunity to gain skill in articulating thoughts and feelings. As you work with your group, remind them of how important this skill can be, both for their lives today and for the future. Talking about what is "inside" is good practice for quality friendships, for getting along with coworkers, for marriage and partnerships, and for being parents. Explain that sharing their thoughts and feelings in a group can also help them discover what they have in common and to understand that they are not as different or as "weird" as they might believe. Finding out what they think and feel through talking moves them along in the process of self-discovery. Group discussions can help them answer a vital question: "Who am I?"

General Objectives

- Group members make progress in defining themselves as individuals, separate from (but still connected to) family and friends.

- They learn to articulate thoughts and feelings.

- They discover what they think and feel by sharing thoughts and feelings with the group and receiving feedback from the group.

- Feedback from the group helps them clarify and evaluate their opinions, beliefs, and values.

- They apply what others share to their own self-assessment.

FOCUS Identity

Personal Strengths and Limitations

- Through articulating personal strengths, group members affirm their capabilities and potentially enhance their self-esteem indirectly.

- By sharing their personal limitations with peers and getting feedback, they learn that others have weaknesses, too, and that having limitations is not shameful.

- They increase their self-awareness and ability to assess themselves realistically.

- They learn to value their unique strengths and to see that there are many kinds of valuable personal characteristics.

- They learn that they do not have to apologize for either their strengths or their limitations.

Suggestions

1. Direct group members to list on paper their personal strengths. Tell them to think of the things they can "count on" or "have confidence in" or "trust" about themselves, both as they interact with others and when they are alone. You might also ask, "What do you think other people value in you?" Model this activity by sharing your own list and/or by offering suggestions from this list.

organized	good listener	poised, not easily "rattled"
responsible	kind	good with animals
compassionate	energetic	common sense
personable	even-tempered	intelligent
athletic	eager learner	good with plants
helpful	good dancer	uncluttered, orderly with belongings
good sense of humor	not moody	know myself well
good friend	patient	witty, good sense of humor
mechanical skills	verbal or mathematical skills	strong physically
physically fit	musical or other artistic talent	strong emotionally
good with elderly people and/or young children	good with technology	good cook
optimism	good at blogging	
hard worker		

Tell the students that recognizing their capabilities is good practice for the future when they will need to speak or write about themselves with confidence during job interviews, on scholarship and award application forms, and on college entrance essays.

2. Encourage group members to share their lists.

<table>
<tr><td>Important</td><td>Adolescents usually are willing to share their lists, even when the group is just beginning and before it has developed a good level of trust and comfort. Contributions help to build a group. However, be sure to remind group members that they always have the right to pass on any aspect of group meetings they feel uncomfortable responding to.</td></tr>
</table>

3. Direct group members to list on paper their personal limitations. Tell them to think of the characteristics, habits, and "flaws" that interfere with things they want to do; that cause problems in their relationships; that keep them from being their best. Model this activity by sharing your own list and/or by offering suggestions, such as the following:

procrastinator	bad-tempered	bossy	perfectionistic
physically unfit	a gossip	disorganized	arrogant
poor math skills	impatient	irresponsible	lazy
poor handwriting	messy	mean	suspicious
little common sense	a poor listener	critical	deceitful
can't follow directions that aren't in writing	naive	easily depressed	manipulative
	blame others	poor sense of direction	moody

4. Encourage group members to share their lists.

5. Don't be surprised if the group lists more limitations than strengths. If time permits, and if limitations did indeed dominate, invite the group to comment on this.

6. For closure, ask which strengths and limitations seem to be common in the group. Ask, "How did it feel to talk about your strengths and limitations with the other group members?" Dispose of the sheets or add them to the group folders.

FOCUS Identity

Three Selves

This session is best placed after the group has met enough times to give credibility to comments about the strengths of those who have difficulty identifying any.

Objectives

- Group members appraise themselves in the presence of supportive peers.

- They thoughtfully compare their real, their disliked, and their ideal selves and assess how different or similar these three selves are.

- They receive helpful feedback from the group and learn how others see them.

Suggestions

1. Have the group complete the "My Three Selves" activity sheet (page 55). Tell them that they may use adjectives, descriptive phrases, or sentences to describe themselves.

2. Encourage them to share their lists.

3. Ask the group to study their lists. Ask questions like the following:

   ~ Are your lists for "The Way I Really Am" and "How I'd Like to Be" fairly similar or very different?

   ~ How comfortably can you live with the parts of yourself you don't like (on a scale of 1 to 10)? (Other possibilities: What would you like to change about yourself? How could those changes affect your life? Who do you know who has the undesirable traits you listed? Encourage descriptions, not names.)

   ~ Are the traits listed under "How I'd Like to Be" possible for you? For those that are possible, what can you do to move in those directions?

   ~ To what extent can you accept the qualities you noted as your "real" self? What would help you accept who you are at this point in your life?

4. As individuals read their descriptors, encourage others to comment. Can they offer feedback, support, and validation for what has been listed? Encourage them to give feedback for positive attributes. If someone's lists are entirely negative, invite group members to give feedback that shows appreciation for some positive aspect of the person that has been demonstrated in the group.

5. For closure, ask the group to comment on what was valuable about this session. If appropriate, commend the group for their honesty and supportive comments. Dispose of the sheets or add them to the group folders.

My Three Selves

Name: _____

List adjectives, phrases, or sentences under each heading.

THE WAY I REALLY AM

1. _____
2. _____
3. _____
4. _____
5. _____

THE SELF I DON'T LIKE

1. _____
2. _____
3. _____
4. _____
5. _____

HOW I'D LIKE TO BE

1. _____
2. _____
3. _____
4. _____
5. _____

The two lists that are most alike for me are

_____

_____

If I could "try on" a new image, I think I would like to be

_____

_____

FOCUS Identity

....

Does the Stereotype Fit?

Objectives

....

- Group members learn about the problems, limitations, and dangers of thinking in stereotypes.

- They learn about themselves by considering how they do and do not fit stereotypes that are applied to them.

Suggestions

....

1. Especially if group members are relatively young, find out if they understand the word *stereotype*. Ask for volunteers to define the term and give examples. If necessary, define it for them. You might say, "A stereotype is an idea that many people have about a particular group of people. It is a way of describing the people in that group without really knowing anything about them as individuals. For example, you may have heard that rich people are snobs or poor people are lazy. These are stereotypes. They affect the way we think about rich people and poor people. They affect the way we treat them. Stereotypes also affect the way we think about ourselves, especially when we are aware that others are stereotyping us."

2. Ask the group to think about how they might be stereotyped at school. If needed, provide a few examples to get them started: "jock/athlete," "nerd," "pretty, not smart," "underachiever," "rebel," "brain," "country," "only child," "doctor's kid," "snob," "extra," "rich," "skater," "bully," "Christian," "Muslim," "liberal," "conservative," "LGBTQ," "popular." (You might even ask them to write various labels on an index card or small sheet of paper.) Terms for various social groups at school are likely to change from time to time. Encourage the group to think of some labels that are new (such as those related to drug use, ethnicity, culture, interests, or religion). To model, share a stereotype that has been used to describe you at some point in your life.

3. Encourage group members to share how they think they might be stereotyped by others, either positively or negatively. Ask them how they fit each stereotype— and how they do not. Then invite the rest of the group to comment about those stereotypes. This interaction may be the most complex part of the meeting. Do not hurry it. Encourage the students to ask questions as each person shares and to make discreet, supportive comments. Trust that adolescents are interested in the opinions of others.

4. Continue by asking one or more of the following questions. You may want to move around the group in order, so that each member has a chance to be heard.

   ~ What do you wish people understood about you?

   ~ What do you wish your classmates understood about you?

   ~ What do you wish your teachers understood about you?

   ~ What do you wish your parents understood about you?

   If time permits and the group seems interested, invite discussion about feeling misunderstood.

5. For closure, either summarize the session yourself or invite members to tell what they learned or felt during the discussion. Ask if anything they heard surprised them or caused them to change their thinking in some way.

FOCUS Identity

Going to Extremes

Objectives

- Group members learn that most people—even those who seem the most secure—are somewhat distressed about being *too* something.

- They learn to articulate their own concerns about being *too* something.

- They hear how others view their *too* characteristics and learn that others may even consider some to be advantageous.

Suggestions

1. Usually responses need no modeling from the facilitator. However, in case the *too* concept is not easily grasped by someone in the group, you might introduce the topic by sharing a *too* characteristic of your own. Perhaps you believe that you are too stressed, disorganized, impatient, restless, or nice.

2. Invite the group to share their self-perceptions regarding *being* too much or too little in some way, or *doing* too much or too little in some area. Or have the group list their extremes on a small sheet of paper or index card and then share them. Complete this suggestion before moving on to #3. On the board or a large sheet of paper, list some examples if group members find the task challenging:

shy	talkative	active	tense	excitable
loud	clumsy	busy	intense	emotional
lazy	easily distracted	moody	nice	easily upset
lonely	people-pleasing	worried	pessimistic	driven
nervous	sensitive	people-oriented	rebellious	depressed

3. Ask the group how these characteristics may, in fact, have some advantages. Give them several seconds to ponder that possibility, and then move around the circle, focusing on each member's earlier comments.

   For example, shyness might be perceived as "mysterious," a positive and intriguing trait that some people find attractive. Shy people may be more comfortable alone than extroverts are. They might be able to work more quietly and effectively on a long-term project than a highly social person can. They probably think before acting. They may be better at finding strength from within, instead of relying on others to help them through hard times. Ask how many consider themselves to be shy. Reframing (putting a supposed negative inside a positive frame) shyness may be quite important to quiet group members.

4. If group members listed their qualities on paper, and if they feel comfortable sharing what they wrote, have them exchange lists with the person sitting next to them. Have each student write or comment on the possible advantages of the other person's extremes.

5. For closure, ask for summary statements about *too* characteristics and other bothersome traits. Ask (one question at a time), "What did you learn from each other today? What are some things you have in common? How did it feel to discuss being '*too* . . .'?"

FOCUS Identity

. . . .

Learning Styles

Background
. . . .

Some people prefer to learn by listening, some by seeing, some by doing. Some like information to be presented in order and in a structured environment, while others seem to thrive in an active, richly textured, unpredictable environment, where information and stimulation come from many directions at once. Some students need to like the teacher in order to do well; for others, this is irrelevant to their learning. Some students are easily distracted; others focus easily. Some sit in the front; others head for the back. Some like group work, and others prefer to work alone.

When teaching style and learning style are at odds, problems may result. However, both the teacher and the student may be unaware that some of the problems may be related to their differing styles. Similarly, when teaching and learning styles are a match, good progress is likely. Teachers are encouraged to teach to different learning styles. Nevertheless, some teachers teach largely in their own preferred style. They need to be encouraged to teach in their unpreferred modes, as well, in order to accommodate preferred learning styles that differ from their own.

It is a common assumption that disciplinary referrals are often kinesthetic learners, referred by nonkinesthetic teachers, yet few teachers examine whether an adjustment in teaching method might improve the situation. Long-term projects and written work are often difficult for such students, especially when hyperactivity also is an issue. Yet these same troublesome kinesthetic learners might nevertheless enjoy school, have good health, and do well in life as adults.

This session can help students understand why they appreciate some teachers more than others, and why they might be having trouble in some classes. After becoming informed, they might become more assertive in asking teachers to modify teaching methods in specific ways in order to help students like them. Middle schoolers might be reluctant to approach teachers themselves; nonetheless, new understanding of their learning preferences might help them make sense of their discomfort in certain classrooms.

You may want to keep a record of the various learning styles that become apparent through the continuum exercise used in this session. Such information can be valuable in advocating for changes in the classroom for underachieving students if you are a school counselor or if you consult with a school counselor. Another benefit of self-awareness is that even young students can figure out ways to adjust to teachers' varying teaching styles. Perhaps the group can brainstorm suggestions.

Objectives

- Group members learn about various teaching and learning styles.

- They become more aware of their own preferred learning styles.

- They learn why they may experience difficulties in certain learning situations and consider ways to adapt to styles different from their preferred style.

Suggestions

1. Introduce the topic with some ideas from the background information. Point out that differing teacher and student styles sometimes cause problems in learning. Explain that learning style can also affect which courses students choose, which teachers are preferred, and which kinds of assignments are easiest to accomplish.

2. Have the group line up along one wall of the room (or form an angle at one corner, with the walls being the two sides). Tell students they have just formed a continuum (a line that can show how something differs in degrees—like a nondigital thermometer). Designate one end of the continuum as 10, "a lot," and the other end as 0, "not at all." Explain that you are going to read a series of statements about learning styles. As you read each statement, students should physically move to the point on the continuum that best represents where they feel they belong.

3. Read aloud statements from "Learning Styles: A Continuum Activity" (page 63). (Choose items that are developmentally appropriate for your group.) After each statement, and after group members have found their places on the continuum, select two to four members to explain why they placed themselves where they did. Be sure to ask a variety of students to report during the activity. If time is short, perhaps select only half of the statements for this activity. (NOTE: This kind of activity needs to move along quickly, and it is best not to spend too long considering individual statements. Hearing and considering each statement and then moving physically likely enhance self-awareness even without discussion, although this activity can also provide a valuable opportunity to develop skills in verbal expression.)

4. For closure, ask the students if they can make a summary statement about themselves as a group. (You might routinely make a quick comment after hearing student explanations of their placement on the continuum. For example, "As a group, you clearly prefer to learn by seeing things.") If they need help, ask questions like the following:

   ~ Were there some preferred learning styles that most of our group had— where most of you bunched together high on the continuum?

   ~ Would you say that, as a group, most of you like teachers and classes to be quite orderly or not so orderly?

   ~ As a group, do you seem to prefer to learn in a variety of ways (listening, seeing, doing) or primarily in one way? (If the latter:) In which way?

   ~ (If #16 was part of your activity:) As a group, are you easily distracted?

~ (If #9 and #20 were in your activity:) As a group, do you prefer working in groups or working alone?

~ Think about the three main preferences for how you like to get information: raise your hand if you learn best by doing . . . by seeing . . . by listening.

It may be interesting to ask how your management of the group suits their individual or group styles. Is there anything you as leader should/could try to do differently? Finally, you might encourage group members to try to strengthen their unpreferred modes. The more flexible they are, the easier it will be for them to feel comfortable and learn in all types of educational and employment situations.

Learning Styles: A Continuum Activity

1. I prefer to learn by doing—building, measuring, drawing, mixing, or fixing—instead of by listening or viewing.

2. I prefer to learn by listening—teacher presentations, speakers, or audio recordings.

3. I prefer to learn by seeing—written material, on-screen material, videos, interactive whiteboard demonstrations.

4. I need to write something down to remember it.

5. I like to know what to expect in a class. I like having a routine.

6. I like to know *why* I need to learn something in a class.

7. I prefer teachers and classes that are highly organized.

8. I like classrooms that have many interesting and colorful things on the walls and elsewhere around the room.

9. I like to work in groups.

10. I like to argue and debate about things in class.

11. I can stand having information coming at me from many directions at once.

12. I like to have my teachers know me well.

13. I like to have teachers call on me and give me attention in class.

14. I learn best when I like the teacher, and I don't do as well when I don't like the teacher.

15. I easily accept authority in others.

16. I am easily distracted.

17. I like to sit in the front of a class.

18. I feel anxious and agitated when a class is disorderly.

19. I like to show what I know in class.

20. I prefer to work alone.

21. I can work and concentrate in the midst of a lot of noise or activity.

22. I try to do well in school because I don't like to be criticized.

23. Most of my teachers like me.

FOCUS Identity

What Defines Us?

Adolescents receive many messages about themselves. Comments from parents, siblings, extended family, friends, teachers, coaches, peers who like them, peers who don't like them, doctors, counselors, psychologists, various media, and any number of other sources may be received as personal definitions. Test scores and grades also "talk." Not all of these messages are positive and encouraging. Loving, nurturing, and patient parents send messages to their children—but so do angry, preoccupied, frustrated, alienated, competitive, perfectionistic, abusive, or neglectful parents. Negative messages may leave permanent scars.

This discussion provides an opportunity for teens to think about who or what has defined them. Other group members and a leader who listen without judgment can send positive, supportive messages that might contribute to a new or altered definition for some.

Objectives

- Group members learn that messages from significant people in their lives have the potential to affect how they see themselves, for better or for worse.

- Within the supportive group environment, they examine messages that have had an impact on how they see themselves.

Suggestions

1. Introduce the session with ideas from the background information. Ask the group to think about individuals in their lives who have made either positive or negative comments that have affected them—their parents, siblings, other relatives, teachers, coaches, friends, enemies, competitors, and so on. Be patient as they think about this request.

2. Invite the group to write down the nicest, most positive message(s) anyone has ever given them. They might also write down the most powerfully negative message(s) anyone has ever given them.

3. Encourage the group to share what they have written. Respect the wishes of those who may prefer not to share the negative messages. Throughout, simply listen and acknowledge their messages with a nod and a smile (or a wince). Or you might contribute brief comments such as "Yes, that's positive!" or "Wow. That must have hurt!"

4. When this discussion slows down, ask the group to think about the negative messages. Ask, "How have those messages affected you? How could you hear such messages less powerfully now? What could you say to yourself now? (Or) How have you managed not to let them be part of your personal definition?"

5. On separate sheets of paper or index cards, write each of the following strengths/limitations: common sense, creative, insightful, good ideas, good with words, mathematical, artistic, musical, social, mechanical, sensitive to others, leader, and strong in life—no matter what. Spread the cards out on the floor and have group members stand in a circle around them. Ask each member, in turn, to list up to three that are strengths for them. Then ask each member to give at least one that is definitely not a strength. After everyone has reported strengths and limitations, ask group members to give one strength they depend on and are glad they have. Where, especially, does it help them? This should give group members an opportunity to affirm one or more strengths and also to discover that everyone has limitations.

6. For closure, ask for a volunteer to summarize the main point(s) of this session. Is there anything group members will continue to think about in the days and weeks ahead? What were some feelings they had during the session? Perhaps they could each make one brief statement that would be at least a *part* of their personal definition at this point in life (for example, "I am a person who is strong in life, no matter what, and has a lot of common sense").

FOCUS Identity
Should Test Scores Define Us?

Peer conversation that centers on grades and test scores quickly becomes narrow and competitive. But students may feel somewhat defined by these subjects in a competitive academic environment. In school and probably elsewhere, academic achievements are seen as "good." For students who do not function well in the classroom, the definition they may sense from grades and scores is "I am not good." If they are known to have a high level of intellectual ability, they might be called underachievers, so defined because of their grades.

The more others emphasize test scores, the more students become preoccupied with them. However, no single test can assess the broad range of traits and abilities that help make a person appreciated, productive, or even well-known. All tests are imperfect measurers and may be affected by any number of factors, including test anxiety, fatigue, stress, low verbal skills, learning differences, room temperature, distracting sounds, attitude toward test-taking, cultural experiences, and cultural values that do not embrace competitively displaying one's knowledge. A test score may also be affected by the gender and manner of the examiner to some extent.

However, tests can indeed be valuable in indicating who might benefit from special programs. Scores can give decision-makers reason to check out a student further. Great discrepancies among subtests might indicate potential for frustration in the classroom and can be used to determine where special help or curriculum modifications might be beneficial. Ability tests may identify highly able students who otherwise would be missed because of poor grades. Yet, while tests and grades have their place, and though both are here to stay, students should not let either define them. Test and other data need to be kept in perspective. It is important to acknowledge that teachers are human and may use subjective methods to grade students, especially when quantitative measures are not possible. They may also use differing performance criteria. For instance, some teachers reward creativity; some discourage it.

Objectives

• Group members put grades and test scores into proper perspective.

• They learn that no test is a perfect measure of anything, that grades are not perfect representations of what a student has learned, and that no one should be defined by either test scores or grades.

Suggestions

1. Ask, "What things in school can tell others who we are?" (Expect comments about school achievement, test scores, skills, talents, behavior, friends, and peers in general.) If appropriate, remind them that teachers are fallible, grading systems are imperfect, siblings and peers may have hidden agendas, some students do not test well, and even ability tests cannot accurately measure valuable strengths such as creativity, common sense, social skills, leadership, personal problem-solving ability, intuition, mechanical skills, artistic skills, or sensitivity to others. Emphasize that they should never let any person or number determine who they are and will be.

2. Ask questions about grades:

   ~ What are grades for?

   ~ What do they tell about a student? (Expect references to learning, intelligence, work ethic, class participation, attendance, cooperation, or ability in a certain area.)

   ~ If your school suddenly decided to stop giving grades, how would this affect your school performance?

3. Find out how students feel about group achievement tests that are given annually in schools, or the kind given to test aptitude for college (consider also the military aptitude tests that are often given in high schools). Ask the following:

   ~ How do you feel about _____ tests (whatever tests are given locally)?

   ~ What are those tests supposed to measure (what has been learned in the curriculum)?

   ~ What helps a student to do well on them?

   ~ What might affect performance on these tests? (Past course selection, verbal ability, feelings about tests, how much a student's parents and culture value tests, learning differences, poor small-motor skills, discomfort with computer-based testing, hyperactivity, atmosphere of the testing room, test anxiety, illness.)

4. Initiate a discussion about intelligence and testing in general. You may find it helpful to read one or more of the following statements. Or pass them out on individual slips of paper and have volunteers read them to the group. (Adjust vocabulary level, if necessary, for your group.)

   ~ A person does not have to be "brilliant" to be successful in life. In fact, those who are "comfortably bright" can do just about anything, career-wise, if they are motivated, persistent, emotionally stable, and able to figure out how the work world functions. There are many kinds of careers and jobs, and finding work that matches ability and interests can help a person feel satisfied.

   ~ Answers on tests do not usually show *how* a person thinks.

   ~ Working slowly on a test does not indicate a "slow mind." Students who take more time may, in fact, be able to consider each question in more ways than most other people can. A slow pace on a timed test can therefore result in a low score for someone even with high ability.

~ Most tests rely a lot on reading/verbal ability. A student's strengths might be in other areas. A disability can affect reading ability.

~ Intelligence and achievement tests usually do not measure creativity, leadership, ability to communicate, sensitivity to others, common sense, or the likelihood of having a satisfying life in the future. They also do not measure motivation, a strong work ethic, ability to work with others, and perseverance, which are important contributors to life success.

~ No single test should "define" anyone.

5. If appropriate for the grade and ability level of your group, explain that standardized achievement tests mostly measure two kinds of knowledge: verbal and mathematical. Parts of *ability* tests fall into the categories of verbal, quantitative, and spatial abilities. Grades usually reflect only a few of these abilities and may demonstrate knowledge, but not understanding. Various cultures value abilities differently from each other, and tests do not always test what a culture values highly and what would be seen as success in that culture. We need to keep "intelligence" in perspective and appreciate that a wide variety of abilities contribute to a healthy society.

6. For closure, ask each group member to say one sentence about what he or she learned about tests, and one sentence about why test-taking skills are important. Affirm, however, that there are many wonderful personal qualities that are not measured by tests, and therefore a test score should not be anyone's "total definition."

Identity

Giving Ourselves Permission

Background

This session works well with many age levels, as long as group members are capable of some abstract thinking. Participants can say as much or as little as they wish in reporting what they have checked on the activity sheet. This session also moves any group ahead in open sharing, since it is quite thorough, and many aspects of a person are revealed in just a few moments—safely. Finally, it is a potentially empowering exercise, since it clearly focuses on a person's own power to grant (or not grant) permission to the self.

If your opportunity to lead a particular group is limited to only a few sessions, this should definitely be among them, since it promotes group bonding.

Objectives

- Group members recognize that they are in charge of how they respond to their various environments.

- They become aware that they could perhaps enhance their lives by giving themselves permission to do, say, or experience more.

- They learn that there are many common limits that individuals place on themselves.

- They experience a sense of community within their group.

Suggestions

1. Hand out the "Giving Myself Permission" activity sheet (page 71). Explain that students may interpret each item however they wish.

   However, some teens may not be accustomed to thinking of "being selfish," "being angry," or "making mistakes" in anything but negative terms. You may want to point out that "being selfish" can mean taking care of important personal needs; "being angry" is better than "stuffing" anger and feeling sad instead; "making mistakes" is human—and a perfectly normal way to learn.

2. In this exercise, it is important for you to model for the group. Fill out the activity sheet yourself and read down your list, prefacing all or many of your items with, "I would like to give myself permission to . . ." in order to impress on them that it would be possible for you to make a change if you had the necessary courage and will. Limit your checked items to ten, in order not to take up too much group time. Checking ten will also give students permission to check more than just one or two. Pause for a second or two after each item so that the group has a chance to register it.

It is also good to offer a one-sentence explanation for each checked item. Throughout, it is important that you role model honesty and vulnerability. (I typically include "feel good about my body," not only because that is true for me, but also because it gives permission to group members to check that common and significant concern of young people.)

3. Give the group a few minutes to complete the activity sheet; it should not take long. Remind them that they will mark what they are *not* doing at this point in their lives. Tell them that they may add items to the list if something they want to give themselves permission to do is not included.

4. Encourage group members to share their lists. If you go around the circle, begin with a volunteer and then move in whatever direction will allow shy or unsure individuals to wait before sharing. As you modeled in suggestion #2, they should simply read down their lists, prefacing perhaps every fourth item with "I would like to give myself permission to . . ." and pausing briefly between items. Encourage the group to listen carefully as each student shares his or her list.

You may want to tally student responses in the margins of your own sheet. Tell the group you will do that and that you will ask them, in the end, what items were checked most often.

5. After each person shares, ask the group if there is anything they would like to know more about or if they heard anything that surprised them. For example, it is probably news if a star athlete wants to "feel good about my body," if a high achiever wants to "be intelligent," or if a rebel wants to "achieve." If there is a dramatic insight or revelation, you yourself might encourage the group to respond and offer support. You may also want to ask for some elaboration on one reported item per group member, if appropriate. As always, each group member has the right to choose not to comment further. Remind them that they can set a boundary and say, "I'd rather not," which is also an important skill to practice.

6. Before closure, ask the group which items were reported most often. Verify their responses with your tally (for example, "Yes, more than half of you checked that one").

7. For closure, ask group members to summarize the session. Ask one or more of the following questions—rhetorically, if you prefer.

~ How was this topic for you?

~ What did your group have in common?

~ Were you surprised at anything?

~ What one item from your list could you give yourself permission to start working on immediately—today?

Dispose of the sheets or add them to the group folders.

Giving Myself Permission

Name: _____

I would like to give myself permission to . . .

- [ ] have fun
- [ ] take risks
- [ ] focus on *now*, instead of focusing so much on the future
- [ ] be angry
- [ ] be talkative
- [ ] be quiet
- [ ] be kind
- [ ] love
- [ ] be loved
- [ ] feel good about my body
- [ ] be intelligent
- [ ] be selfish
- [ ] make mistakes
- [ ] achieve
- [ ] follow my own path
- [ ] show others that I am upset
- [ ] be happy
- [ ] be sad
- [ ] be free to "just be"—and not worry about others' expectations of me
- [ ] accept authority in others
- [ ] live okay in a less-than-perfect situation
- [ ] be comfortable when alone
- [ ] stop a bad behavior or a harmful habit
- [ ] be imperfect
- [ ] relax
- [ ] be "bad"
- [ ] be "good"
- [ ] say difficult things to someone
- [ ] take charge of my life
- [ ] admit that I have conflicting and opposite (good and bad) feelings about someone in my family
- [ ] _____
- [ ] _____
- [ ] _____

FOCUS Identity

Time and Priorities

- Group members become more aware of the dominant U.S. culture's preoccupation with time.

- They consider how this preoccupation affects them personally.

- They examine how they use their time outside of school.

- They assess their ability to set priorities and use time wisely.

Suggestions

1. Start the session by asking the group to brainstorm all of the compound words or phrases they can think of that include the word *time*. (You may want to list their words and phrases on the board or a large sheet of paper.) Some examples follow:

saving time	taking time
making time	arranging a time
losing time	gaining time
overtime	time clock
time sheet	time-and-a-half
flex-time	part-time
full-time	leisure time
in time	on time
a reasonable time	in good time
high time	against time
time-share	timer
timekeeper	time-tested
standard time	daylight saving time
timetable	time to go
time-out	time off
time's up	out of time
real time	time limit
making good use of time	

2. Offer the observation that language reflects what a culture emphasizes. Other cultures may not have so many words about time—or so many clocks.

3. Depending on the ability level of group members, encourage them to give specific examples of time constraints on their lives. After they have shared, ask questions like the following:

~ How does our preoccupation with time affect our lives? (After some discussion, ask, "Are you able to relax when you need to?")

~ How able are we to be patient with things that take a long time? (Possible areas to pursue: What about long-term relationships? long-term projects? reading long books or watching long movies? learning new things that cannot be learned overnight, such as a language?) Are you involved in anything long-term?

~ How do you feel about the idea that "more" always means "better"? That "faster" always means "better"? Where might we see this in our society? How many of you often feel that you are overextended, overbusy, overscheduled, often late, or often worried about time?

4. Invite group members to consider how time affects them personally. If discussion moves in a negative direction, ask, "What changes would you like to make in the way you look at and use time? What in terms of time, and use of time, would help you feel better about your life?" Again, consider ability when phrasing or including questions.

5. Introduce the concept of prioritizing activities. Hand out the "Pieces of the Pie" activity sheet (page 74). Ask group members to divide the first "pie" into segments representing the average time they spend each week on the various parts of their lives, including working, sleeping, eating, studying, being in school, hanging out with friends, relaxing, and being with family.

6. Invite the group to present their pie charts. Ask questions like the following—of individuals or of the group—to generate discussion:

~ According to your pie chart, how do you use time?

~ How do you feel about that?

~ How good are you at taking care of your responsibilities? your needs? your relationships?

~ What are some parts of your life that you would like to give more time to? less time to?

~ What could you do to improve the way you spend your time?

If time permits, tell the group that they may use the other "pie" on the activity sheet to show how they would like to spend their time. Discuss the differences between the first and second pie charts.

7. For closure, ask the group for their "timely" opinions about this session. Was it "time well spent"? Dispose of the sheets or add them to the group folders.

Pieces of the Pie

Name: _____

Divide this "pie" into pieces showing how much time you spend each week in school classes, participating in extracurricular activities, sleeping, eating, studying, hanging out with friends, relaxing, watching television, playing video games, using the computer or the internet, participating in social networking, talking on the phone or text messaging, exercising, and interacting with family. Divide your "pie" into whatever areas represent your life.

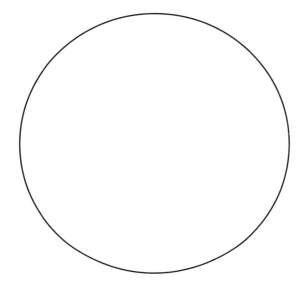

Divide this "pie" into pieces, showing how you would *like* to spend your time.

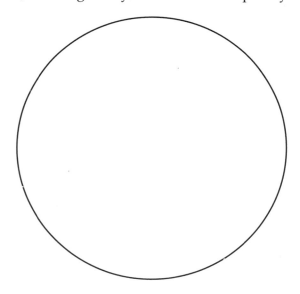

FOCUS Identity

Risk-Taking

Background

Thinking about adolescence often brings risk-taking to mind—social, academic, health, and safety. This session is an opportunity for teens to talk about concerns associated with becoming increasingly autonomous. Adults who care may worry since peers have increasingly more influence on teens' behavior and thinking—not uncommon at this stage. Focusing a small-group session on risk allows interaction without the bravado and posturing likely to appear in large-group discussions—and with less preaching from adults about dangers. Concerns can be expressed genuinely.

Cautious, compliant, anxious teens probably take few risks that are potentially dangerous, and their caution helps them avoid impulsive decisions that put them at risk. They can easily argue against stepping into unknown territory, even when not much is at risk. Other adolescents are risk-takers, gravitating toward uncertainty, not afraid of chaos and drama, and not letting dangers dissuade them from diving in. They may give little or no thought to possible consequences. They prefer the new, the different, the unknown—whatever can't be totally controlled. Most teens land somewhere between these two extremes. Most have heard about risks, especially related to drugs including nicotine and alcohol. But they may not normally talk about the risks. They may also not be aware of the risk involved in using some substances (for example, e-cigarettes, marijuana, caffeinated energy drinks, and recreational use of prescription drugs possibly sold by peers at school).

Objectives

- Group members learn that personalities differ in regard to risk-taking.

- Group members develop an understanding of their tolerance for or pull toward risk-taking so that they can consider these as they face greater risks and make choices accordingly.

Suggestions

1. Invite the group to brainstorm what comes to mind when they hear the term *risk*. Then ask them about their personality in regard to risk-taking (perhaps on a scale of 1 to 10, with 10 being "take a lot of risks"). Ask group members to report their scaled number and give an example of a situation that reflects their self-assessment. When all have reported, ask them to think about what they heard from the group: Are they mostly risk-takers, not-risk-takers, or does it depend on what kind of risk is involved? How do the risk-takers make sense of their risk-taking? How do the

not-risk-takers make sense of theirs? Make the point that personalities inclined toward risk-taking probably differ greatly.

2. To give students time for further self-reflection, distribute the activity sheet "My History of Risk-Taking," page 78. Explain that the "When begun?" column on the form is asking for the school level (P = preschool; E = elementary; M = middle school; H = high school) when the risk-taking first appeared. If some members seem to be struggling with the sheet, you might mention these risk-taking examples to provoke thought:

   ~ social: starting a conversation with a peer not known well; moving at lunch to sit with someone sitting alone; deciding to spend less time with friends who behave dangerously; making a big change in appearance; joining peers involved with alcohol, smoking, or other drugs; becoming known as someone who gossips; talking negatively about friends; being honest with opinions; socializing *without* alcohol

   ~ academic: taking a challenging class outside of your usual academic comfort zone; choosing a creative option for a project; not doing schoolwork; being disruptive in class or at school; not responding well to school authorities; avoiding hard courses because of anxiety or to protect academic record

   ~ health: signing up for a 5K race; trying a new sport; joining a mindfulness class in the community; eating too much; not eating enough; drinking too much soda; eating mostly junk food; not getting enough sleep; spending too much time online or playing video games; developing addictions to nicotine, alcohol, marijuana, or other drugs (you might also mention the long-term effects on the brain and one's ability to self-regulate when substances are used in adolescence)

   ~ safety: offering to drive an impaired and belligerent friend home from a party; walking to class with a lonely or vulnerable classmate; calling parents when a gathering is uncomfortable or dangerous; going into dangerous social situations alone; having sex with multiple partners and without protection; walking alone at night; driving too fast; driving while under the influence of drugs or riding with someone impaired by alcohol or other drugs

3. Invite the group to draw a line graph on paper representing their risk-taking history (preschool, elementary, middle school, high school). If they describe dangerous or dramatic behavior, ask them what was going on in their family, school, classroom, and social life at that time and how they felt about themselves. For those with little risk-taking, avoid suggesting that low risk-taking is strange. Perhaps they are not similar in risk-taking across all areas of their life—or they are simply impressively wise and mature or quiet, observant, not gregarious, not assertive in personality, or different in neurological "wiring."

4. Ask group members about current risk-taking (perhaps on a scale of 1 to 10, with 10 being "high level of risk-taking") among their peers. If they claim they do not know, encourage them to make assumptions. Then ask the group to make sense of the assumptions, especially if the scaling varied widely.

5. Invite them to consider the difference between dangerous and smart risk-taking. When is it advantageous to take social risks (for example, initiating conversation, befriending a new student)? to take academic risks (signing up for a course known to be "hard" or unpopular, easing up on perfectionistic homework habits in favor of being more social or more involved in activities)? Taking health or safety risks is usually not positive. You might invite the most social group members to talk about how they start conversations and keep them going. You might encourage the least social to study how social peers in the classroom engage in conversation—and then practice in low-risk contexts—*if* they want to make changes. If appropriate, ask "catastrophe" questions such as, "What would be the worst thing that could happen if you tried to start a conversation and it didn't work?"

6. For closure, invite students to write, on the back of their activity sheet or line graph, five short statements, up to five words each, starting with *I* or *we* and summarizing the discussion. They then might read the statements aloud, like a poem.

My History of Risk-Taking

	Example	Consequence	When begun?
Social risks			
Academic risks			
Health risks			
Safety risks			

FOCUS Identity

In Control, Out of Control

Objectives

- Group members consider the issue of control in their lives.

- They discuss what it means to be "in control" and "out of control."

Suggestions

1. Introduce the topic by asking what comes to mind when thinking about feeling "in control." Group members might mention the following:

   academics
   social situations
   leading something
   playing a sport
   private space at home
   competition
   music
   conversation
   sleeping
   eating
   taking care of brothers and sisters
   babysitting
   having money from a job
   cleaning

   Especially if you are working with a large group, write the responses on the board or a large sheet of paper, or have a few students write the list. Leave room to write responses for suggestion #2, perhaps in a second column.

2. Now ask the group what they associate with being "out of control." Here they might mention some of the categories from suggestion #1 and others as well, such as these:

strong emotions	feeling intimidated
being "outclassed"	fears
depression	anxiety
abuse	family rules
dating	food
conflict	anger
arguments	alcohol and other drugs

being around someone of another gender

being around someone with an unusual gender identity

being in a group of peers doing something dangerous

"addiction" (including to caffeine, chocolate, eating, not eating, exercise, video games, television, cell phone use, internet use, pornography)

Common ground will probably emerge. Invite the group to share incidents from their lives when they felt out of control. Modeling discretion, share one or more incidents from your life. You might say, "I feel comfortable sharing this. There are some other situations I wouldn't be comfortable sharing. Share whatever feels comfortable for you." It is especially important to offer such guidance to young adolescents, although I have learned that group members of all ages generally share discreetly, according to their level of trust in the group.

3. Move the discussion toward what it means to have a sense of control in one's life. Ask questions like the following:

~ What does it mean to feel a sense of control in your life?

~ To what extent do you feel that you have control in your life? sometimes? often? always? a lot? a little?

~ What helps you to feel in control?

~ Without giving a name, do you know anyone who seems to have a good amount of control in life? What has given you this impression of this person? What words would you use to describe this person?

~ What are your thoughts about people who seem to be in control? (Someone may mention that everyone probably feels a lack of control sometimes, that those who *seem* in control may not *feel* in control, and that people can learn how to present an image of being in control in various situations.)

~ How might adults and kids differ in feeling in control in life?

~ What are some examples of being "in control" in a negative way? (Examples: Controlling others, using threats and other kinds of bullying, being abusive, using intimidation, manipulating, having temper tantrums.)

~ What are some things in life that people do not have 100 percent control over? (Possibilities: Health, environmental changes, feelings, other people, taxes, death, safety.)

4. Invite the group to share what they would like to feel control over and perhaps what they could do to gain more control. They might mention some of the following:

counting to ten before responding when angered

using relaxation techniques

talking about feelings

getting a good education

being independent, on one's own

having a good relationship
paying more attention to health
being more careful with money
becoming and staying healthy
getting a good job
becoming financially secure
becoming an adult

5. For closure, ask a few or all to describe what being "in control" means to them personally. Perhaps their thoughts and feelings changed in the course of the discussion.

FOCUS Identity

Measuring Self-Esteem

Background

An important part of adolescence is developing a personal identity—figuring out who one is. To do this, young people may try on various images and check out the responses of peers, parents, and teachers. They may become self-critical, gauge their worth against the standards of their peer culture, dream impossible dreams, or identify with superheroes, movie stars, musicians, or sports stars. When they make mistakes, are embarrassed, or feel "different," their sense of self may be affected.

Many adolescents do not express their lack of confidence and their doubts about themselves. Many (perhaps most) do not seek out trusted adults to talk with. This session gives students a chance to talk in a safe and supportive group of peers about what they think of themselves. Group members can give feedback. Teens often listen more intently to peers than to adults.

Low self-esteem has a ripple effect in a young life. It affects relationships with peers and family. It can play a role in a number of behaviors, from shyness and poor classroom participation to cruel gossiping, bullying, and intimidation of peers and siblings (even though those aggressive behaviors do not necessarily reflect poor self-esteem). It can contribute to abusive relationships, as well as to misuse of alcohol and other drugs and other dangerous and self-destructive behaviors, including self-injury or self-mutilation, disordered eating and eating disorders, and activities that affect the brain's oxygen levels to produce an altered state.

Appearance alone does not tell us whether teens "know who they are" and what they think of themselves. All teens, regardless of achievement, ability level, or personality, can benefit from this discussion.

Important

It is best to place this session far enough into the group experience that positive comments have credibility. When such comments are made early in the life of the group, they may not be believed, since "that person doesn't know me well enough to say those things about me."

Objectives

- Group members consider their sense of self in a supportive group setting.

- They consider the sources of self-esteem.

- They become aware that low self-esteem can negatively affect life as an adult.

- They brainstorm ways to improve their sense of self.

- They practice giving and receiving life-enhancing comments.

Suggestions

1. Introduce the topic by asking group members to define *self-esteem* (perhaps "how people see or value themselves"). After a brief discussion, hand out the "Rating My Self-Esteem" activity sheet (page 86). Give students a few minutes to complete their sheets.

2. Have them tell how they determined their self-esteem ratings. Ask questions like the following to generate group discussion:

   ~ What contributed to your (physical, intellectual, social, emotional) self-esteem rating?

   ~ How much have comments by others affected your self-esteem?

   ~ What personal standards have you set for yourself (physically, intellectually, socially, emotionally)?

   ~ What are the (physical, intellectual, social, emotional) standards of your peer group?

   ~ What are your family's (physical, intellectual, social, emotional) standards?

   ~ What do you tell yourself in each of the four areas? (Give them the term *self-talk*.)

3. Invite the group to consider where self-esteem comes from. Ask questions like these:

   ~ How much is positive self-esteem "given" to us through praise, gifts, and attention versus coming from somewhere else? How much of low self-esteem comes from others' comments or actions?

   ~ How much choice do we have in how we respond to others' comments about us?

   ~ How do we develop positive self-esteem? (If group members do not mention the following, contribute them to the discussion: Learning how to do things for ourselves, gaining skills through meeting challenges. Invite them to comment on these ideas.)

   ~ Are self-esteem and self-sufficiency the same? How are they alike and different? (Adjust this vocabulary to your group's ability and language level.)

   ~ What kind of parenting do you think helps children to develop positive self-esteem?

   ~ How do you know you're okay? How do you know you're valued? (Be aware that some individuals may indicate that they do not know they are valued. If that occurs, encourage the group to offer support—especially if the individuals have previously demonstrated that capacity.)

4. Ask whether and how adult life might be affected by low self-esteem. If they do not come up in discussion and if they seem appropriate for your group, introduce the following as areas that can be affected by low self-esteem:

   ~ marriage and partnership (feeling inadequate; being abused or abusive; being competitive, critical)

   ~ parenting (feeling inadequate; being abused or abusive; inability to be close to one's children; alienation; rigidity; fearfulness; isolation; pessimism)

   ~ social relationships (feeling inadequate; tendency to dominate others or be dominated by them)

   ~ relationships at work (inability to compliment and support or have compassion for others; gossiping; being nonassertive; being self-absorbed)

   ~ career direction and success (feeling inadequate; inability to make necessary career moves; lack of focus)

   ~ productivity (preoccupation with one's flaws and inadequacies; lack of a can-do attitude)

   ~ contentment and satisfaction with life (low or nonexistent)

5. Have the group brainstorm ways to start improving their self-esteem now. Following are some suggestions:

   ~ Give yourself compliments and praise instead of relying on others to do it.

   ~ Receive and accept approval instead of rejecting it. "Parent" yourself. Do for yourself what others have been unable to do for you. (This is especially important for teens who have grown up with chaotic, depressed, abusive, neglectful, or substance-dependent adults who may not have been able to parent well.)

   ~ Do something you know you're good at, and then congratulate yourself on a job well done.

   ~ Try something new. Even if you "fail," congratulate yourself for being brave enough to take the risk.

   ~ Accept and acknowledge all of your feelings, even the "bad" ones: anger, guilt, inadequacy, disappointment. (Point out that no feeling is "bad" in itself. All feelings make sense. However, feelings are connected to thoughts, and we can work to alter our thoughts about emotional situations. Also point out that it is how feelings are expressed—with behaviors—that may cause problems. We can work to change the ways we *express* our emotions.)

6. Ask students to write down at least one positive comment about everyone in the group (including themselves). Then, focusing on one student at a time, invite members to share their positive comments about him or her. If time is short, you will have to move this activity along fairly quickly. Let the comments stand alone; allow them to be heard, but do not discuss them. You might suggest that each person wait to hear all comments from the group before saying a simple, "Thank you."

7. For closure, thank the group for sharing, for articulating their concerns in personally sensitive areas, and for being generous and thoughtful in their comments. Dispose of the sheets or add them to the group folders.

Rating My Self-Esteem

Name: _____

In each of the following four areas, rate yourself on a scale of 1 to 10, with 1 being "very low" and 10 being "very high."

PHYSICAL

     1   2   3   4   5   6   7   8   9   10

INTELLECTUAL

     1   2   3   4   5   6   7   8   9   10

SOCIAL

     1   2   3   4   5   6   7   8   9   10

EMOTIONAL

     1   2   3   4   5   6   7   8   9   10

Now give yourself an overall rating.

     1   2   3   4   5   6   7   8   9   10

FOCUS Identity

Making Mistakes

Objectives
- Group members share their feelings about making mistakes.
- They hear the message that making mistakes is being human.

Suggestions

1. Begin the meeting by saying, "Close your eyes and think about the last big mistake you made in front of at least one other person . . . Imagine the scene . . . You have just made the mistake . . . Who is there with you? . . . What are you feeling? . . . Are you expecting someone to say something to you about the mistake? . . . Does this happen? . . . What else happens? . . . What is your response—to the other person's comment or to the silence? . . . How do you feel? . . . How long does this feeling last?" After perhaps half a minute, tell the students to open their eyes.

2. Briefly share a pertinent experience from your own life—a time when you made a mistake and someone said something about it. Explain how you felt. Then encourage the group to share their experiences. Let them respond to and support one another, perhaps adding comments about similar experiences. If that does not happen spontaneously, model an appropriate response—acknowledge what is shared without treating it like a catastrophe, give eye contact, and reflect the tone of the speaker (for example, lighthearted, serious). Indicate that you have been paying attention by reflecting a feeling (for example, "I can hear your embarrassment" or "That must have been scary"). If an error had dangerous repercussions, you might say, "Wow, I'm sorry you had to experience that—a difficult time." In order to involve others in the discussion, you might ask, "Does that remind any of you of an experience you've had?"

3. Afterward, ask the group how they felt during the exchange. (Relaxed? Apprehensive? Close to one another? Uneasy?) Then ask questions like the following:

   ~ How did it feel to share your mistakes?

   ~ How would you describe the atmosphere here during the sharing? (Open? Honest? Supportive?)

   ~ What did the sharing contribute to our group? Did it affect your feelings about anyone?

4. Initiate a general discussion about mistakes by asking questions such as the following:

   ~ How do you usually feel about your mistakes? (Perhaps on a scale of 1 to 10, with 10 being "no problem.")

   ~ Are you ever around someone who seems to enjoy pointing out your mistakes or "pouncing" on them? How much time do you spend around this person?

   ~ What happens at home when you make a mistake?

   ~ What happens when you make a mistake around your friends?

   ~ Do you know any people who typically laugh at their mistakes?

   ~ What might happen if someone tried to avoid making mistakes at all costs? (Perfectionism is linked to fear of error, low risk-taking, unreasonable standards, self-criticism, lack of joy when doing/making something, being preoccupied with others' opinions.)

   ~ What is a healthy attitude about making mistakes? (If not mentioned in the group, comment that we can forgive ourselves, apologize when our mistakes hurt others, laugh at our errors, not think of them as catastrophes, and put them behind us.)

5. For closure, invite the group to create a motto or slogan about mistakes, which can be used as self-talk in the future. If they seem stuck, offer examples such as "I have the right to make mistakes," "Nobody's perfect," and "I'm human and make mistakes." Thank the group for sharing their personal experiences.

FOCUS Identity

Heroes

Objectives

- Group members think about whether they have heroes.

- They consider whether the heroes of today are different from heroes of the past.

- They consider whether their heroes reflect their personal values.

Suggestions

1. Introduce the topic with the following observation (spoken slowly, in these words or your own): "Some people believe that young people today, unlike young people of the past, don't have heroes. Or, if they do, their heroes are poor role models. I don't know what the word *hero* means to you. Is it someone who inspires you or serves as a role model for you? Is it someone who has accomplished something you admire, has qualities you admire, has helped you personally, or has overcome some problem or adversity? Your heroes (if you have them) may be real or fictional, young or old, living or dead. Write a list of your heroes. If you don't have any heroes, list people you respect or admire. If you can't think of any heroes—or any people you respect or admire—write 'none.'"

   Or simply ask the group to list heroes without giving any suggestions about how to interpret the word.

2. Encourage group members to share their lists. Ask them to pause briefly between the names on their lists so that others have a chance to think about them. If they like, they may tell why they listed each one in turn, or they might wait until they have read through their lists and then comment generally on their reasons for listing those individuals.

3. When all have read their lists, ask the group to point out any similarities in their lists. Perhaps several in the group named one or more of the same people as heroes. Or perhaps the heroes they listed have characteristics or traits in common. Then encourage more discussion with questions like these:

   ~ Have your heroes changed over time?

   ~ Did you have different heroes when you were younger? Or have some of your heroes stayed the same for many years?

~ Have all of your heroes had similar traits? Do they represent what you value? Do they have traits that you have? What traits of your heroes do you wish you had—if any? Do heroes reflect what we value?

~ (For those who wrote "none" on their lists) Was there a time when you had heroes? (If anyone says no, accept that with an affirming okay.)

4. If you introduced the session by reading the observation in suggestion #1, ask, "Do teens today have different kinds of heroes than their parents or grandparents did?" If several in the group wrote "none" on their lists, ask, "Do you think having no heroes is typical for kids your age?" If so, invite them to suggest possible reasons.

5. For closure, ask, "If, in fact, heroes reflect what we admire, what might you say about what you value as a group, judging by the heroes you listed?" Then, "Do you think the values of the group are similar to the values of most people your age today?" Dispose of the sheets or add them to the group folders.

FOCUS Identity

Having Fun

Background

Although this topic may seem odd, and although most of your group may already seem to know plenty about it, it merits attention. Some teens socialize a great deal without having fun. Some have parents who believe having fun is not appropriate in school—or in life. Some may appear to be having fun, but in fact are envious of those who *really* seem to be enjoying life.

Some teens do not make time to relax and have fun—and may not know where to start to do either. They may be unable to enjoy the present moment. Some may be too angry or frustrated to have fun. Some may be too depressed even to imagine fun. Some may translate *having fun* as dangerous, harmful, destructive, or self-destructive behavior. Some may feel isolated and distressed because they have no one to have fun with. Some, of course, may have fun doing what others might see as work.

This session brings a seemingly light topic forward for serious discussion. In this stressful age and society, everyone probably needs to talk about fun, think about how to have it, and affirm and celebrate it when it is happening.

Objectives

- Group members learn that having fun is part of a healthy, balanced life.

- They become more aware of whether and how they have fun.

- They brainstorm ways to have creative fun that is not dangerous.

- They recognize that it is possible to have fun as an adult—even at work.

- They recognize that it is possible to have fun as a teen—even when at school, and even while learning.

Suggestions

1. Begin by having the group define the word *fun*. What does it mean to them? Accept their responses without comment (but show respect and receptivity with your facial expression).

2. Encourage them to share what they normally do for fun. Where do they go? With whom? How long do they spend on the fun? How often do they do fun activities?

3. Continue the discussion by asking questions like the following:

~ How much do you include fun and relaxation in your life? (Perhaps on a scale of 1 to 10, with 10 being "a lot.")

~ (For those who include it) How are you able to set aside time for fun and relaxation?

~ (For those who do not) Help us to understand why you don't do this. (You might want to ask questions about feeling no permission to have fun or pressure not to have fun. Be aware that some members might not feel the need to have fun in the ways described by others in the group. They may feel quite comfortable and balanced as they are.)

~ What do you *enjoy* doing?

~ How do you feel after doing whatever you do for fun?

~ How did you learn to have fun? Who has modeled "having fun" for you?

~ Do adults have fun? Do the adults in your life have fun?

~ On a scale of 1 to 10, with 10 being "very," how much is your fun unhealthy, destructive, or dangerous?

~ How often do you feel restless and bored, with nothing to do?

4. Introduce the concept of *creative* fun—fun that is not dangerous or destructive. (This focus is especially important if some in your group are involved in unhealthy, unsafe activities, or if many complain about being bored and having nothing to do.) Invite the group to brainstorm ideas for enjoyable activities that meet the following criteria:

~ It's something I can do with a friend or in a group. People interact.

~ People talk and laugh together.

~ It doesn't hurt anyone, including me.

~ It helps people get to know each other better, maybe even become friends.

~ It doesn't involve alcohol or other drugs.

~ It brings out the best in everyone involved.

Make the connection between having fun and being childlike. You might say something like this, "Some people think that having fun is just for kids. Think of things you did as a small child that were fun for you. Is there anything from your past that you're still doing for enjoyment today—or that you *could* do today, as a teen? How could you make it appropriate for your age group?"

This discussion may not be easy for some groups. You may need to guide them and to think, beforehand, of some possible directions. For example, I recall a group of young girls, already involved with the corrections system, drug use, promiscuous sex, shoplifting, and "crank calls," who eventually considered splitting the cost of ingredients for baking a cake or some other dish and then following (or trying to follow) the recipe as a group. Or dancing in one of their living rooms—just them. Or renting a movie and seeing how many feelings are in it, or how women and men are portrayed. Or finding a safe playground to "act like a kid."

5. Invite the group to look ahead to the future by asking questions like these:

   ~ Is it okay for adults to have fun?

   ~ How do the adults you know have fun—if they have fun?

   ~ Can work be fun? Do you know anyone for whom work seems like play—someone who seems to enjoy his or her job?

   ~ When you picture yourself as a young or even as an older adult having fun, what do you see yourself doing? (NOTE: Encourage the group to imagine activities other than drinking, if their responses are mostly centered around alcohol use.)

   ~ When you're an adult, how will you balance work and play in your life—having both?

6. For closure, either summarize the session yourself or ask the group to tell what they have heard from the members. Compliment them for taking this subject seriously, and wish for them balanced lives that include fun, relaxation, and laughter.

FOCUS Identity

Each of Us Is an Interesting Story

Background

This session can help group members sort through the various "threads" of their personal history, affirm the richness of their lives, and appreciate that all of life's experiences—pleasant or painful, delightful or difficult—combine to make each one of us unique and interesting. What we experience in our lives leads to wisdom, strength, resiliency, vision, compassion, and complex emotions.

No one is bland or boring. Everyone's story is textured. Our life stories are quilt-like—original, colorful, one of a kind. Whatever metaphor you choose (or students suggest), the idea that each of us is an interesting story can begin to cast a positive light on all life situations, including those that are challenging or difficult.

Since the "My Story" activity requires at least ten minutes to fill out, and each student in the group should get the group's full attention when presenting his or her story, you may want to divide this session into two, depending on time available. If you present this topic over two sessions, be sure to collect the activity sheets after the first session for use during the following session. In addition, because a trustworthy group environment is particularly important in this session, delay using this session until your group is well established and has developed a sense of respect and safety.

Objectives

- Group members learn that each of them is a "story" that is worth recording, hearing, and learning about and from.

- They experience that sharing parts of their personal story helps to build bridges to others and forge bonds of friendship and support.

Suggestions

1. Introduce the topic with some ideas from the background information above. Hand out the "My Story" activity sheet (pages 96–97). Tell the group that they will spend part of this session completing it. Instruct them to look at the various parts of the activity sheet as you read through the following guidelines.

   ~ Treat your life as a story. Pretend that you're writing your autobiography or a novel based on your life.

   ~ Don't worry about writing complete sentences. Brief notes are okay.

   ~ Be clever and creative, and use humor if you like, but take this activity seriously.

Ask if anyone has questions about any part of the activity sheet. Then allow enough time for the students to complete the sheets. They can add items as they listen to others later. Be aware that some may finish quickly, and some may want time to write many details. Begin the discussion when perhaps one-third of the group seems done.

2. Invite the group to share their stories one at a time. Tell them that they may share all or part of what they have written, elaborating or omitting according to what they are comfortable with.

3. If group members share difficult situations, experiences, or facts, or if anyone becomes distressed while sharing or listening, offer support (for example, "That sounds like a difficult time") and encourage the other students to do likewise. Remind the group that all parts of a person's life contribute to a complex, interesting, multidimensional person. Affirm all experiences—pleasant and unpleasant, positive and negative (for example, "You have a very interesting story").

4. For closure, thank the students for their stories. Affirm their rich, complex, varied, and interesting lives. Celebrate their uniqueness as individuals. You might also ask how this session felt to them. Dispose of the sheets or add them to group folders.

My Story

Name: _____

Pretend you are writing a book about your life.

1. The title of the story of my life is _____

   _____

2. The heroes in my story (people who have helped me) are _____

   _____

3. The "bad characters" in my story (children, peers, adults who hurt me or were not nice to me) are _____

   _____

4. The adults I have most appreciated are _____

   _____

5. The turning points (when things changed a lot) are _____

   _____

6. The most dramatic times (lots of emotion, big things happening) are _____

   _____

7. The most clear memories I have are _____

   _____

8. Blank times (no memory, hardly any memory) are _____

   _____

(continued)

My Story (continued)

9. I would like to reward my heroes with _____
_____

10. I would like to punish my bad characters by _____
_____

11. The person who has understood me the best is _____
_____

12. The person who has been my best friend is _____
_____

13. The best neighbor my family has had is _____
_____

14. The person who helped me feel better when I was sad is _____
_____

15. The person who gave me good advice and helped me grow up is _____
_____

Identity

. . . .

When We Need Courage

Background
. . . .

This session gives group members an opportunity to share an incident from their lives that required courage. Confronted with danger—physical or psychological—they found the strength they needed to face it, even if they were afraid. They may not have realized at the time that they were being courageous, perhaps because they were preoccupied with the situation and were concentrating on surviving the crisis. Now, looking back, they can notice the strength they showed. This is an especially positive experience for adolescents, who may feel that most of the events in their lives are largely beyond their control, or even that they are victims.

Objectives
. . . .

- Group members recall times when they were courageous.

- They recognize that courage is needed for honest self-assessment, as well as for times when they are faced with a danger or threat.

Suggestions
. . . .

1. Introduce the topic with ideas from the background information above. Ask group members to think of times when they needed courage to face a threat, danger, or difficulty in their lives. If they need help, focus on one of the following questions at a time:

   ~ Has there ever been a time when your family was in danger because of problems within the family or threats from outside of the family? (For example, a family crisis, a serious illness or accident, parents getting divorced, the loss of a job, financial problems, a natural disaster.) How did your family survive (if they did) the dangerous time?

   ~ Has there ever been a time when you confronted someone you were afraid of or were intimidated by? (For example, someone who was bullying, someone who threatened you or a sibling, someone with a reputation for violent behavior.) How did you find the courage to do that?

   ~ Has there ever been a time when you faced a danger or threat alone? Would you be willing to share the experience with the group? (Remind them that it is all right not to share.)

   ~ Were you ever caring for a child or an animal who suddenly needed help or protection? What did you do?

~ Have you ever had to stand up against peer pressure in a difficult situation? How were you able to do that?

~ Have you ever had to stand up to a parent or other adult when it took great courage to do so? What did you do? How did you find courage to do that?

~ Can you remember a time when it would have been easy to avoid doing something difficult, but you found the courage to get it done?

Allow time for group members to share and respond to each other's stories. Model positive, affirming responses (for example, "That's so impressive" or "That must have been very difficult to do"). Afterward, ask, "How did it feel to recall times when you were courageous?"

2. Turn the discussion to the relationship between courage and self-assessment. Ask questions like the following:

~ Compared to responding to danger, do you think it takes more courage, or less, to take responsibility for actions, accept consequences, or admit mistakes? Can you think of a time when you have done that?

~ What kinds of changes in someone's life require courage? (For example, getting out of an unhealthy relationship, saying no to unhealthy or risky behavior, asking your family for help with a problem.)

~ How much courage might it take to feel unpleasant feelings? Can you think of a time when you did that—instead of avoiding those feelings?

~ How much courage might it take to put the past behind you and get on with your life in the present? Have you ever done that? Do you know someone who has done that?

~ How much courage might it take to be appropriately angry at someone who has harmed you in some way—and to let that person know you are angry? Can you think of an example from your life?

3. Ask if anyone in the group is in need of courage right now or will be in the near future. If one or more individuals choose to share a situation that requires courage, listen supportively (for example, "It makes sense that you are worried and frightened" or "We'll hope for the best for you") and encourage the other group members to show support. Remind the group about confidentiality.

4. For closure, commend the group for the courage they have shown in the past— and in the present—and thank them for sharing their stories with the group. You might also say something like this: "You probably know each other better now than you did at the beginning of this session. That happens when people share some of themselves discreetly, as we did today. I appreciate your trust in the group. We will be trustworthy in response."

FOCUS Identity

A Prisoner of Image

Background

A teen who is perceived as a rebel, risk-taker, joker, or social outcast may feel stuck in that role. A bubbly, buoyant, energetic student may feel constrained from expressing sadness. Mr. Nice Guy may be tired of being nice. The class comedian may yearn to be taken seriously. The brain may wish to ask a "stupid question," but may not feel allowed to do so.

It is possible to be a prisoner of one's image—so that no other behavior seems acceptable. It takes courage not to do what is expected of us. For the student burdened with a bad reputation, it can be especially difficult to escape.

Objectives

- Group members consider the image other people have of them.

- They consider whether they pay a price for living up to an image.

- They imagine what would happen if they did not live up to their image.

Suggestions

1. Introduce the topic by asking group members to think about these questions: "What's your image? How do other people see you? How do others picture you?" You might mention some of the images from the background information above.

2. Tell them about someone you have known, or give an example from your own life, to illustrate how someone can be "imprisoned" by an image.

3. Ask the group to think of times when they had an image to live up to. If they need help, read aloud some of the images from the list that follows. Ask, "Can anyone identify with these? What has been your unique image? What part of your image serves you well—and you wouldn't want to change it? What part of your image would you like to change—if any?"

class clown	someone who can handle anything
high achiever	cool
underachiever	in control
anti-school	compliant, follows rules
cynical	defiant, daring
winner	easily hurt and upset
loser	

After group members reveal their images, ask questions like the following:

~ What might someone sacrifice if always living up to an image?

~ What might happen if you didn't live up to your image? (Possible directions: lose identity, be teased, surprise friends.)

~ Has your image ever caused problems for you?

~ Does anyone in the group not fit the image you had of them prior to being in the group?

4. Ask the group if they would like to know what image others in the group have of them. If some or all are willing to find out, continue. For each member who volunteers, invite the other students to describe what they believe that person's image to be, reminding them to be sensitive to how their comments might be received. Then ask the individual, "How did it feel to hear how others see you? Do you think their views of you are accurate? Do their views of you limit you in any way?" Keep this discussion focused on image. Delay a detailed treatment of this topic until "How Others See Us" in the Relationships section (page 169), or combine that session with this one.

5. For closure, ask for a volunteer to summarize the session. What about it was thought-provoking?

FOCUS Identity

Feeling Free

Objectives

- Group members think about the meaning of personal freedom.

- They consider what contributes to feeling free.

Suggestions

NOTE: If your time is limited, you may want to begin with suggestion #4.

1. Begin by inviting the group to think of people who seem to be free. These should be people they know personally—friends, relatives, children, adults. (Perhaps they could list these on a sheet of paper.) Ask students to describe these people to the group. Have them explain what "freedom" means in each case.

   This part of the discussion may move far away from the concept of personal freedom. Let it find its own course. Your group will likely express important feelings and thoughts, and this should always be a goal of each session—not whether they are "right" or "wrong" in their perceptions. As individuals offer examples, the group's definition of *freedom* might even change.

2. Invite the group to think about what they just heard. Ask questions like the following to stimulate discussion:

   ~ What is the age of most of the people you named?

   ~ Are they married? single? with a partner? intelligent? educated? lacking education? at peace with themselves? active? passive? aggressive? assertive? nice? not nice?

   ~ Are they involved with others? uninvolved? living with rules? living without rules? making a contribution to society? destructive to society? neutral regarding contribution?

   ~ If they are adolescents, are they living with their parents? foster parents? relatives? on their own? successful at something? unconcerned with success? financially secure? not concerned about money?

   Finally, ask group members what conclusions they can draw about freedom and feeling free, based on the discussion so far. If members can handle abstract discussions, ask them if guidelines and social rules get in our way or help us to be free.

3. Turn the focus to group members with questions like the following:

~ Do you feel free? If you do, how does that feel? In what ways do you feel free? If not, how does that feel? In what ways are you not free?

~ If you don't feel free, what would help you to feel more free?

~ What is the relationship between making choices and freedom? (Possibility: When we have choices, we have freedom in those areas.)

4. If time allows, ask the group to fill out the "Freedom of Choice" activity sheet (page 104) and share their responses.

5. For closure, emphasize the points made in items 7 through 10 on the activity sheet. Then ask for volunteers to summarize the session. Wish for them good choices in life as they exercise their freedom to choose. Dispose of the sheets or add them to the group folders.

Freedom of Choice

Name _____

1. I can't _____

   _____

   I can't _____

   _____

2. I won't _____

   _____

   I won't _____

   _____

3. If I could _____

   I would _____

4. In my life, I'm in charge of _____

   _____

5. I'm not in charge of _____

   _____

6. When _____ and _____

   _____ happen, I'll probably feel more free.

7. These are the choices I've made lately that show I have the freedom to choose in my life:

   _____

8. This is what I've done lately that shows I take responsibility for my choices:

   _____

   _____

9. Times when I have allowed others to make choices for me are _____

   _____

10. A time when I chose *not* to make a choice was when _____

    _____

FOCUS Identity

Success and Failure

Background

The words *success* and *failure* are tossed around a lot at all age levels. But what do they mean? Does money make one successful? Does education? Does respect? Does lack of money, education, or respect mean failure? Who defines those words for us? Do people view success and failure differently, depending on their ethnic and socioeconomic backgrounds?

All adolescents wrestle with these terms and the feelings connected with them. This session gives students a chance to talk about their unique present and future expectations and possible anxieties regarding success and failure.

Objectives

- Group members learn that their peers' definitions of the words *success* and *failure* vary.

- They consider that success and failure do not have to be connected to money, grades, athletic abilities, or popularity.

- They think about the future and what might contribute to feeling successful as adults.

Suggestions

1. Introduce the topic by asking for examples of successful adults. Then ask the group to define the terms *success* and *failure*. Their definitions and interpretations may vary considerably and generate discussion.

2. Invite the group to apply the terms to various aspects of school life—academic, extracurricular, social. Ask questions like the following:

   ~ Can a student be successful and not be well-known in school?

   ~ Can a student be successful and not be liked in school?

   ~ Can a person be successful but feel like a failure?

   ~ Does success depend on other people knowing about it? Does failure?

   ~ When might success "go to someone's head"?

   ~ When might "failure" be especially devastating?

   ~ When have you experienced success?

   ~ When have you experienced failure?

~ Has anyone ever used the term *failure* to describe something you've done?

~ Who and what have influenced how you interpret the words *success* and *failure*?

~ Who do you want to tell when you feel successful? Why? How important is that person to you?

~ How much do you worry about failure?

~ Is it important to learn how to fail? Explain your answer.

~ Do *success* and *failure* mean the same thing to everybody? Are there gender differences in how these terms are defined? If so, how do the definitions differ?

3. It is difficult for some teens to think about the future—perhaps because the present is so demanding or paralyzing or because the future is simply too far away and hard to imagine. Shift the focus to adulthood with questions like the following:

~ Do *success* and *failure* mean the same to adults as to teens?

~ What might help you feel successful when you are thirty? forty? fifty? retired? (Possibilities: Being respected; knowing that you have done your best; being able to put talents and abilities to use; being content; having a successful relationship with someone.)

~ What could contribute to your feeling like a failure when you're an adult?

4. Encourage the group to think of success in general terms. How does society view success? What is it to most people? Satisfaction? Wealth? Social status? Children and grandchildren? A comfortable home? What do students hear and see on various media that affects how they define success? To whom do they compare themselves when assessing success or failure?

5. For closure, ask one group member or a few to define the terms *success* and *failure* again. What did they hear during the discussion? Did any comments surprise them? Did they all agree?

FOCUS Identity

Being Alone Versus Being Lonely

Background

Some adolescents—and adults, too—are afraid to be alone. Social media can connect them meaningfully to others, but may also exacerbate feelings of isolation and fears of being left out. A solitary weekend evening may be uncomfortable at best and anxiety-laden at worst. They may believe that the rest of the world is busily and happily having fun while they're left behind, or they fear that spending weekends alone is their lot for the rest of their lives. On the other hand, some adolescents—and adults—love solitude and quietness and savor it as a time for renewal apart from the pressures and demands of life. Solitude can help people reflect and tune in to themselves.

Perhaps the differences in how people perceive being alone are related to predisposition toward introversion or extroversion. Introverts tend to find sustenance from within and appreciate time alone to recoup their energy, while extroverts tend to prefer people contact for sustenance and renewal. However, it is undoubtedly more complex than that. Some in both groups feel insecure and afraid when they're alone. Maybe those feelings urge them to be social.

Whether simple or complex, emotions connected to being alone versus being lonely are worth discussing, especially while young. There is value in just talking about them.

You may want to research this topic before leading this discussion, particularly in regard to introversion and extroversion. However, as always, it is best to let the students teach you about their world, their perceptions about themselves in various environments, and their feelings, rather than focusing on informing them about the concepts here. Regardless, it is important to affirm both introverts and extroverts. There is no "good" or "bad"—just different.

Objectives

- Group members learn more about themselves by thinking about how comfortable they are when alone.

- They practice articulating their feelings about being alone versus being lonely and discover similarities within the group.

- They explore possible benefits of being alone.

- They consider ways to alleviate loneliness.

1. Introduce the topic by asking the group to define the terms *alone* and *lonely*. (This focus usually generates discussion without an activity. However, if your group likes to write, they might create a poem from the prompt "When I'm alone . . ." If they like to draw, they might draw a nondigital thermometer to show the degree of anxiety they associate with being alone and being lonely.)

2. Begin a discussion by asking questions like the following:

   ~ How easy is it for you to be alone? (On a scale of 1 to 10, with 10 being "very.")

   ~ Who are you when you're alone? (Encourage group members to describe themselves. For example, a worried, anxious eighth grader who would rather be with friends; a calm, content girl who is social in school, but enjoys being alone and quiet at home; someone who likes having time just to relax.)

   ~ How comfortable are you when walking down the halls in school alone? shopping by yourself? attending an event alone? eating alone? (Perhaps on a scale of 1 to 10, with 10 being "very.")

   ~ How do you feel about being at home alone on a weekend night? on a weekday night? (If being alone is associated with insecurity and fear, what are the fears?)

   ~ How do you feel about silence? What are you likely to do when you're home alone and the house is quiet?

   ~ How would you describe your parents' attitudes about solitude and quietness? How can you tell? How do you think your siblings or friends view solitude?

3. Turn the group's attention toward possible benefits of being alone. Ask questions like the following:

Important

As always, there are no right or wrong responses to any of these questions. Simply let group members respond, encourage them to be honest and genuine about their feelings, and actively listen to what they say.

   ~ Does being alone always mean being lonely? Can a person be social, but also be lonely?

   ~ Can loneliness have a purpose or a positive result? (Possibilities: Inspire someone to make changes and reach out to others; result in creative expression in the arts.)

   ~ Is it possible to become dependent on relationships, socializing, and being around other people?

   ~ How can a person use time alone, now and then, for personal benefit?

4. Encourage group members to explore ways to alleviate loneliness and/or give themselves permission to be alone.

5. For closure, ask a volunteer to summarize the session. Thank group members for contributing to the discussion and wish them well as they endeavor to become increasingly more comfortable with themselves, whether with people or alone.

FOCUS Identity

A Personal Symbol

Objectives

- Group members think about who they are and what they value.
- They communicate a personal symbol thoughtfully and sensitively.

Important

At the session immediately preceding this one, instruct group members to bring something to the next session that symbolizes them. Explain that this should be something that represents who they are or what they value or that "sums them up." The symbol cannot be a word, even though words are symbols. Rather, it must be something they can touch, hold, and show to the group. If it cannot actually be brought to the group, a photograph or drawing will do. You might mention some things that students in the past have brought or bring something that represents you (a photo that sums up important aspects or a special place; a gift representing a special relationship; a piece of music representing an important talent; a book representing a lifetime of adventures; a ball symbolizing well-roundedness; a teddy bear representing security).

Clarify the assignment as needed, according to group members' level of abstract thinking. Tell them that you trust them to take the assignment seriously and give it some thought. Reassure them that when they present and tell about their symbol, they will be treated with sensitivity and respect. If they have trouble thinking of something to bring, invite them to see you individually for help.

Although this activity is appropriate for any group, it works best for groups that are fairly similar in ability.

Suggestions

1. Begin by asking the group to display their personal symbols and explain what they represent. Remind students to be courteous and respectful during this show-and-tell, since it involves some degree of risk for everyone. If some members forget to bring a symbol, allow them to draw their symbol while the others tell about theirs, and have these students share their symbols/drawings last. As many in the group as possible (and as many as are willing) should participate in this activity. It makes sense that some students might forget to bring a symbol, since they are not used to bringing something to group meetings. However, sustaining the focus to a second session, for the sake of 100 percent participation, may not be productive, since group members may forget again. Therefore, work with only what is offered in this session.

2. Ask, "Is there anyone who would have had a much different symbol a few years ago?" Allow time for discussion. Then ask, "Is there anyone who would probably have brought the same symbol to group a few years ago?" Again, allow time for discussion.

3. For closure, thank the group for sharing their symbols and for giving the assignment careful thought. If appropriate, tell them that you appreciate knowing them better now, as a result of hearing about their personal symbols, and that they probably now know each other a bit better as well.

FOCUS
Feelings

FOCUS Feelings

....

Adolescents deal with intense emotions. Someone special pays attention to them. They are invited to a most important party. They get a good grade on a tough assignment. Compliments come their way for something they wear. They do well in gym class. They fall in love. These are the great times, when the ride is on the upswing. It is easy to smile and laugh and be lighthearted then.

But with other experiences, the roller coaster rolls downhill. The social climate at school can be competitive and unpredictable, and relationships change. Rough language may be aimed in their direction. They feel disappointed, sometimes devastated, when things do not work out as hoped. They experience losses and transitions at home, and they grieve. They say and do things they know they should not, and they feel guilty. They experience the rush of romantic love, and they suffer when relationships end. They also have strong feelings if their parents' relationship ends, and they experience anxiety as parents remarry and families blend. They perceive that holiday celebrations are not what they used to be. They are no longer children, and their family may have changed considerably.

Then there are the perplexing mood swings that many experience. Adults may not realize that seemingly insignificant events may feel like major traumas to teens. Adolescents feel intensely, and they do not have the wisdom from experience to know that nothing stays the same—situations change, time heals, and feelings pass. They may believe that no one feels as they do, and they are lonely in their distress. If they lose heart, they may flirt with dangerous behaviors and may develop serious problems with alcohol and other drugs. Sometimes they show their feelings, and sometimes they do not.

It is good to talk about feelings. Building that skill will probably help future relationships—with friends, coworkers, partners, spouses, and children. Learning to identify and accept feelings helps us stay balanced and integrated in a complex world.

General
Objectives

- Group members feel emotions in the present, affirm them, and talk about them with a group of supportive peers and a concerned adult.

- They look at past emotions and gain perspective.

FOCUS Feelings

....

Mood Swings and Mood Range

Background
....

This session sets the stage for the sessions that follow in this section. It is helpful to look at mood range. On a scale of 1 to 10, some individuals experience the full range, some a narrow range, some a moderate range, some a range that stays buoyantly above 5, and some a range that never rises above 5. It is interesting for teens to consider their own and each others' fluctuations in morale, particularly during this time of their lives, when mood swings seem to be the norm. Do families have unique ways of expressing emotions? Do some families thoroughly guard their emotions? Do all people have intense emotions, but only some express them intensely? Do some fear emotions? Do family members differ in mood range? Do we protect ourselves from having "1" feelings by narrowing our mood ranges, thereby ruling out "10" feelings as well? These are interesting questions for teens to ponder.

Compassionate parents want to protect their children from feeling bad. But such protection takes away opportunities to practice surviving bad times. Everyone needs to learn to deal with their feelings and the world. Preoccupation with keeping children happy may lead to children's fearing the "bad" and depending on others to provide stimulation and happiness. Children need to learn that it is all right to feel bad—and that bad feelings are survivable. One way to move past them is to feel them and go *through* them (like a tunnel). That can include talking about feelings. Much emotional energy is spent keeping the lid shut tightly on uncomfortable emotions.

It can be beneficial for adolescents to hear about others' mood ranges. This session also gives them an opportunity to express concerns about moods, including sadness and depression.

Objectives
....

- Group members learn that mood swings are common in their age group and that mood range varies widely from person to person.

- They feel less strange after listening to shared experiences and thoughts about moods.

- They practice positive self-talk as a way to cope with downswings in mood.

- They consider that they might have some choice about their own range of mood.

- They consider how mood range may affect life and vice versa.

1. Ask the group what they have heard or know about mood swings during adolescence. They might mention that mood swings are fairly common for teens. Depending on what is offered, you might mention that many things probably contribute to mood swings:

   ~ rapid physical growth

   ~ hormonal changes

   ~ being aware of and concerned about romantic relationships

   ~ social changes and conflicts

   ~ complex relationships

   ~ greater awareness of, and frustration about, family stressors

   ~ the tug-and-pull of beginning to separate from parents and explore the world

   ~ the bumpy process of forging identity

   ~ family style of coping with stress

2. Ask the group for suggestions about how to cope with mood swings. Ask questions like these:

   ~ What do you do that helps you survive your mood swings?

   ~ How are your parents coping with your mood swings?

   ~ What strategies have adults suggested for dealing with them—for themselves and for you?

3. Pass out sheets of paper and ask group members to draw a line representing their moods during the past week. Some lines may be evenly and moderately rippled, some may have sharp peaks and dips, and some might be almost flat (high or low). Invite the group to display their lines and describe the changes in their moods, if any.

4. Introduce the idea of self-talk. Invite group members to close their eyes and repeat silently one or two of the statements listed below. If there is time, and if you think it would be helpful, go around the group first and ask which statement(s) might be most helpful for them—today or on a daily basis. Whether their mood is up or down at the moment, practicing positive self-talk can help them prepare for future situations.

   ~ "I have a right to be imperfect."

   ~ "I have a right to make mistakes."

   ~ "(She/He/They) (has/have) a right to be imperfect."

   ~ "I will feel better soon."

   ~ "I'm really stronger than I feel I am right now. I'll get through this."

   ~ "I've gotten through times like this before."

   ~ "I'm learning."

~ "They said middle school (or being a teen, or growing up) was tough. Yes, it is. But I'm surviving it."

~ "I need to be patient (kind, gentle, understanding, tolerant) with myself."

~ "I'm not alone. Others my age are riding this same roller coaster."

~ "I'm okay."

5. Ask what their mood is on a scale of 1 to 10, with 1 being "very bad" and 10 being "fantastic." Invite them to comment on what might have contributed to their mood. You may want to spend time discussing some of their situations, but be sure to allow time for each person to report. Even if only five or ten minutes remain when this discussion seems to be winding down, go ahead with the next suggestion.

6. Ask questions like these:

~ What is your usual range of moods, perhaps over one week's time? 1–10? 3–7? 5–9?

~ When are you likely to go up or down?

~ How often do you swing up? down?

~ How often do you feel sad or depressed for no apparent reason?

~ How has your mood range changed over time, if at all?

7. Invite the group to think about others' mood ranges. Ask questions like these and encourage members to respond discreetly:

~ How similar are you to other family members in mood range?

~ How similar are you to your friends in mood range?

~ Whose mood range is (most) like yours? Whose is (most) different?

~ How do you feel about those people?

~ How much control do you feel you have over your mood range?

8. Prepare for closure with these questions:

~ How did it feel to talk about mood swings (and/or mood range)?

~ Were you surprised by anything that was said? What surprised you?

~ Was the discussion helpful? (Closed questions like this often elicit a few nods that provide a positive ending, especially when no time remains for further discussion. If there is no rush, make it an open-ended question: "What in the discussion was helpful?")

Dispose of the sheets or add them to the group folders.

FOCUS Feelings

Unfair!

Objectives

- Group members focus on situations that seem unfair.
- They gain skills in articulating feelings about them.
- They have an opportunity to vent frustrations about the adult world.
- They practice seeing unfairness from a different perspective.

Suggestions

1. Begin by asking the group to brainstorm—and perhaps list on the board or a large sheet of paper—things in life that seem grossly unfair. Tell them you want to hear about situations, institutions, or people that provoke intense emotions about unfairness. (Be prepared for anything from school, court, corporate, and political systems to gender issues and typical wages for teens. Group members might also mention specific actions by adults in their lives, including parents, teachers, and school principals.) Then ask these rhetorical questions about their list to provoke thought:

   ~ Are any of these the result of poor adult judgment or behavior?

   ~ Are any of these problems common across society?

   ~ Are some associated with strict limits or rules?

   ~ Are some unavoidable—that is, "necessary evils"?

2. Change direction with some of these questions:

   ~ How do you react when things seem unfair? What do you feel?

   ~ What feelings cause problems for you? What kinds of problems?

   ~ How do you release your frustrations? Where?

   ~ Do you tell anyone how you feel? Who do you tell?

   ~ How long does the feeling of unfairness last?

   ~ How do you usually handle intense feelings?

   ~ How well does that work for you?

3. Put unfairness into a somewhat different light, especially if your group likes to deal with the abstract. Ask these questions:

~ How do you think "unfair" actions by adults might help you move into adulthood? (Possibilities: They give teens something to react against and help them clarify their values. They give teens a chance to assert themselves and gain confidence.)

~ What advice would you give to someone your age about how to deal with unfairness?

~ What is a smart way to deal with unfairness? (Possibilities: Figure out how to get the system to work for you. Decide to let it go instead of dwelling on it. Find someone to talk to about it. Become a political activist. Talk directly to whoever is being unfair and ask for what you believe is more fair.)

4. In your own words, convey these thoughts to your group: Most people would probably agree that it is the job of parents to set wise limits for their children and encourage impulse control. Protecting and nurturing means firm and consistent guidance and discipline. Children are owed that.

Then, pose some of the following questions:

~ Can you think of something unfair your parents said or did that turned out to be wise?

~ Can you think of times when your parents did something you didn't like that was important for your safety or growth?

~ Can you recall a time when a parent, relative, teacher, or coach made a demand of you that was unfair (and might have been an abuse of power over you)? How did you feel about that? How did you respond?

~ Have you ever been given great responsibility—for example, for taking care of the family, for making family decisions, for being a "parent" to others in the family (including being a parent to a parent), or for doing most household chores? If so, how have you handled that? How have you managed to accomplish that? What are your feelings about that? What have you learned through that? (Even though such situations represent an inappropriate hierarchy within the family, a teen may believe that there is little or no choice about assuming adult responsibilities. Teens may also feel quite mature as a result.)

~ In general, how fairly or unfairly have the adults in your life treated you?

~ Would you like *more* rules and limits in your life? (Preface this by saying that some adolescents do, in fact, wish for more guidance and limits. Invite the group to consider reasons for such wishes.)

5. Ask these questions:

~ What are you owed as adolescents—by your teachers, by your parents, by your employers? (They may think this is just a manipulative question, meant to convince them that they are owed nothing. Quite the contrary. The adults who are responsible for them *do* owe them—care and nurturing, protection, and guidance.)

~ Is it helpful to talk about fairness and unfairness? How is it helpful? (Possibilities: It can be helpful to find out what upsets others: two people with the same agenda might be able to change a situation. Even when situations seem unchangeable, there is less loneliness in knowing that others care and may have similar problems. There is also benefit in learning how to put strong feelings into words. Sometimes that's how we find out what we think and feel. Maybe we don't know we feel something is unfair until we apply that word to it—and find that it fits.)

6. For closure, ask someone to summarize what has been discussed, or tell the group what you yourself have heard. Thank group members for their honesty and helpful sharing, if that is appropriate. You might also ask the following questions:

~ What did you feel during the discussion?

~ What did you think about during the discussion?

Affirm the teens as a group. Tell them, "You have a lot of potential as a group," or "It's good to see you developing as a group," or something more appropriate.

FOCUS Feelings

Disappointment

Background

This session provides another chance for group members to practice articulating thoughts and feelings and to let down the mask that adolescents, like others, wear in order to appear at ease and confident and hide insecurities. All in your group have experienced disappointment, as all people inevitably do, and all have survived. It is usually not difficult for adolescents to recall long and short moments of disappointment. They will probably welcome the chance to hear others' stories of coping. Perhaps they will recognize the value of learning to deal with disappointment—and of not having others protect them from it.

Objectives

- Group members articulate experiences of personal disappointment and express their feelings about those experiences.

- They recognize that disappointment is part of life.

- They learn that experiencing disappointment can potentially build resilience.

Suggestions

1. Begin by asking, "What is *disappointment*?" After group members have shared definitions and examples, ask them if they have experienced it a lot, an average amount, not much, or hardly ever.

2. Encourage them to share moments of disappointment in their lives. First, ask them about disappointments in school—at any age, including the present. Then ask if they have had disappointments in friendships or relationships or at home. (An option here, especially with early adolescents, is to provide paper and a pencil or marker, direct them to draw a disappointed face, and list at least three disappointments underneath it. You might also construct a questionnaire for group members to complete, based on the questions below.) Ask questions like the following, allowing time for elaboration:

   ~ How did you handle the disappointment?

   ~ How did you react? What did you feel?

   ~ How long did it take to move past the disappointment, if indeed you are past it?

   ~ What did you learn about yourself or about feelings in the process?

~ What did you learn about coping? What advice about disappointment can you offer to others?

~ Should someone have protected you from disappointment? (If the examples are related to material desires or to academic, social, or not-being-selected kinds of situations, the answer is likely to be no. However, be aware that negligence or abuse by adults in their lives or loss-related disappointments may warrant a "yes.")

3. If #2 did not already move in this direction, ask group members to think about possible effects of experiencing disappointment. Some may mention negative effects on motivation, self-confidence, faith in people, and trust in relationships, besides feelings of powerlessness and pessimism. However, others might speak of maturity, increased confidence and resilience (perhaps define and discuss *resilience)*, increased drive to succeed, or compassion for others. Ask questions like these:

~ When and how have you helped yourself get over a disappointment? (Perhaps they talked to a good listener, used positive self-talk, immersed themselves in an activity, or tried again. Counseling is also a possibility.)

~ How much disappointment is normal? Can there be too much? too little?

~ What have you experienced connected to competition in school or other places? What are possible results from always winning? from always losing? from being in competitive situations?

~ What can be gained through overcoming disappointment?

4. For closure, ask the group what has been thought-provoking for them during this session. Thank them for sharing, commend them for expressing their feelings well, and wish them a life with just enough disappointments to help them build resilience and develop a can-do attitude.

FOCUS Feelings

The Light Side

Background

Having a sense of humor can make life more enjoyable and help us survive complicated situations. A sense of humor can mean having an eye for the ridiculous, the ability to respond with delight to comical situations, or the ability to laugh at ourselves. Humor can also be a way to cope. From the most grim childhoods can come nationally known comedians, joke-tellers in the break room at work, and nimble conversational wit. Laughter is helpful and healthful.

This session can be used simply as a break from heavy topics or as a serious discussion on the function of humor. Your particular group's needs and abilities should be your guide. If your group normally has difficulty sustaining dialogue because one or more comedians use humor to avoid serious conversation, you might prod group growth by addressing it as a serious topic. It also may be helpful and productive to discuss how humor can be hurtful. Sometimes we are uncomfortable with other people's humor, and we don't know why.

Objectives

- Group members appreciate the role of humor in daily life.

- They consider their own sense of humor.

- They consider how humor can help people cope with difficulties.

- They consider how humor can be hurtful.

Suggestions

1. Ask questions like these to begin:

   ~ Who do you know who has a sense of humor you appreciate?

   ~ What do you like about that person's sense of humor?

   ~ How would you rate your own sense of humor on a scale of 1 to 10, with 1 being "practically nonexistent" and 10 being "terrific"?

   ~ Does your sense of humor show, or is it kept mostly inside—seen only in chuckles or smiles?

   ~ How often are you around people who have a good sense of humor?

   ~ What kind of sense of humor are you most attracted to?

2. Back up a bit. Pursue these ideas:

~ What is a "sense of humor"? (Depending on the developmental level of your group, the following might be helpful for provoking thought: Does it mean joke-telling? responding to situations in a particular way? making terrible, gross, uncomfortable things seem funny? warmth and sensitivity? comfort? repartee? dry wit? practical jokes on people? satire? irony?)

~ Describe your sense of humor.

~ Do people learn to have a sense of humor, or is it natural?

3. Invite the group to consider the function of humor. Ask these questions:

~ What can humor do for us? How can it help us? (Possibilities: It can help us cope with stress and relieve tension. It can help us not take ourselves and others too seriously. It can provide a balance to seriousness.)

~ Can you think of examples where humor (your own or someone else's) has been helpful for you?

~ Can you think of examples where humor (your own or someone else's) has been hurtful? offensive? a put-down? critical? Can you remember a practical joke that caused great discomfort for you or someone else?

~ What about the possibility that humor can interfere with, or shut down, conversation? Some people use humor in tense situations, like when emotions in a group feel uncomfortable. Can you think of examples of this? Have you ever been frustrated by someone who continued to joke when you wanted to be serious? (Point out that there are times when it is preferable to let uncomfortable emotions be expressed rather than covering them up and "pretending them away.")

~ What is sarcasm? (Possibilities: Mocking, ironic, intending to unsettle, sending a negative message about something or someone.) Can you think of examples of it, including when you have used it yourself? Can you think of examples when someone has been sarcastic to you?

~ What might be some good guidelines for telling jokes? (Point out that a joke-teller's audience may include those with sensitivities and differing views related to gender, gender identity, culture, age, religion, politics, physical characteristics, sexuality, sexual orientation, socioeconomic status, and occupation—to name only some considerations.) (Possibilities: Never use humor to hurt, harm, or cause discomfort. Avoid jokes that callously put down any group. Use good taste and be cautious with language and content of jokes.)

4. Ask if anyone has a joke to share. You might also ask the following:

~ Is there a particular kind of joke that is popular with your friends lately?

~ Do you enjoy hearing jokes? What kinds?

~ Do you know any families who joke a lot among themselves?

~ Do you know any families who banter with each other, being critical in a teasing way, connecting with each other in that way?

5. For closure, ask for a volunteer to summarize the session, or ask what was enjoyable, interesting, or thought-provoking. Did the discussion provoke any strong feelings? As your closing statement, affirm humor as complex and interesting, and affirm laughter as good for health.

FOCUS Feelings

Anger

Anger is a powerful emotion. It is full of energy, and it demands release. It can be expressed in violent outbursts, aggression, cruelty, vindictiveness, or obvious sullenness—but also undramatically with quiet words or even silence. It can be expressed both effectively and ineffectively. Ineffectively, it can provide short-term control, but have long-term repercussions. Anger can hurt, and it can be perpetuated. It can also be bottled up, not articulated, stuffed, and turned into sadness and even physical and emotional problems when it goes on for a long time. Angry individuals may be defensive and aggressive. The target of anger may not be the person or situation actually provoking it. On the other hand, anger can positively and productively be directed toward, and find a voice in, political and social action.

Anger can throw people off balance. People can also be discounted when they are angry too often and too intensely. Sometimes anger is not allowed in a family. Many girls and women do not feel permission to be angry—or to express anger. Sometimes they don't even recognize it as anger. It may be expressed in another form, like depression.

Anger can tell us a lot. If we pay attention to it, we can discover what we feel— and even what is contributing to the anger. For instance, something may not be comfortable for us. Perhaps our needs are ignored (by self or others); we feel taken advantage of or taken for granted; we are not assertive enough; we feel "stuck"; or we feel that someone is crashing through personal boundaries. When we can identify the "parts" of anger, we can do something to help ourselves. We can change something—if not the situation itself, then maybe our responses to it. We might ask for help from someone outside of the situation who can be objective. By understanding our behavior, and by learning to assess our feelings accurately, we can make anger a positive force. By learning how to express anger in clear and productive ways, we can enhance our relationships with others and feel empowered. Several options are available in the suggestions for this session.

Objectives

- Group members learn to acknowledge and articulate feelings of anger and to recognize unresolved anger.

- They learn that anger *is*—in other words, it is not something that one chooses or should or should not feel.

- They have a chance to speak about anger-producing situations—at home, at work, at school, or among their peers.

- They learn that they have much in common with others their age regarding anger.

- They learn that all *feelings* are okay, but not all *behaviors* are.

Suggestions

1. Introduce the topic. Hand out copies of "Being Angry" (pages 127–128) and ask the group to fill out the activity sheet with brief responses, anonymously. Assure them that they will not be asked to share all of their answers. When they are done, invite them to share whatever they are willing to.

   Encourage the group to respond, ask questions, and offer suggestions. You may want them to concentrate on only one of their situations—that is, just *a* or just *b*. If some members prefer not to share either one, they may ask to pass (which should always be an option). The group should not press anyone to share. Some may prefer to name the situation, answer yes or no to the other questions, and not elaborate. Fast, able readers may be able to read down all of their answers for *a*, for example, in statement form ("It lasted a day," "Yes, it happens often," and so on).

2. (If the following activity was done during an earlier session, do not repeat it here.) In addition to the above, especially if your group members are young teens, have them fill in an outline of a human form with colors (perhaps from yellow to red or even black) representing various levels of anger according to where angry feelings are felt in the body (for example, in the head, in the clenched jaw, in the stomach, in the heart, in tense shoulders). Group members can then take turns describing how anger feels and where their bodies reflect anger. Perhaps each can also use a metaphor to describe the feelings (for example, flooded, white-hot, cold).

3. Another option is to bring children's books that focus on anger and invite members to read through them and critique them regarding whether the books accurately portray anger and whether they would have been appealing and helpful to members at a younger age. (For a list of suggested books, see the Recommended Resources, page 279.)

4. Go around the group and invite each person to finish this sentence: "The time I was most angry in my life was when . . ." They may elaborate on the intensity of what they felt, if they wish. Assure them that they have the right to pass, as always.

5. Share with the group some of the background information. Encourage the group to read about anger, talk about it, understand it, and ask questions about it throughout their lives. Use some of the following additional thoughts about anger to generate discussion. Or use these ideas to create a handout for discussion.

   ~ Anger is "energy." As a feeling, it's not bad or immoral. We should pay attention to it. It can tell us what needs to be changed.

   ~ We can channel anger constructively into healthy competitiveness, such as in sales and athletics.

~ We can channel anger constructively into political action, protests, social causes, and efforts to right a wrong that has hurt a person or group.

~ Destructive anger hurts people and things; constructive anger channels the energy into positive action.

~ We express anger in many ways—silent withdrawal, moodiness, foul language, insults, criticism, manipulation, tantrums, and violence, for example. We can also use earnest, heartfelt, rational words to express anger.

~ It's possible to be angry with someone we love. It's also easy to point anger at those who simply happen to be around—especially at home.

~ We need to understand why something "pushes our anger button."

~ We can be frightened of our own anger. It threatens our sense of control.

~ Learning how to deal with anger while we're young is important.

~ Women and girls may feel less permission than men and boys in our society to be angry. They may feel sad when anger would be more appropriate. Males may feel more permission to be angry than to be sad, and therefore may express anger when they feel sad. Ideally, all people would feel permitted by society to be angry and sad.

~ Talking about strong feelings with a good listener is helpful. If we can express feelings to someone who hears and accepts them, and if we feel heard, we can begin to move beyond those feelings. Talking about strong feelings with the target of the feelings is even better. An objective third person may be needed to help, both to listen and to respond in helpful ways. Counselors can serve that function.

6. Ask, "Is there someone you're angry with often? Do you argue a lot or exchange angry words? Do you find yourself saying the same things over and over? Maybe there's a way to break that habit." Encourage them to try something different next time. For example, instead of defending themselves or attacking the other person, they might respond by calmly saying, "I hear you. I know you're angry." Point out that changing a pattern in this way is a personally powerful thing to do. When the other person feels heard, he or she might be more willing to listen in return. Eventually *both* people may feel heard, which can help to resolve conflict and diminish anger.

7. If time remains, ask, "How did you learn to 'do anger'? Did someone show you how?" (Some group members may propose that ways to express anger are inherited. Ask them to consider instead that they might learn how to "do emotions" by observation. This suggests that they can also learn new ways to express anger.)

8. For closure, invite the group to summarize the discussion, offer thoughts, or share feelings that surfaced. Encourage them to be alert to angry feelings during the coming week and to share observations at a later meeting. You might also conclude by asking which statements in #13 on the questionnaire they feel are true, especially if you have discussed anger in those terms. Dispose of the sheets.

Being Angry

1. Briefly describe the last two times you were angry.

   a.   b.

For questions 2–12, your "a" answers should relate to the situation "a" you described in question #1, and your "b" answers should relate to situation "b."

2. What caused each situation?

   a.   b.

3. How did you act? (Did you say anything? Were you aggressive? assertive? Did you do something physical? hurt anything or anyone? cry? yell? leave? withdraw? show your temper?)

   a.   b.

4. How long did your angry feeling last?

   a.   b.

5. Did you feel that something or someone was being unfair?

   a.   b.

6. Did you feel that you were being attacked, invaded, or harmed somehow?

   a.   b.

7. Does this angry situation happen often for you?

   a.   b.

8. Did you or someone else bring up "old garbage" that had nothing to do with the situation? If so, what?

   a.   b.

(continued)

Being Angry (continued)

9. Is your anger about the situation done, or is it likely to come up again?

   a.   b.

10. Was the anger connected to something that goes on and on, but is rarely discussed?

    a.   b.

11. Did you "talk out" your anger later with someone who was not involved in the situation?

    a.   b.

12. Have you discussed your anger with the person or persons involved in the situation?

    a.   b.

    If not, what would you like to say to that person or those persons?

    a.

    b.

13. Check what you believe about anger. You may check more than one response.

    ☐ Anger is one of many strong feelings that everyone feels sometimes.

    ☐ Anger is a bad feeling.

    ☐ Anger is a good feeling.

    ☐ Anger always hurts someone.

    ☐ Anger is always dangerous.

    ☐ Anger can be expressed in many ways.

FOCUS Feelings

....

Fear, Worry, and Anxiety

Background

....

It isn't just young children who are afraid. Adolescents also have fears and anxieties. They may worry about certain school situations, like giving a speech, performing in a concert, or having no one to eat lunch with. They may worry about the safety, health, or job security of their parents or about their own health and the possibility of death by accident, gang violence, random or targeted shootings, fire, natural disaster, or terrorism. They may wonder and worry about HIV/AIDS and other sexually transmitted diseases—and even life-threatening hospital infections. They may worry about internet predators. They may fear bullying at school or online and/or abuse at home, even being afraid to go home after school if home is dangerously unpredictable. For all, there may also be anxiety about romantic relationships, getting along at work, or parents fighting. All may feel anxiety about the future—because it seems bleak, because it carries heavy responsibilities, or because it is simply an unknown. They may have vague social and sexual anxiety and may wonder and worry about their sexual orientation, even before they leave elementary school.

It's normal to feel anxiety when facing new or challenging situations. When anxiety is a catalyst for growth, it can improve a person's quality of life. When someone is able to embrace anxiety and not avoid challenging situations through escapism, addictions, or hysteria, life can be an adventure. In contrast, anxiety may preoccupy someone so much that it limits life activities and some freedom is lost. Life satisfaction is probably related to the ability to adapt to change. Being able to deal with anxiety is part of being adaptable.

Young people of all ages experience anxiety, and school, community, and college and university counselors are seeing more and more of it. For some students, anxiety is a constant, vague dread of what might lie ahead. Perfectionists often are anxious about the next challenge, which they believe must be done perfectly. College-bound students may "catastrophize," worrying that today's fatigue will impact papers, tests, grades, extracurricular performance, and, ultimately, college selection and acceptance to preferred institutions. They and others who are chronically anxious about the future may have trouble relaxing in the present. It may be difficult to imagine getting over all the hurdles between present and future. And, of course, those are seen as a formidable whole, not as a series of conquerable, manageable steps.

Teens need encouragement to pause and appreciate the present—and even laugh a little about themselves and their anxieties. Helping them gain insight about personal responses to various situations can also be beneficial. In this "age of anxiety," they need to name their dread—in a place where it is safe to talk. Ideally, they will be able to accept normal anxiety as potentially motivating and find ways to lessen whatever anxiety depletes energy and limits life. Talking about fears can help teens find support and cope.

Objectives

- Group members communicate honestly about their worries and fears.

- They learn that anxiety is part of being human.

- They learn that others their age also have worries and fears.

- They practice identifying and distinguishing between rational and irrational fears, and between productive and unproductive anxiety.

- They consider ways to diminish irrational fears.

- They practice articulating concerns about the future.

Suggestions

NOTE: There are probably too many suggestions here for just one session. Choose direction according to what you think your group would benefit from most. It is also possible to split this into two sessions: a fear focus and an anxiety focus, perhaps, even though there is considerable overlap between these areas. Another option is to let the activity sheet be the focus for a follow-up session.

1. Hand out copies of "Being Afraid" (page 134). Have the group fill out the activity sheet, anonymously, as a way of tuning in to past and present fears. Depending on trust and age level, invite members to share some of their responses—perhaps just #1, #2, and #3 if you think they might be hesitant to share the others. For #1, they might mention bad dreams and barking dogs, heights and depths, fire and water, spiders and snakes, or being lost, for example. Then move away from the activity sheet and ask questions like the following. Having filled out the sheet may help them articulate responses to the questions here and later in this meeting.

   ~ Have some of your early fears continued until today? Which ones?

   ~ Were some of your early fears provoked by specific things that happened to you? (You may want to let yes or no suffice here if group members do not offer examples quickly, since you might seem to be prying if you ask for specifics.)

   ~ What did you do when you were afraid?

   ~ Who comforted you? (If no one) How did you make it through that time? (Perhaps they learned to cope, became strong, and learned to rely on themselves.)

2. Move the discussion into the present. Choose questions from the following that are appropriate for your group's age, maturity level, and context:

   ~ What kinds of fears do kids your age have? (This general question lets group members put the question at arm's length for a moment, but it may still result in personal examples.)

   ~ If you have fears, what do they feel like? (You may want to encourage similes and metaphors—like "heavy weights," "lurking monsters," "a hand around the heart," "a knot in the stomach." You also might give one of your own metaphors as an example.)

   ~ What are some times when you get "butterflies" in your stomach, feel that your heart stops for a moment, or feel that you can't breathe—because you are anxious?

   ~ Which fears and anxieties are vague—not about a specific person, thing, or situation? (Possibilities: About the future, relationships in general, or being criticized or evaluated—by anyone, anywhere.)

   ~ Which fears are real and specific? (Perhaps a parent's unemployment, a family member's poor health, a bullying situation, an asthma attack.)

   ~ How much do you worry about violence at home? on the street? at school? Do you ever feel unsafe?

   Let the discussion move freely in any of these directions. Complex situations may come up, sharing might be spontaneous, and group members may immediately respond to each other. Encourage them to share feelings. If they tell a story about something fearsome, ask about their feelings related to the story or reflect feelings you hear yourself (for example, "That does sound scary"). Tell them to put specific words on the feelings (for example, "What did scary feel like?"). Focusing on feelings is practice for effective communication in relationships and for coping with stress. Focusing on feelings also helps prevent long narratives by individuals, which limit broad participation within the group.

3. Eventually ask group members for examples of fears that are real—things that could really happen. After they offer ideas, say, "These may be *rational* fears, because they make sense and there might be real danger or discomfort." Then ask them to list some fears about things that are *not* likely to happen. Afterward, say, "These may be *irrational* fears, because they are not reasonable." Then ask these questions:

   ~ When do you worry most about things that are *unlikely* to happen?

   ~ Have these fears ever stopped you from doing important things? What things? What other feelings do you have when you worry or are afraid?

   ~ What could you do to make these fears bigger? (Example: Worry even more, even every waking hour.) smaller? (Examples: Self-talk in an encouraging way; look at the fears and figure out why they're so powerful; label them as irrational.)

   ~ What would be different in your life if you didn't have irrational fears?

4. Ask the group to define *anxiety* (vague worry and concern). Then invite the group to share what they worry about by asking, "What are vague worries that sometimes occupy your thoughts?" Perhaps each group member can share three things.

Going around the group, ask students to rate their general anxiety/worry level on a scale of 1 to 10. (Especially for young teens or with middle schoolers, you might draw and copy a "worryometer," similar to the "procrastometer" in the "Procrastination" session on page 40. Numbered degrees might be "I worry all the time," "I worry every day," "I worry most of the time," "I worry a lot," "I'm sort of a worrier," "sometimes I worry," "I worry once in a while," "I hardly ever worry," "I can't remember worrying," "I never worry.") Then ask how anxiety/worry affects their lives:

~ How much does your anxiety keep you from doing something?

~ How much of your free time is spent thinking anxious thoughts?

~ What are the catastrophes you worry about—terrible things that might happen if you do or don't do certain things? (You might ask for an example of a small worry—like a bad grade—and then catastrophize as a group: "What's the worst thing that could happen if you got a bad grade?" "Then what might happen?" "And then?")

~ How much does your personal well-being depend on whatever you're concerned about?

~ (Ask those with low levels of anxiety) How do you view some of the worry-filled situations that others have shared here? What advice would you give them?

5. Introduce the idea of "productive anxiety"—worry that helps people get a job done or take care of personal care and safety. Ask the following:

~ What are some things you worry about that help you get things done? (Possibilities: Assignments; tests; locking the door at night; not losing a wallet or house key; preparing for a performance.)

~ Can you think of some examples of excessive, unproductive worry? (Possibilities: Social situations in general; criticism; imperfection; mistakes; "what ifs"—like moving, parents divorcing, fire, natural disasters, death, not measuring up in the future, not having a best friend, getting sick.)

6. Ask students to think of several things they felt quite anxious about a year ago. They might even write them down so that they can study them for a moment. Then ask these questions:

~ How many of those situations turned out all right?

~ Which ones were not worth worrying about? (Similar situations in the future will probably also work out all right.)

~ Which are still concerns?

7. Invite the group to think about whether worry and anxiety can be learned. Ask, "Who taught you to worry as you do (whether productively or unproductively) by showing you how to do it?" (Worry and anxiety may have genetic origins, but to some extent, these tendencies can probably be made worse by others' modeling them.)

8. Turn the group's attention to self-talk as a tool for coping with anxiety. Begin by asking these questions:

   ~ What are some things you tell yourself when you're facing situations that are frightening? What goes through your head?

   ~ What are some things you could tell yourself that might help you handle these situations better?

   Explore the idea of changing anxious self-talk to positive self-talk. Encourage the group to come up with positive, rational statements to replace the following:

   ~ "I've got to get an A on this test."

   ~ "I'm not going to be able to remember what to say."

   ~ "I'll be crushed if she says no."

   ~ "I know I'm not going to do well in the game."

   ~ "If I don't get a job, I'll have a miserable summer."

   ~ "If we move, I'll never see my friends again. And I'll never make new friends."

   ~ "If no one asks me to dance, I'll never be able to show my face in school again."

   ~ "If we break up, I'm going to die."

   ~ "If I wear those jeans, everyone will laugh."

9. For closure, ask someone to summarize the session. Was anything surprising? What was helpful? Wish the group a relaxing, only-productively-anxious time until the next meeting.

   Thank them for their honesty, if appropriate. Dispose of the sheets.

Being Afraid

1. As a little child, I often was afraid that

   a. _____

   b. _____

   c. _____

2. Later on, I had these fears:

   a. _____

   b. _____

   c. _____

3. Of the fears I listed in #1 and #2, these were *rational* (they could really happen):

   a. _____

   b. _____

   c. _____

4. Of the fears I listed in #1 and #2, these were *irrational* (they were highly unlikely to happen):

   a. _____

   b. _____

   c. _____

5. My *rational* fears at the present time (real fears of real possibilities) are

   a. _____

   b. _____

   c. _____

6. My *irrational* fears at this time in my life (fears of things that probably could never happen) are

   a. _____

   b. _____

   c. _____

7. Of the fears I listed in #5 and #6, these take up the most energy:

   a. _____

   b. _____

   c. _____

FOCUS Feelings

When We Were at Our Best

Background

This might be a light, upbeat session. On the other hand, for teens who have low self-esteem, or who might be in particularly difficult situations, it may be distressing. In either case, it has the potential to affirm personal strengths, especially when a group has established a good level of trust.

Objectives

- Group members affirm their own and each other's personal strengths and worth.

- They recall a time when they were at their best.

- They explore ways to recapture their best selves.

Suggestions

1. Pass out sheets of paper and invite group members to write something positive, personal, and appreciated about each of the other group members. They may mention something about personality, warmth, kindness, acceptance of others, ability to listen, faithfulness in attendance, energy, creativity, insights, deep thinking, unusualness, assertiveness, sensitivity, smile, or eye contact, for example. Be aware that, especially if some group members have not been showing a positive side, it may be difficult for others to affirm them. Giving the just-mentioned suggestions at the outset will help.

2. Holding the focus on one person at a time, invite the rest of the group to offer affirming statements.

3. Invite them to remember a time when they were at their best. If your group likes to write down ideas before sharing them, ask them to list a few of the characteristics of this "best self."

4. Ask each group member in turn to share the context of this positive period in their lives. Following are directions that may be followed if they don't appear spontaneously:

   ~ How old were you?

   ~ What helped you to feel so good?

   ~ What kinds of comments were others making about you?

   ~ How was the rest of your life affected by your being at your best?

~ What were you doing for yourself at that best point in your life?

~ If these best parts of yourself haven't been showing lately, where are they?

~ What could *you* do (or what would help you) to bring your best parts to light again? (Encourage them to think about what they can do for themselves, rather than focusing on what others can do for them. We cannot control others—only ourselves, and how we respond to situations.)

Suggest that the group problem-solve together for the last question, if that seems appropriate. Be careful, however, to validate whatever negatives they might bring up as preventing the best self from surfacing again. Do not minimize their difficulties. To validate their feelings and difficulties, you might say, "Yes, it sounds as if you're in a challenging situation right now"; "That sounds like a lot of pressure"; "It's hard to remember the best of ourselves when our world seems out of joint." Then affirm the best parts from the past (for example, "You were a good friend and your friends enjoyed being with you"). Remind group members that their best parts were real—and are still part of them. Express confidence that they will be able to have them again, especially since they have gained strength in managing difficult situations since then.

5. For closure, tell the group that it was good to hear about their best selves. Ask for summary comments about feelings, thoughts, or the discussion in general. How was it to talk about this topic as a group? Dispose of the sheets or add them to the group folders.

FOCUS Feelings

....

Happiness

Background

I recall a poster about happiness that was displayed prominently in a room I once taught in. I do not recall the exact words, but it compared happiness to a butterfly. It escapes us if we chase it, but it may come and sit on our shoulder when we are not preoccupied with pursuing it.

That is a nice thought. But many adolescents have doubts. Some wonder if happiness actually exists anywhere. For others, happiness is familiar. They might not feel it every day, but they have faith that it will come again—like a butterfly.

Happy is a word that adolescents use often, whether describing the feeling of a moment or telling how they wish they could feel. This session can move in many directions.

Objectives

- Group members learn that there are many ways to view happiness.

- They consider whether happiness is something to be achieved, whether it is a choice, whether it can be pursued, and whether it might sometimes be there, unnoticed.

Suggestions

1. Begin by asking, "What does *happy* mean to you?" Encourage students to describe feelings and give examples of times they have felt happy. (If your group likes to draw, invite them to draw a picture representing "happy." You can probably begin the discussion before everyone has completed the picture. You might ask them to make a statement or two about their picture to the group.) Then ask these questions:

   ~ Do things like success, love, security, quietness, contentment, rest, competence, weather, faith, friends, favorite activities, or gifts "make" us happy?

   ~ Is happiness related to anything particular? Or does it simply "happen"?

Important

Be alert to those group members who may actually be saddened by a discussion of this topic. Some may be cynical and pessimistic about happiness. Encourage them to express their feelings (resist any urge to "fix" or judge their attitudes). Give them time to think complexly. Validate their feelings—that is, don't express doubt about their feelings, but rather affirm their feelings (for example, "That does sound sad" or "I can hear your frustration"). It is important that they feel heard and not shut down. If their thoughts affect the mood of the group, comment about that (for example, "I'm sensing that hearing her say that just changed the climate in here") and discuss it, but without judgment. Those who are not "happy," whatever that is, probably are aware of the power of their feelings and may be hesitant to speak. The group can practice listening attentively and affirming them.

2. Ask questions like the following after group members have shared their thoughts:

~ How often do you think about happiness—where you might even mentally use the word *happy*? (Perhaps on a scale of 1 to 10, with 10 being "every day.")

~ Are any of you usually buoyant and upbeat? (To those) How much do you think about happiness?

~ (Depending on the response to the preceding question) Do you think that upbeat people think about happiness *less* than people who are *not* upbeat— or more? Do unhappy people think about happiness a lot? Is that possible? What do you think?

~ Does anyone here *not* think about happiness much? (To those) How often do you *feel* happy?

~ Does anyone here feel distressed about not feeling happy often? (If so) Can you remember times when you were happy? What was different then?

~ What do you connect to "happy thoughts"?

Important

Be prepared for the mention of altered states—through alcohol, inhalants, or other drugs, for example. If so, explore that kind of happy—that is, short-term effects, escapism, danger, addiction, or poor coping habits that are counterproductive. Sexual activity might also be seen as a route to happiness. Affirm that the sexual drive is certainly powerful and is fueled by feelings and desire for feelings. Group members might consider that sexual activity can also be a potentially dangerous way of coping with stress and pursuing happiness, especially if it is seen simply as a means to that end. It is important, if either of these areas comes up, to hear students' thoughts and opinions first before offering your adult views. Be aware that students will be watching your responses. By responding rationally, without preaching, you will provide them with an opportunity to express feelings, come out from behind bravado, and be young and vulnerable. In some cases, that opportunity might be rare. It is always important to enter the adolescent world and hear adolescent concerns, and not make assumptions, before giving adult opinions, observations, and guidance—and then perhaps only if requested. There is great potential value in simply giving a group the chance to express their perspectives and get feedback from peers and you. Moving quickly to advice or judgment will likely stifle important and respectful discussion. You do not have to advise or evaluate anything here.

3. Continue the discussion by asking questions like these:

  ~ (After telling the group about the poster mentioned in the background information) What do you think about happiness being like a butterfly?

  ~ Is it possible for a person to choose to be happy, even in bad circumstances? What are you basing your opinion on?

  ~ Can a person in a reasonably good situation choose *not* to be happy? If so, have you seen examples where this seems to be the case?

  ~ How much control does a person have over moods? What are you basing your opinion on?

4. If someone brings up the topic of depression, the group might pursue that spontaneously. Prepare yourself by reading through the "Sadness, Depression, and Dark Thoughts" session (pages 153–158) in advance of this session. If depression is not mentioned, that topic is best delayed.

5. For closure, ask someone to summarize the discussion, or ask one or more of the following questions:

  ~ What have been the main ideas in our discussion today?

  ~ What were your feelings during the discussion?

  ~ Was happiness a good topic to discuss? Why or why not?

Compliment them, if appropriate, on expressing thoughts and feelings well during the discussion. Note that being aware of feelings and being able to describe and express them clearly will probably help them in future relationships, besides helping them emotionally.

FOCUS Feelings

Coping with Change, Loss, and Transition

Background

Many situations and events involve loss: the death of a loved one; the death of a pet; the loss of a friend because of a move; the loss of childhood; the loss of innocence; the loss of security and trust; the loss of family "the way it used to be"; an accident, illness, or other situation that changes the ability to do favorite things; a relationship that does not work out; the shattering of an image (one's own or someone else's).

Grieving is certainly not just for losses through death. Every change, even positive change, leaves something behind. Something is lost. For every loss there is grief, which may or may not find a way to be expressed. With every loss comes a time of transition: to life without the person, the pet, the place, the friend, the family the way it was, the trust, the relationship. The transition period may be uneven, as new resources and new life rhythms are found.

This session gives teens an opportunity to share experiences related to loss and transition. Perhaps they can find common ground, comfort, and hope through that communication. Not all members of a group will have experienced difficult transitions. However, those who have will probably feel support from the group, and those who have not will gain understanding and compassion for those who have.

Objectives

- Group members learn that many life experiences involve loss.

- They learn that it is helpful to share such experiences discreetly with others.

- They gain hope through hearing how others have successfully navigated transitions.

Suggestions

1. Introduce the topic with material from the background information or ask the group to brainstorm life experiences that involve change and loss.

2. Hand out copies of "Experiencing Loss" (pages 142–143) and ask the group to complete the activity sheet with very brief responses, anonymously. Use the questionnaire to start discussion. You might take one part of question #1 at a time and ask for volunteers to share what they have written. Be sensitive to the fact that some members might not feel comfortable sharing their answers. Simply state that they can decide what would be appropriate to share. You might also ask each member to list *all* parts of #1 that were answered with yes.

3. As each student reports responses, ask some of the following questions. (If someone's loss is in the present, adjust the questions accordingly and omit the last two.)

~ Do you remember your feelings at the time of the loss? What were some that you recall?

~ If your emotions were huge and strong, how did that affect you?

~ Who was available for support—if anyone?

~ What was the hardest part of going through that experience?

~ What did you have to learn to do?

~ What did you do for yourself to help you through it?

~ How long did it take for you to move past the intense feelings of loss?

~ What advice would you give to someone just beginning the same transition?

You might offer the following general suggestions for dealing with loss, if the group does not mention them:

~ Go ahead and feel.

~ Try to understand that feelings help us to start going through a difficult experience. We have to go through them—like a tunnel—and can't go around or over or under them. Feelings can be painful, but they move us forward, and we can survive them. They are an important part of healing. Struggle has a purpose, in the view of experts who have studied it. It helps us develop into stronger, wiser, more compassionate, more "advanced" people.

~ Talk to a friend or an adult, someone you trust. Or talk to a counselor.

~ Find ways to keep going. Distract yourself. Keep busy with activities. Make plans for your altered life. Reach out to others.

~ Remember that time *does* heal scars, and though the memory will remain, it will gradually lose its intensity.

4. For closure, ask a few group members to summarize what they thought or felt during the discussion. Dispose of the sheets.

Experiencing Loss

1. Have you ever experienced loss through . . .

. . . the death of someone you were close to?   Yes ☐   No ☐

Who? _____

. . . the death of a pet?   Yes ☐   No ☐

What was the pet's name? _____

. . . moving away from friends?   Yes ☐   No ☐

Who were they? _____

. . . having friends move away?   Yes ☐   No ☐

Who? _____

. . . losing trust in someone?   Yes ☐   No ☐

Who? _____

. . . losing trust in something?   Yes ☐   No ☐

What? _____

. . . an illness or accident?   Yes ☐   No ☐

What happened? _____

. . . a change in your family or life that made it

different from what it used to be?   Yes ☐   No ☐

What was the change? _____

. . . the loss of a special friendship?   Yes ☐   No ☐

Who with? _____

. . . being disappointed in a special person?   Yes ☐   No ☐

Who? _____

(continued)

Experiencing Loss (continued)

... loss of innocence, or childhood, or the past?   Yes ☐   No ☐

Which one? _____

... the loss of feeling secure?   Yes ☐   No ☐

When? _____

... a major change in your life?   Yes ☐   No ☐

When? _____

... another kind of loss, not mentioned above?   Yes ☐   No ☐

What? When? _____

2. Pick three of the circumstances described in #1. What feelings do you recall from that time?

a. _____

b. _____

c. _____

How long did it take before you felt better?

a. _____

b. _____

c. _____

FOCUS Feelings

It's Complicated

When we ask a troubled student, "What's going on?" the response might be, "It's complicated." This response, in itself, does not provide information about specifics, but it may have to suffice. Adolescents, regardless of age, ability, and social status, may assume that complex circumstances, many-layered problems, or relationship concerns at school or at home, for example, are simply beyond description or impossible to resolve. Limited language for talking about problems or feelings, lack of experience with explaining difficult situations, concerns about making something more difficult with family or peers by talking about it—any number of possible constraints might keep an important conversation from happening. But students need to have these conversations, sooner or later.

This session provides an opportunity for group members to sort out complicated situations if trust and safety in the group have developed. Remind group members that when talking about complicated issues in the group, they need to be discreet—respecting others' privacy by not mentioning names, not hurting someone inside or outside of the group, choosing carefully what to say—but they also need to help the group understand a concern by offering their thoughts when comfortable doing so. Group members can learn from each other, support one another, and practice expressing themselves within normal social constraints. Learning how to talk about complex topics helps students develop useful skills for current and future relationships.

Objectives

- Group members observe and gain skills related to expressive language.

- They realize that complicated situations are common among peers.

- They feel support in the shared experience of talking about concerns.

Suggestions

1. To generate thoughts about the topic, ask the group for examples of complicated situations students may find themselves in, such as with family members, friends, peers, bosses or administrators, teachers, or coaches. Give each student an opportunity to provide one to five examples. Assure them that they can repeat what someone else has given as an example. Perhaps ask a group member to make a list as examples are given—or write them down yourself—perhaps on a whiteboard or a large sheet of paper. Encourage group members to listen carefully because you will ask them later what were the most common types of situations.

Ask the group what were some themes they heard. What kinds of complicated situations were mentioned most often? What situations were they surprised to hear about?

Ask for additional examples they thought of while listening to others and add these examples to the list.

2. Invite group members to draw on a half sheet of paper or sculpt with pipe cleaners something that reflects the complexity of "what's going on" for them at the present time. Then, invite members to talk about how the drawings or sculptures represent the complexity of their situation or situations. *Resist the impulse to probe beyond what students initially explain.* Thank them for giving the group something to think about.

3. Ask the group *when* they are likely to think about complicated situations—for example, when riding on a bus or in a car, when trying to sleep, when listening to music, when walking, when sitting in classes. If someone has no complicated situations to be concerned about, celebrate that sincerely and respectfully.

4. Ask students some scaling questions:

   ~ How complicated does your life feel right now on a scale of 1 to 10, with 10 being "extremely complicated"?

   ~ On a scale of 1 to 10, with 10 being "quite often," how often do you talk, or how much would you like to talk, about complicated situations with a trusted adult? with a friend? (Invite those who gave ratings of 5 to 10 to describe the qualities of the adults and friends, without naming, that make these people good listeners.)

   ~ On a scale of 1 to 10, with 10 being "It would really be good if I could do that," how much do you need, or would like, to talk about a complicated situation with someone? (Avoid probing if little or no information is offered. Instead, perhaps say, "I wish you well.")

5. For closure, ask for comments summarizing what it was like for members to think, hear, and talk about complicated situations. Invite anyone feeling high anxiety about a complicated situation to stay after the meeting or to contact you before the end of the day to discuss possible resources or, if you are a counselor, to "be heard" in private. If you are not a counselor and your group meets in a school, encourage these students to see a school counselor or accompany them to a school counselor's office.

FOCUS Feelings

When Parents Divorce

Background

Some group members probably have experienced divorce in their families. For some, it might have occurred when they were toddlers; others may currently be in the uneven period that often follows it, including being in the throes of custody battles or being pressured to decide which parent to live with. Some might have experienced divorce more than once. Feelings and behaviors related to separation and divorce may include loss of concentration, acting out, sadness and depression, anger, or sense of loss. It is also possible that the process is undramatic and uneventful, with little or no acrimony.

Divorce is not abnormal or unusual in current society. Of course, divorce is not an ideal and often involves considerable upheaval. But it is unfair and inaccurate to characterize all divorced families as unstable and "broken"—that is, not functioning. It is also unfair and inaccurate to assume that all single parents are inadequate in child-rearing—or that all so-called intact families parent adequately. In many cases, divorce stops abuse and mutual destruction that even counseling cannot alter. In such situations, those who divorce and can address important personal needs may be healthier than they were before. People can do harm by staying together.

What are some possible reasons for the high divorce rate? Media messages create unrealistic expectations about marriage. A mobile society deprives couples of the support of extended family and long-term friends. Couples are often not adept at communicating personal needs in relationships. Couples grow and change in different ways, at different speeds. Too few go for counseling *early*, when adjustments can be made more easily than later, when pain and anger reign.

Often, young adults marry without first forming separate identities and clear ego boundaries. When something goes wrong, they are unable to deal with imperfections in themselves or their partners. They cannot look at their relationship in parts and address those that need fixing. People who are not healthily separate individuals tend to form and leave relationships quickly. They continue unhealthy patterns that are familiar to them and that reflect their poorly defined sense of self. They are not committed to changing those patterns and often lack the skills needed to change them.

Whatever the reasons for a divorce, it is never easy for those involved, particularly the children, who also likely do not receive the same benefit as the adults. How children cope and thrive following a divorce depends, in part, on what parents do to avoid the tensions that can linger when the *emotional* divorce is left unfinished. Sometimes divorce escalates conflict instead of stopping it, with rancor and vindictiveness going on for years. Long and expensive court battles are hurtful for everyone involved, since the focus stays on what is wrong. Mediation or work with both legal and mental health professionals can help make the process less destructive. When parents can maturely separate spousal issues from parental issues, they may be better able to keep the children in mind in the midst of the stress of divorce.

There are many similarities between death and divorce in how people react. Divorce means change, change means loss, and loss means grief. Grief needs mourning, a process that can take years. It is important to feel the feelings rather than push them away, since they can remain toxic and affect the future if they are not allowed to run their course.

It is important to help children of any age understand that good people do divorce, that children are not responsible for parents divorcing, that it is difficult when a child is asked to be a messenger between Mom and Dad, that it's easy to idealize the absent parent and have conflict with the custodial parent, that proper preparation for divorce can lessen many fears in children, that even adult children can feel devastated by their parents' divorce, and that the need for co-parenting after a divorce does not necessarily end when children are grown up. Under most circumstances, children deserve some sort of consistent contact with both parents.

Adolescents may find normal confusion about sexuality exaggerated by divorce. In addition, children of divorce sometimes are afraid of marriage, stay in unhappy marriages, or repeat unhealthy patterns from the past. Discussion groups can help students to learn important communication skills, encourage exploration of feelings, and ultimately help to prepare them for long-term relationships.

Important	Some group members might welcome a discussion of divorce; others may not. Especially when the group has not been organized specifically for "divorce support," you need to be sensitive to various situations in addressing this topic. You might even give general permission at the outset of this meeting for individuals to remain silent, if they prefer.

The comfort/trust level of the group, how recently group members have been affected by divorce, and the number who have been affected will likely determine how much, and if, they share and interact during this discussion. During the previous session, in order to know what to expect, you might have them tell you on paper if their parents are divorced and, if so, when the divorce occurred; if they are in a "new family"; and if they are willing to talk about their feelings and experiences in the group. Explain that you will be addressing the topic soon, but they will be in charge of whether they share anything about their experiences, and you will not ask them about divorce unless they indicate their willingness to be asked. Mention that those who have not been affected by divorce may learn more about it and become more sensitive to those who have, and that everyone can benefit by hearing what others have to say. To help to avoid indiscreet sharing about current tensions of parents/guardians, emphasize that the focus of the discussion will be on changes, feelings, and adjustments for kids after divorces occur—not on marriages in general.

If your group is large, or if it consists of an entire classroom, it may be more difficult for students to share their thoughts and feelings regarding this sensitive and emotionally charged topic. In fact, this topic may not be appropriate for interactive discussion in a large group. A counselor might do an informative presentation on divorce instead.

Objectives
. . . .

- Group members learn how young people respond to divorce.
- They learn how children of divorce adjust to their altered families.
- They learn that it can be helpful for children of divorce to share feelings about their experiences.

Suggestions
. . . .

1. Familiarize yourself with the background information provided and organize an introduction to the topic that is appropriate for your group. Acknowledge the inevitable changes and loss that result from divorce; perhaps mention general dilemmas for children regarding divorce; note that adjustments to new family and living situations take time; assume that the divorce probably remains a significant memory; and affirm that good people sometimes have difficulty living together. You might even refer to how common divorce is in your school or institution, since many children in divorced families are unaware of that and may feel that no one can understand their situation. In a comfortable small group, support from those who have "been there" can be valuable for those currently experiencing divorce.

2. There are many potential directions for this discussion. If you followed the suggestion in "Important," you might say, "Last time, some of you wrote that you have experienced divorce. If you are willing to share some of your experiences, your thoughts might help others in the group to better understand what divorce means." If some group members have indicated that they are willing to share, ask the following questions:

   ~ How did various members of your family react to the divorce? (Here, you might have group members draw quick outlines of each member of their family and fill in each with a color that represents a reaction.)

   ~ How did you react?

   ~ What roles did your family members have before and after the divorce? For example, who was the leader? helper? bill-payer? house-cleaner? dishwasher? car-fixer? family "taxi"? cook?

   ~ How did roles change because of the divorce?

   ~ How have your life and your responsibilities changed since the divorce?

   ~ How much of a surprise was the divorce for you?

~ What feelings and attitudes have you gone through since the divorce?

~ How much and what kind of contact do you have with the parent who doesn't live with you?

~ What have you learned about yourself in this experience?

~ What strengths have you discovered in yourself?

~ What advice would you give someone going through divorce now?

Ask the group members who are willing to share if others may also ask them questions, especially those who are in need of assurance or advice. Encourage discretion (for example, "Think carefully about your questions, and be sensitive to feelings and the need for family privacy") and, if necessary, intervene (for example, "Is that question too personal?"). Some answers may generate helpful discussion.

3. For closure, thank the group for sharing and for offering support, if that is appropriate. Remind them that talking about feelings is important for healing and also as practice for their own relationships in the future. To obtain feedback for yourself and future planning, ask them how valuable and/or comfortable the discussion was.

FOCUS Feelings

Dealing with Holidays and Family Gatherings

Background

After (not before) a holiday break from school, one involving family get-togethers and anticipation, this topic can help group members tie up some feelings about what they experienced and address some of the developmental issues that are involved. Holidays bring out the best and the worst in extended families. They also bring into sharp focus the adjustments required when families break up, are re-formed in new configurations, or are joined by new in-laws in the family circle. These are changes experienced by many teens.

Adolescents sometimes feel caught in the middle at gatherings, suspended as they are between childhood and adulthood. Perhaps they cannot just happily play with the cousins, as they used to, because these age-peers have grown up and have different interests, and it's not enough simply to talk about toys, games, and food. Maybe the teens are not interested in the adult conversation, either. The traditional holiday event may not have the wonder and color that it used to. In addition, older adolescents often work many hours at jobs over the holidays. Some may have to travel to one parent's distant home—and meet his or her new spouse. Holiday get-togethers may be painful reminders of loss and how things used to be. The week after the holiday break might not be full of happy memories.

This focus can be valuable for gaining perspective. Expect a variety of experiences and feelings—from "best ever" to "worst possible." Be prepared that some group members might not have been with any family at all.

Objectives

- Group members learn that any frustration or sadness they experienced over the holiday break was probably shared by several others their age.

- They put their feelings into a developmental perspective.

- They learn to articulate complex and varied feelings associated with the holidays.

Suggestions

1. Have the group begin by reporting how they are feeling at the present moment on a scale of 1 to 10, with 10 being "terrific." They may give some reasons for their emotional state. This is a good way to direct attention to feelings, since that is the focus of the session. It is also another chance for group members to practice talking about feelings.

2. Ask the group to tell about their holidays—what was fun, what was stressful, what new experiences they had, where they went. Or, as an alternative, have them list on paper one or two times of good feelings in any context, and one or two moments of stress, and share some of these.

3. Move the focus to interactions with family members. If some individuals in your group celebrate at times other than during this season, encourage them to think back to the last extended-family gathering they experienced. If someone indicates no extended-family contact (which might be because of vacation travel, economic circumstances, family accident/illness, family dissension, discomfort with extended family, extended family in another country), make a calm, validating comment (for example, "So your holiday situation wasn't typical, didn't fit the stereotype" or "So something major interfered" or "It was just your immediate family that got together"). Ask questions like the following of those who had family gatherings:

   ~ Which relatives attended your family gatherings?

   ~ What kinds of relationships do you have with them?

   ~ Do you see them often otherwise?

   ~ What were some changes in them since the last time you were together?

   ~ Had anything changed in how you felt toward these people?

   ~ How would you describe your extended family (including brothers and sisters, parents, aunts, uncles, cousins, grandparents, stepfamilies, foster family)? How would you describe how they are when they get together in a large group? (If positive) Who is particularly enjoyable for you? What kinds of things do you do together? (Here, you might ask, "If we were your extended family at a holiday gathering, what would we all be doing right now?")

4. Focus on the feelings brought out by group members' holiday experiences. In fact, if the discussion seems to be focused solely on happenings, foods, and descriptions of people, you may want to steer it purposefully toward feelings. Ask these questions:

   ~ How did you feel at these gatherings? (Possibilities: Happy, sad, revved up, disappointed, nostalgic, loving, affectionate, grateful, excited, inspired, comfortable, uncomfortable.)

   ~ Were any feelings connected to your life in the past? (Possibilities: Loss of childhood, loss of the "old family," loss of familiarity, loss of "place," loss of comfort, loss of a relative, loss of a sibling to marriage.)

   ~ Sometimes kids feel stress from too much family, too many work hours, or adjustments to new family situations. Do any of these apply to your holidays this year?

Encourage group members to give examples or situations for each feeling they identify, but respect any reluctance to share. Affirm that the holiday world usually is not "tidy," just as families are not.

5. Ask, "How would you describe the perfect holiday for you? Which family members would it include? Which family members would not be there? Why? What would you want to do? What wouldn't you want to do?"

6. Steer the discussion toward growing up—and what that means in terms of making adjustments to the holidays. Ask questions like these:

   ~ How were the holidays different for you this year compared to last year?

   ~ How were *you* different?

   ~ Was there a difference in what interested you?

   ~ Were you treated differently from in the past?

   ~ Did you behave differently?

7. For closure, ask someone to give a one-sentence summary about holidays and family gatherings for people their age, based on what has been shared during this session. Were there any discoveries or insights about adolescent experiences? Were there common feelings and experiences?

FOCUS Feelings

....

Sadness, Depression, and Dark Thoughts

Background

Only in the last few decades has the topic of depression been freely discussed. What used to be largely closeted has been much researched in recent years, with significant breakthroughs in treatment. Advances in the understanding of brain chemistry and the chemistry of stress have led to a number of effective drug therapies, with the media helping to raise consumer awareness of varying levels of potential side effects and also vulnerabilities associated with the time between initially taking a drug and having the drug have a positive effect. Cognitive therapy that works to change the way people think about themselves and situations in their lives has also been effective, and generally it is understood that counseling and medication together are more effective than medication alone. People still experience depression, and much of it goes untreated, but more and more are getting help.

Like many adults, young people use the term *depression* loosely. Sometimes they use it for "being in a bad mood." Perhaps they are referring to a normal, situational unhappiness that will soon go away. Or they may use it to indicate a moderate level of clinical depression characterized by fatigue, changes in sleep patterns and weight, physical pain, difficulty with memory, withdrawal from friends, lessened interest in favorite activities, and a general feeling of hopelessness. At this level, they might also "act out." As they try to improve their mood, but the depression remains, they can become vulnerable to alcohol and other drugs. Thoughts of suicide are not uncommon.

Because mood swings are so common during adolescence, it is difficult for adults to know when to be concerned about depression. It is also hard to recognize the early signs. Because young people are so concerned with remaining socially acceptable, they often keep smiling, even when in emotional pain. They know that depression is difficult for others to be around. There is a tendency for others to withdraw, just when focused attention is crucial. In addition, adolescents are often reluctant to ask for help. When they do ask for help, they may be disappointed. Others might respond, "All you need to do is get up and get on with your life," or "It doesn't make sense for you to be depressed when you have so much going for you," or "What do you mean— depressed? You don't know anything about it!" But for the clinically depressed, there is little or no energy to move ahead, no matter what others say.

There seem to be several varieties of depression, according to current thought. They include a mild, chronic category; minor and major depression; depression associated with an event or situation; cyclically recurring depression; low periods that alternate with highs; and even a depression involving a perpetually gloomy and negatively critical outlook. Clinical assessment of depression usually includes questions about frequency, duration, and severity. Treatment varies, depending on the kind and level. Depression may even be related to physical illness. Whatever is involved, it is important to treat it early. It is important that people feeling "depressed" be checked out by a qualified professional if their feelings are interfering with normal life.

Depression is common in Western cultures in general.[1] The fact that females suffer from serious depression at a higher rate than males may be in part because women pay greater attention to moods and dwell more on depressing interpretations of events around them and because they are more likely to experience chronic strain and have a low sense of mastery.[2] Men may distract themselves with activity, but male alcoholism may be equivalent to depression in females, the result of society's giving males and females different "permissions." Females could learn from males how not to dwell on their emotions, and males could learn how to deal with negative feelings in a healthy way, instead of, for example, with aggression and violence. However, it is important to remember that not all females and not all males fit the majorities described here.

Suicide is near the top of the list as a cause of death among adolescents and young adults. According to the Centers for Disease Control and Prevention, suicide ranked second as cause of death for ages 10–14 and 15–24 in 2016, and almost all states have reported alarming increases in suicide in recent years. (For more information about these statistics, see the National Institute of Mental Health website at www.nimh .nih.gov.) Consequently, this topic should be included in any program focused on adolescent concerns. However, many adults are fearful of bringing up the subject—even with those who are clearly suicidal. The adults may have a vague awe of the depth of feeling that precipitates suicidal thoughts, or they may be wary of what they themselves may have to handle if they begin a dialogue on this heavy topic. Teachers, parents, and even counselors often harbor a concern about "planting the idea" in those who may be "just depressed," and they also worry about the possibility of cluster suicides when there has already been one. Though understandable, those concerns should not preclude discussion of this important topic. No research has shown that talking about suicide increases its likelihood.

Contributing to thoughts of suicide in young people in general are family problems, loss, abusive relationships, the breakup of relationships, sexual and other physical abuse, emotional abuse, earlier abuse that rears its head with increased sexual awareness, concerns related to sexual orientation, and alcohol and other drug abuse. When more than one of these factors are present in a student's life, hopelessness can set in. No matter what the situation is, those who contemplate suicide feel that there are no

1. G. L. Klerman and M. M. Weissma, "Increasing Rates of Depression," *Journal of the American Medical Association* 261 (1989): 2229–2235.

2. S. Nolen-Hoeksema and C. Corte, "Gender and Self-Regulation," in *Handbook of Self-Regulation: Research, Theory, and Applications*, edited by R. F. Baumeister and K. K. Vohs (New York: Guilford Press, 2004), 411–421; S. Nolen-Hoeksema, J. Larson, and C. Grayson, "Explaining the Gender Difference in Depressive Symptoms," *Journal of Personality and Social Psychology* 77 (1999): 1061–1072.

other options. They might not want to die, but they feel like nothing will change and life is too painful as it is. Children and adolescents do not have an adult perspective. They may not believe that change is not only possible, but inevitable. Life is not static.

Discussion groups are an ideal forum for discussing the troubling phenomenon of suicide, which can usually be seriously and productively addressed if there is a good level of trust. Those who struggle with depression may find comfort in knowing that they are not alone and perhaps will ask for help. Those who have not experienced it can learn about it and feel compassion for those who have. Wise peers can also be an important line of defense for troubled individuals.

Adolescents do not treat the subject of suicide lightly. Many have been around suicidal peers or family members. They may have known someone who died from suicide. Assess the age and maturity level of your group carefully as you decide whether and how to address this topic. Certainly it must be handled sensitively—and yet in a matter-of-fact manner. Your ability to be calm in discussing this topic with them will be appreciated and may be crucial. You will model that such topics can indeed be discussed.

This session can easily be divided into two sessions, one on depression and one on suicide.

Important

Assess the maturity and trust levels of your group when deciding if, and how, this topic should be addressed. It is most appropriate for older adolescents, although depression and suicide can occur even at young ages, and certainly middle schoolers can benefit by receiving pertinent and appropriate information about these topics. The format is most appropriate for small groups, rather than for full classrooms. If you decide not to use this session with your group, use the information in it to raise your own awareness. You might also pursue information about depression and suicide through an internet search, including of academic databases. See also the Recommended Resources, page 279.

Objectives

- Group members become more knowledgeable about depression.

- They learn that everyone experiences ups and downs, which are part of growth, change, and life in general, but feelings of depression should not be treated lightly when they interfere with normal activity.

- They learn how to identify, describe, and express feelings and thoughts associated with sadness.

- They are exposed to information about suicide.

- They learn that even sad and scary topics like this one can be discussed.

- They learn that it is important to ask for help when experiencing unrelenting sadness.

- They learn that they should seek help for suicidal persons.

Suggestions

1. Introduce the topic of depression by connecting it to stress. (The first few sessions in the Stress section may be helpful to you in preparing for this session.) Ask the group, "Do you feel stressed a lot? About what?"

2. Use parts of the background information to introduce depression (but do not read that section aloud), or invite a local mental health professional to speak to your group. If you are a degreed mental health professional, your group will benefit from your expertise. If you are not, you may want to do further reading on depression in preparation for this session. When dealing with topics like this one, it is important not to claim to be an authority or to speak with authority, unless, in fact, you are an authority. Resist the impulse to share examples from your own personal history. Instead, introduce information by citing credible sources and remind the group (if this is the case) that you are simply a layperson who believes it is important to raise awareness about depression. As always, there is great value in group members' simply talking about this topic, with no adult "teaching" or "fixing." Being informed yourself may help you to counter misinformation from the group during the discussion.

3. Ask the group to fill out the "Feeling Bad" activity sheet (pages 159–160) with brief responses. Explain that they will not be sharing the whole questionnaire with the group, and they may choose not to share at all. In any setting, make a general comment, when they finish, that if they have been feeling deeply sad over a period of time, they may see you in private for suggestions about getting assistance. (If in a school, and you are not a counselor, it is appropriate for you then to offer to go with the student to the school counselor, who can evaluate, communicate with parents, and make an outside referral, if warranted.) Give group members specific times when you are available. Tell them that if they don't feel comfortable coming to see you, they should see someone else (such as a school counselor, parent, grandparent, mentor, or youth leader who can help them get assistance). You can also give them local crisis-hotline phone numbers. Talk with the student about your need to contact a parent if they are a danger to themselves. If they need to see a community counselor, someone can help them find one—a school counselor, school psychologist, or social worker, for instance.

Important

You are probably a mandatory reporter, and you need to follow protocol for notifying appropriate resources if someone seems to be suicidal. (See "Handling 'Bombs,'" page 12.) If someone responds to your invitation in #3, it is appropriate for you to ask about thoughts of self-harm and if he or she has a plan—and the means—for self-harm. If you are working in a school setting, and if you are not a particular student's counselor, it is important that you see the counselor *immediately* if there is cause for concern. You might first say to the teen, with direct eye contact, "Should I worry about you? Have you thought of harming yourself?" If you have followed the directive in the introduction to this book about informed consent, the student knows that you will have to follow through if the answers are yes.

4. Use the questions from the handout in a poll-taking manner (with raised hands):

   ~ How many of you have felt down in the last year? the last month?

   ~ How many of you sleep more (less) when you feel bad like that?

   ~ Have you ever felt uncomfortably or frighteningly sad for no apparent reason?

   The discussion is less invasive if you do not insist on an oral answer from everyone. (Then no one needs, self-consciously, to pass.) Be aware that the answers to #4, #5, #7, and #8 might reveal symptoms of depression (see the second paragraph of the background information).

Important   If the discussion or poll-taking leads you to believe that someone is in danger, follow up individually, outside the session, as soon as possible. Ask, for example, "Are you okay? Let's talk a few minutes about the mood you were describing today. I'm concerned."

---

5. Ask the group these questions:

   ~ What do you think adults understand about adolescent stress?

   ~ I've heard that kids your age often assume that everyone *else* is "fine," but not they themselves. Do you ever feel that way?

   ~ There seems to be more depression among adolescents today. What might that reflect about this time in our society? (Possibilities: Life is complex and confusing. People are not patient with problems. Technology can negatively affect personal connection. Media messages, rapid and dramatic changes in society, and the incidence of divorce contribute to feelings of insecurity. Society is mobile, and families often have no extended family nearby for support. Job security of parents seems fragile. Rapid change is likely to continue.)

   ~ How much do you think young children understand (or feel, but do not understand) during times of grief and family stress?

6. Depending on the developmental level of group members, you might share some or all of the following pertinent information, perhaps with a handout or simply by reading the statements slowly, pausing between each one. You might also select only some of these statements and adjust the vocabulary, particularly for early middle schoolers.

   ~ Isolation and alienation contribute to suicide, but the key factor is depression.

   ~ Teen suicide may be the result of easy access to drugs, glamorizing of death by the media, an unrealistic view of death (not fully realizing that it is permanent), pressure to succeed, and lack of family cohesion, among many possible factors.

~ Warning signs of severe depression, with thoughts of suicide, include changes in behavior, appetite, sleeping patterns, school performance, concentration, energy level, interest in friends, attitude toward self, risk-taking, and a preoccupation with death.

~ Most people who attempt suicide send signals first—comments about hopelessness or worthlessness, increased isolation, making arrangements for pets or possessions, or changing suddenly from agitation to peace and calm (because the decision has been made).

~ Anyone who suspects that someone is suicidal should ask direct questions about whether the person has thoughts of suicide or whether he or she has a plan in mind.

~ Anyone who believes that someone is in danger of suicide should immediately notify someone who can evaluate the situation and help to set up a support system and/or referral for professional help (in a school, a school counselor is an appropriate person). This holds true for adolescents, too, when they are aware that a peer is suicidal.

~ Listening and *really* hearing the feelings are keys to helping a suicidal person. If the person is talking about desperate feelings, he or she is asking for help and hoping for change. But teens cannot "solve" this problem for someone else.

~ Promises of confidentiality cannot be kept when someone is a danger to self.

~ Suicide is a permanent solution to a temporary problem. Eventually despair is likely to fade away completely.

~ Suicide can devastate the lives of the surviving family and friends.

7. For closure, ask the group for summary statements, or contribute statements of your own. What was learned? What was felt? How was it to talk about depression and suicide? This topic often leaves groups quiet and in deep thought. Glance at the "Feeling Bad" sheets before filing or shredding them to learn if anyone needs attention.

Feeling Bad

Name: _____

1. Have you felt significantly sad . . .

. . . in the last year? Yes ☐   No ☐

. . . in the last month? Yes ☐   No ☐

. . . in the last week? Yes ☐   No ☐

. . . today? Yes ☐   No ☐

2. What seems to get you down?

_____

_____

_____

3. Do you sometimes feel bad for no apparent reason? Yes ☐   No ☐

4. Do those feelings affect your sleeping? Yes ☐   No ☐

If so, do you sleep *more* than usual? Yes ☐   No ☐

Less than usual? Yes ☐   No ☐

5. Describe "feeling bad." How does this feeling affect you?

_____

_____

_____

6. How long does the feeling last?

_____

_____

_____

(continued)

Feeling Bad (continued)

7. Does there seem to be a pattern to that feeling (for example, every two weeks, once a month, every spring, every January, every holiday)? If so, explain:

_____

_____

_____

8. Does this feeling interfere with school? Yes ☐   No ☐

With your other activities or job? Yes ☐   No ☐

With relationships? Yes ☐   No ☐

If so, explain how it interferes:

_____

_____

_____

9. What do you do to deal with feelings of sadness?

_____

_____

_____

10. Have you ever talked to someone about feeling sad? Yes ☐   No ☐

If so, who? How did you feel after talking?

_____

_____

_____

11. Have you ever written about feeling sad—just for yourself? Yes ☐   No ☐

Have you ever written about it for someone else to read? Yes ☐   No ☐

FOCUS Feelings

Eating Disorders

Background

It is probably accurate to say that, in the United States, much of society is obsessed with physical appearance, particularly with being thin and looking fit. Advertisements equate thinness with sex appeal; most store mannequins do not resemble the majority of people; diets and food products are promoted with weight-consciousness in mind. Positive aspects of this are an awareness of fitness and of the nutritional value of various foods, although this trend stands in contrast to the current prevalence of obesity. Among numerous negatives are that many young people may severely limit their food intake, stunt their growth, develop disordered eating, miss needed nutrients, and put their lives at risk.

Young people hear the media messages. Added to these are the comments that parents, significant others, siblings, and other significant persons make to growing children and adolescents—especially to females. All may be affected by positive messages seen or heard about underweight stars and models in movies and television series, fashion ads, and videos. In addition, coaches, directors, and instructors may blink at bulimia in the interest of having competitive teams, squads, and troupes. If a family overemphasizes appearance and thinness as a value at a time when an adolescent's normal growth conflicts with that value, it may lead to disordered eating or a diagnosable eating disorder, especially for those who are culturally, biologically, or psychologically vulnerable.

Eating disorders may reflect power and control issues; difficulty expressing uncomfortable feelings; anxiety; fear of maturity; dependency; difficulty with problem-solving; childhood trauma; ongoing, accumulated stress; or difficulty with trust, intimacy, and expression of anger. Low self-esteem and feelings of powerlessness may also contribute, with the eating problems then exacerbating the low self-concept. Chronically dieting, addicted, chaotic, neglectful, violent, overprotective, or perfectionistic families; parents, relatives, and peers who tease and call attention to weight; early dieting; and personality or impulse disorders—any of these also can contribute to vulnerability. However, disordered eating may not initially be about weight. Instead, it might reflect a need to control *something* when aspects of life formerly tied to self-worth no longer feel controllable. Eating disorders usually begin during adolescence and can go on indefinitely.

Because they also can be afflicted, males need to become aware of disordered eating. Probably no less than for females, media images of male athletes, actors, musicians, and other celebrities send the message to young boys and men that perfect thinness or perfect brawn is ideal. And dancers and athletes in certain sports are especially vulnerable. They are likely to suppress anger and to have high expectations and a high tolerance for physical discomfort. It is good to raise awareness about compulsive exercising or excessive dieting for athletics, since negative lifelong eating habits may become well-established during years in school sports. In addition, because their comments have impact, and because they may have girlfriends, sisters, mothers, or friends who are vulnerable or already in need of help for an eating disorder, young men need to understand how serious and dangerous disordered eating can become.

Eating disorders are complex, and individual and family therapy is usually basic to recovery, the time required varying with the factors involved. Such disorders can become life-threatening, progressing until heart failure, decreased kidney function, elevated blood pressure, stroke, cardiac arrhythmia, rectal bleeding, loss of normal intestinal function, electrolyte imbalance, enlarged salivary glands, dental enamel erosion, seizures, or depression and suicide result. The medical consequences of eating disorders vary with the type of disorder.

As you discuss this topic with your group, offer these definitions:

~ *anorexia nervosa:* self-starvation and an intense fear of obesity that does not diminish with weight loss; distorted perception of actual body weight, size, or shape; weight loss of at least 25 percent of original body weight.

~ *bulimia:* recurrent binge eating of high-calorie foods, probably without others knowing, followed by depressed mood or self-deprecating thoughts; probable purging, using vomiting, laxatives, diuretics, or highly restrictive diets; frequent weight fluctuations greater than ten pounds.

Before discussing this topic, take advantage of resources in your school or local library or counseling center to become more informed about eating disorders. See also the Recommended Resources section on page 279. Acquaint yourself with hospitals and clinics where eating disorders are treated, especially since they are not plentiful. Some are reluctant to admit persons at extreme, life-threatening levels. You might also be able to obtain some brochures from a medical or mental health facility or some reliable internet information to hand out. Be aware that some internet sites may actually celebrate and promote disordered eating.

As mentioned earlier, obesity also is a major health concern. However, in stark contrast to the eating disorders already discussed here, simple obesity is not automatically a psychiatric diagnosis, since psychological or behavioral factors are not consistently associated with it. Instead, unless psychological factors are involved, it is viewed as a medical condition. It is not clinically discussed as an "addiction," per se.

Like many conditions that are connected to behaviors, obesity is complex. Certainly, in terms of the general culture, lack of physical activity and the availability of unhealthful snacks and fast-food meals are easily to blame. However, genetics, body type, metabolism, occupation, a sedentary lifestyle, fitness, family environment, and culture have all been discussed, depending on context. Obesity is not easy to explain, even though it might be easy to see. Even with a media culture preoccupied with thinness and buff bodies, and with talk and reality shows carving up "the willing guilty," it is important not to pathologize obesity and make simplistic assumptions about the behaviors or psychological health of individuals struggling with it. It also is important not to assume that self-knowledge and knowledge of associated risks are enough to provoke someone struggling with obesity to make dramatic changes. Change probably means a long-term, lifelong commitment, which is not easy for anyone with firmly established behaviors in any area of life.

With these cautions in mind, it is encouraging that insurance companies, businesses, and other institutions are promoting lifestyle changes related to eating habits, physical activity, and weight in the interest of a healthy workforce. They would cheer your including obesity in this session with teens. However, be aware that obesity is no more comfortable for teens to discuss than are anorexia nervosa and bulimia nervosa—certainly for those who are struggling with it. Obesity also is highly visible, in contrast with these two disorders. Given the sensitivity of teens about appearance, discussion of obesity needs to be carefully facilitated. It will be important that you not single out any group member to illuminate how obesity feels or affects life. It also will be important that tactless comments, if they occur, be "processed" immediately. The groups promoted in this book are not meant to encourage confrontation or intervention, since the emphasis is on prevention and development. As always, it will be valuable to stay focused on inviting group members' views (for example, of fitness, eating habits of people their age). If someone who is overweight offers insights, that will be a welcome bonus, but should not be expected.

Important	One option for dealing with this topic is to invite a local clinical expert on eating disorders to make a group presentation, with discussion following. The purpose of this session is definitely not to do therapy with those who have an eating disorder. In fact, it is highly unlikely that group members will reveal even that they are worried that they may have a serious problem. As a general admonition, simply encourage group members, if they are concerned, to seek professional help immediately if they have concerns about themselves and to seek help for anyone they know who seems to have an eating disorder. Encourage individuals to see you privately for referral possibilities and have resources available, or, if you are not one yourself and in a school setting, refer them to the school counselor.

Objectives	• Group members become better informed about eating disorders.
	• They explore possible contributing factors to eating disorders.
	• They consider how media and social pressures are associated with eating disorders.

Suggestions	1. If you have invited an expert on eating disorders to make a presentation to your group, follow the presentation with discussion.
	2. If this will be entirely a discussion session, introduce the topic by asking what the group knows about eating disorders. Caution them against mentioning anyone by

name, or describing someone, even though a personal experience or the experience of a friend may have provided general knowledge that can be shared. Add to what they report with material from the background information. Remember that discussion among peers, in your presence, is in itself potentially valuable and, therefore, you should not assume that your purpose is to "teach." You may be surprised by their understanding of eating disorders, but be prepared to hear a great deal of misinformation. If the latter, wait until it would be appropriate to gently ask if they would like some current information. Present it calmly, without preaching. Listen to their concerns.

3. Be prepared for these possible digressions in the discussion:

   ~ societal pressures regarding appearance

   ~ extreme clothing, jewelry, body piercings, and tattoos

   ~ expectations from families and significant others

   ~ concerns about control in life

   ~ the incidence of eating disorders among certain groups of students

4. You may want to offer additional information during the discussion, if you think it would be helpful:

   ~ The "ideal weight," by American standards, has become lower and lower over the years.

   ~ Women need a fat level of approximately 22 percent of their body weight in order to menstruate normally.

   ~ Bingeing is the body's natural response to excessive dieting. The more one diets, the more one feels the need to eat. The best defense against binge eating is to eat—and to eat sensibly, healthfully, and regularly.

5. If you wish to broaden the discussion to include obesity, ask these questions (you might decide to address this suggestion before moving into the discussion of #2):

   ~ In general, how does our society feel about food and weight? How "big a deal" are they to most people? How do kids your age feel about food and weight?

   ~ What have you noticed, lately, on television, about food and weight? (Possibilities: Attention to healthful cooking, fitness, health risks associated with weight problems.)

   ~ (If the consensus is that teens have poor eating habits or lifestyle) What do you think would help kids your age eat more healthfully or have a more healthful lifestyle? (Possibilities: More physical movement, less time with video games and online, less fast food, fewer soft drinks, more family dinners together, more attention to cooking healthfully.)

6. For closure, offer some kind of summation appropriate to the session, or ask group members to summarize the discussion.

FOCUS Feelings

Cutting

....

Deliberate physical self-harm, without suicidal intent, is the focus of this session. Self-injury/self-mutilation can take many forms: cutting; intense scratching or rubbing of the skin; burning the skin on arms, torso, or legs; biting oneself; or head banging. This behavior may occur only a limited number of times or may be repetitive and compulsive.

Any young person can be involved in this kind of self-harming behavior. Many adolescents are familiar with the phenomenon, and therefore it deserves attention. Although the behavior is usually secretive, self-injury can become competitive, with students—even in middle school—trying to outdo one another with dramatic revelations and suggestions of "bravery." Online forums and internet chatrooms may add to that spiraling effect.

Some "cutters" and other self-injurers may seem rebellious or stressed out, and others may appear to be doing well socially and academically. However, the behavior of self-injury often reflects anxiety and depression, isolation and alienation, rage and powerlessness, and failure to cope with highly stressful situations. Those who self-injure may feel unable to stop the behavior. When life seems out of control, and emotional pain feels overwhelming, self-injury can bring a feeling of relief; emotions then take physical form—visible and controllable.

This session is not meant to encourage group facilitators to try to stop self-injurious behaviors. School and other proactive, prevention-oriented groups are not appropriate for intervention, and school counselors' caseloads make long-term therapy infeasible and inequitable. Mental health professionals might address this behavior by helping clients to improve problem-solving and coping and replace self-injury with other ways to express emotional pain and stimulate the senses. The discussion here is an opportunity for students to talk with peers, in the presence of a nonjudgmental adult, about this behavior—one that probably seems strange and frightening to parents and teachers, who may respond simplistically with "That's horrible. Stop it!" Sometimes adults become punitive. Self-injury may be difficult to unravel, since complex emotions are involved.

It is important to control the impulse to moralize. The emphasis of this session is on raising awareness. Talking and listening can help troubled adolescents to normalize emotions, make genuine connections, and develop skills in expressive language.

Those who are not self-injuring and who are not inclined to do that can become more informed about the phenomenon, gain compassion for troubled peers, offer support, and also gain skills in healthy forms of self-expression. This session requires more time than a brief meeting, but a class-period length will probably be enough.

- Group members learn about the phenomenon of self-injury.
- They gain some perspective about emotional pain.
- They learn skills related to healthy expression of emotions.

1. Invite individual group members to make a list on paper of ways they express extreme emotions. (Possibilities: Crying, screaming, withdrawing, sulking, sleeping, eating, running, listening to violent music.) Ask the students to share their lists, if they are willing. This activity might spark discussion, which leads easily to the focus of this session.

2. Ask group members what they know about "cutting" and other forms of self-injury. Let them share their various understandings before offering any background information. Remind them not to name names if they share information about peers or family. This suggestion may provoke enough discussion to last the entire meeting. It is appropriate for you to ask, after something is shared, "How do you feel about that?" If someone says something shocking, process that (for example, "What was that like to hear that statement?").

3. If group members seem to need more information than they already have, share some details from the background information.

You might want to prepare for this session by learning more about self-injury, particularly related to contributing factors. (See Recommended Resources on page 279.) However, it is important that you not present yourself as a clinically trained expert, unless you are such an expert. Self-injury is a complex phenomenon, and offering "truth" about it (that is, strong statements suggesting "*the* cause" or "*the* effect" or "*the* way to solve it," may not only be insensitive to, and judgmental of, group members who may be struggling with the behavior, but also may convey an inappropriately narrow view of something that certainly can be troubling, persistent, and addictive. Professional assistance is often required to stop the behavior. Above all, even if you believe a first-person account might be helpful to the group, do not ask if anyone in the group has self-injured, since shame is likely involved, and it is important not to appear to be prying for details if someone reveals involvement in self-injurious behavior (which is always a possibility). Rather, thank and commend them for their courage in sharing that personal information. Similarly, resist any urge to talk about your own experiences with self-injury. Keep the focus on students and on what they know or wonder about.

4. For closure, thank group members for their serious consideration of this complex phenomenon. Ask what they felt or thought during the discussion. Invite one or two students to summarize the discussion.

FOCUS
Relationships

FOCUS Relationships

· ·

General Background
· · · · · · · · · · · · · ·

Relationships contribute significantly to degree of satisfaction, feelings of self-worth, and balance in life. For some teens, positive and satisfying relationships seem to come easily. For others, relationships are hard both to make and to keep. This section invites students to consider how they relate to others, including peers and significant adults, and how this affects their behavior, choices, decision-making, and view of themselves.

Teens have received powerful messages from adults in their world. For some, the messages have encouraged and supported them, and they may feel secure as a result. Others have heard mostly critical, shaming, or intimidating comments and, as a result, may have trouble relating to people in authority. If the adults in their world have not been reliable, adolescents may feel that if they leaned on someone, they would find no support. In some cases, their families might look to them for crucial support, perhaps to a degree inappropriate for their age. Even some young teens have great family responsibilities. They may be taking care of others' needs, but may not know how to ask to have their own needs met.

A discussion group gives teens an opportunity to discover what they have in common with their peers. They are all negotiating a complex period in their lives. Genuine, open dialogue and interaction can help them feel less lonely, different, or "weird." There is comfort in knowing that others are going through similar struggles. Being supported—in the context of a unique group relationship—can help to fill an important human connection for some. Having a safe place to talk about relationships can nurture confidence, patience, tolerance, and a more positive outlook on life.

General Objectives
· · · · · · · · · · · · · ·

- Students focus on various relationships in their lives and learn to articulate their feelings about them.

- They discover common concerns regarding relationships.

- They have opportunities to help each other with problem-solving about relationships.

- They ponder how relationships contribute to self-worth, goals, and a sense of self.

- Group members consider how others affect their attitudes and behaviors.

- They learn about how others perceive them.

- They identify personal needs and consider ways to meet them.

- They recognize the need for tolerance and compassion.

FOCUS Relationships
How Others See Us

Background

Adolescents wonder how they are seen by others their age. They are critical of others and themselves. They may not have an accurate sense of what kind of image they present to the world. A discussion group provides teens an opportunity for feedback about themselves.

Objectives

- Group members articulate how they believe others see them.

- They learn how they are perceived by members of the group.

- They learn whether others' perceptions of them match their perceptions of themselves.

- They explore the importance of clothing style, facial expression, posture, walk, and other body language in creating impressions.

Suggestions

1. Have group members complete the "How Others See Me, How I See Myself" activity sheet (page 171). Then encourage them to share what they wrote about themselves in Part 1 of the activity sheet. This is one of those rare sessions where, to give "permission," you might model with your own list, looking back to yourself at their age. However, modeling may not be necessary.

2. After each student reads from the sheet, ask if any of the descriptions listed feel uncomfortable or are inaccurate. Ask the group if they heard any discrepancies among the various perceptions. Encourage them to express surprise, disbelief, or support for perceptions that were shared.

3. Discuss how nonverbal messages affect the way people perceive each other and themselves. Ask questions like the following:

   ~ What kinds of nonverbal messages do people send?

   ~ (NOTE: Ask the following questions one at a time.) Are there any specific nonverbal messages which suggest that someone is arrogant? nervous? critical? uptight? happy? content? tired? secure? insecure? confident about appearance? self-conscious? sad? depressed? angry? irritated? frustrated?

4. Direct the group to look at what they wrote in Part 2 of the activity sheet. Unlike in the "Measuring Self-Esteem" and "When We Were at Our Best" sessions, the emphasis here is on first impressions based on physical appearance and nonverbal behaviors. Focusing on one person at a time, invite the others to share what is on their paper about that person. A few minutes might be devoted to that individual. Then ask that group member if there is anything he or she would like to ask the others. (Examples: "Do I seem arrogant?" "Do you think of me as boring and uninteresting?" "Am I too talkative?" "Do you see me as a friendly person?" "Am I okay to be around?" "Have you changed your opinion after getting to know me?") Be aware that this can be a powerful activity. In the safety of the group, each student has an opportunity to hear others' perceptions and to ask important questions.

Important
Regardless of group composition, and regardless of venue, I have repeatedly found that teens take this activity seriously and are sensitive to others' feelings. With that said, however, it is the facilitator's responsibility to protect group members from psychological harm. Therefore, be alert to inappropriate or insensitive comments. If they occur, say something like, "Whoa. Let me ask you as a group how you just felt when he said that to her. Do you have any comments for (the inappropriate speaker) or (the target of the insensitive comment)?"

5. Ask the group whether appearance and first impressions matter. If so, how much? Middle school students are typically quite concerned about the impressions they make. This question gives some group members a chance to say, perhaps genuinely, that appearance and first impressions don't matter. Others may doubt their sincerity. A brief, good discussion might result.

6. For closure, either summarize the experience yourself, perhaps by speaking of your feelings during the exercise, or ask one or more students to share their feelings. Group members might also summarize personal discoveries or insights, particularly about nonverbal messages, first impressions, and whether and how much peers' perspectives matter. Dispose of the sheets or add them to the group folders.

How Others See Me, How I See Myself

Name: _____

PART 1
Complete each sentence with at least three descriptive words.

My mother/guardian thinks I am _____

My father/guardian thinks I am _____

My teachers think I am _____

My friends think I am _____

People who don't know me and who have never heard me talk, but just see me in the halls at school, probably think I am _____

People who know me usually appreciate my _____

I think I am _____

PART 2
List the names of all the people in this group. Leave some space after each person's name. Use the space to write down your first impression of each person, no matter how long ago it was. If you can't recall your first impression, describe what you are told by the person's facial expression and the way he or she stands, walks, sits, talks, gestures, and dresses.

_____

_____

_____

_____

_____

_____

_____

_____

_____

_____

FOCUS Relationships

Encouragers and Discouragers

Background

It is relatively easy for someone who feels satisfied and secure in life to encourage others through good wishes, compliments, and other supportive actions. (And sometimes people are supportive of others in ways they wish others would be supportive of them.) In contrast, it may be difficult for someone who is highly competitive and critical of self and others to offer encouragement. If parents have not modeled encouragement at home, teens may lack the instinct and skills needed to encourage others.

Sometimes it is equally difficult to *receive* support and encouragement. People may be concerned about appearing arrogant or self-absorbed if they accept compliments too readily. Or they may feel unworthy of the compliments they receive because they think poorly of themselves. Whatever the feelings involved, receiving compliments, like giving them, is a learned social skill that becomes easier with practice. A group of supportive peers is a good place to practice.

Objectives

- Group members recognize encouragement and discouragement in their lives.

- They learn about how encouragement and discouragement from others can affect their growing identity.

- They consider their own power and ability to encourage and discourage others.

- They practice expressing support in the form of compliments and accepting compliments gracefully.

Suggestions

1. Introduce the topic. Ask the group to list on paper those people who encourage them and, in a separate column, those who discourage them.

2. Invite the group to share their lists and tell how the various individuals encourage or discourage them. Afterward, you might ask them how they feel when around a particular discourager. Then focus on encouragers: "Who seems to give you unconditional support—no strings attached, no conditions to meet, no 'tests' to pass?" (Pose this question to the entire group, waiting then to see if anyone volunteers a response, rather than asking each to respond. It is possible that most or all in the group may not have such a person in their lives. If that is the case, ask group members how they encourage themselves.)

3. Introduce the idea of giving genuine compliments as a way to encourage others. Ask questions like the following and allow for discussion, as time permits:

   ~ How much are you used to getting and giving compliments in your family? among your friends?

   ~ On a scale of 1 to 10, with 10 being "very," how easy is it for you to *give* compliments?

   ~ How might academic or social competition affect teens' ability to give and receive compliments at school?

   ~ On a scale of 1 to 10, with 10 being "very," how good are you at *receiving* compliments gracefully?

   ~ Are there particular situations and times in your life when it's especially difficult to give or receive compliments?

4. Ask experienced compliment-givers to demonstrate their skills, with the group giving feedback. Ask them also to demonstrate receiving compliments, with group feedback.

5. Acknowledge that it is normal to have mixed feelings about giving and receiving compliments. Present examples like the following, and ask the group for comments:

   ~ We wonder if accepting a compliment will cost us something later. (Will "I like your jacket" turn into "May I borrow your jacket?" Do I owe friendship in return for a compliment? Do I have to remember to return the compliment tomorrow?)

   ~ We feel as if we have measured up to the complimenter's standards, and we worry that we will have to keep meeting those standards. (Does "Great job!" mean "I expect you to keep getting/doing 100 percent"?)

   ~ Some compliments seem routine and not heartfelt. How can we be sure?

   ~ We worry that we are being manipulated. (Is "I like your sweater" meant to ensure your vote in the student council election? Is "You do such a good job of vacuuming" meant to get you to accept that chore every week at home? Does "You're so responsible" mean that you'll soon have to accept more responsibility?)

   ~ We wonder if our reactions are being tested. (When someone says, "Great haircut," are we supposed to smile and say, "Thanks," or do and say nothing?)

   Most of us probably accept the compliments that fit our image of ourselves. Even then, we may feel torn between accepting the compliments gracefully and worrying about appearing arrogant. Encourage group members to accept—and give—compliments when the moment is ripe, for opportunities are quickly lost. Discourage them from automatically rejecting or deflecting compliments or being suspicious of compliment-givers.

6. For closure, have group members arrange themselves in pairs and exchange compliments, with the receiver simply saying, "Thank you." They can then rearrange themselves into new pairs and repeat the exchange, ending the session on a positive note.

FOCUS Relationships

Influencers

Background

This session can be particularly valuable for at-risk teens, since it gives them an opportunity to sort out the influences on their lives (both positive and negative) and to discover which ones provoke strong responses in them (both positive and negative). It is a good topic for all others as well, who may deal intensely with others' expectations and influences.

Objectives

- Group members become more self-aware through reflecting on those who have influenced their values and direction, both positively and negatively.

- Individuals at risk gain self-awareness through considering those who may have influenced them to respond to school, to other people, or to life in ways that are not productive or satisfying.

- Group members gain experience in acknowledging others who have influenced them positively.

Suggestions

1. Begin the session by asking the group to list on paper five to ten people who have had a positive influence on their values and direction. Then ask them to list five to ten people who have had a negative influence on their values and direction. (One or more individuals could be on both lists.) Another option is to have them make a separate column for people they have promised themselves *never* to be like.

   Students' lists of influencers might include peers, family members, teachers, other adults, and older siblings, for example. Their lists may also include people they have read about in biographies or heard about on the news; however, avoid steering them away from their immediate world by suggesting these categories. If you want to discourage their listing video game, television, or movie characters, require that only real people be listed. As always, it is important that you gear discussion to *their* world; therefore, be prepared to hear that high-profile sports figures and pop-culture idols are among their significant influencers.

2. Encourage students to share their lists. Invite them to give a reason for listing each person.

3. Encourage discussion by asking questions like the following:

~ Does your list of positive influencers include mostly those who have influenced your beliefs, what you think is important, or what skills you now have, or mostly people who have influenced your direction for the future? What about your list of negative influencers? What impact have they had on you?

~ How would you describe the group of people you have listed? (For example, mostly family members or people outside of your family? People who are similar to each other or many different types of people? Short-term acquaintances or long-term acquaintances? People you know personally or people you have read about or heard about? Rebels or conformists? Competitive achievers or laid-back types? Optimists or pessimists?)

~ Is there one key individual on your positive list who has influenced you more than anyone else? If so, what might that person wish for you? Does that person know how much you have been influenced by him or her? Are you in contact with that person?

4. Some adolescents may have had few or no positive influencers. If you notice some group members are struggling to fill in that category, encourage them to describe the kind of person they would listen to and be positively influenced by. They may also be willing to tell how the absence of positive influencers has affected them. If they become angry or sad while exploring this sensitive topic, support their feelings (for example, "That makes sense that you feel angry/sad about that") and invite them to help the group understand their experience. Remind the group of the need for confidentiality.

Before the group series ends, you might try to match these teens with adults who were in difficult circumstances as adolescents but have since grown up to be successful, contributing members of the community. Local service clubs might be interested in spreading the word about the need for these models. Perhaps you can arrange some regular contact for a period of time so that the teens can experience some outside-of-school, outside-of-family influence on their self-image, values, and direction.

5. For closure, ask group members to write a note of acknowledgment and thanks to one of the people on their list of positive influencers. You may want to mention that a note to a parent or other close relative can be especially touching and appreciated; in many families, such messages are never shared or are thought of too late. Tell the group that they may then choose to send their notes or not.

FOCUS Relationships

Uniquenesses and Similarities

Objectives

- Group members learn more about how they are different from others and how they are similar.

- Those who feel that no one else is as different as they are will feel more connected to others their age.

Suggestions

1. Introduce the topic briefly.

2. Have the group line up along one wall of the room (or form an angle along two sides). Tell them they have just formed a continuum. Designate one end of the continuum as "10—to a great extent/a lot" and the other end as "0—not at all." Explain that you are going to read a series of statements. As you read each statement, group members should physically move to the point on the continuum that best represents where they think they belong.

3. Read aloud each statement from "Uniquenesses and Similarities: A Continuum Activity" (page 177). After each statement, and after group members have found their places on the continuum, select two to four students (or more, if time allows) to explain why they placed themselves where they did. Be sure not to ask the same few to report each time, and avoid commenting, although your facial expressions and other nonverbal responses can show that you received group members' answers thoughtfully. Hearing and considering each statement and then moving physically to a place on the continuum will deepen self-awareness even without discussion.

4. For closure, ask the group if they noticed any trends. Are they similarly creative, flexible, distractible, and impulsive, or are they perfectionistic, highly focused, organized, and orderly? a balance between both extremes? Can anyone offer a general statement describing the group?

Uniquenesses and Similarities: A Continuum Activity

1. I like tough challenges and feel best when I have to work hard at something.

2. I am cool in a crisis, and I can even lead others in a crisis.

3. I can change direction easily when I am doing something—for example, if suddenly someone wants to do something different.

4. I am organized in every part of my life.

5. I am a dreamer, spending a lot of time in fantasies.

6. I work rapidly in whatever I do.

7. I am a highly creative person.

8. I am a perfectionist in almost everything I do. I like things to be "just right."

9. I prefer to work alone, rather than with others, on most things.

10. I am quick to respond to almost all situations.

11. I am impulsive, and I often wish I would have thought first before doing something.

12. I can work well without encouragement from someone else.

13. I like to work with my hands.

14. I am quite critical of others.

15. I worry a lot.

FOCUS Relationships

Responding to Authority

Background

Many young people do not deal well with authority. When a teen is involved in significant conflict with Dad or Mom, that conflict may carry over into school in the form of resistance to an authority figure of the same gender or with a similar manner. Strict parenting and/or harsh discipline, especially without warmth and support, can also lead to frustration and "acting out" in school or elsewhere.

When one parent is absent, anger over that situation might spill over into conflict with the caretaking parent and may affect relationships with adults in school. If there is no male authority figure in the family, boys may insist, "I basically raised myself. Don't anybody tell me what to do!" They may respond to directives from male teachers, bosses, administrators, coaches, or police officers with automatic and intense resistance. Or they may target female teachers or other authority figures. Male students whose fathers have dominated their mothers may behave according to that model with female teachers. Young girls may have similar problems dealing with authority, depending on their circumstances. However, attitudes toward authority are probably complex in origin. When responding to anti-authority behaviors, adults in authority should remain calm and avoid making assumptions or trying to interpret the situation. Working toward less conflict in a relationship by monitoring their own emotional reactions can be beneficial to both adult and teen.

If parental discipline is arbitrary and unpredictable, a child may be quick to blame "the system" when it seems inconsistent, when it seems to play favorites, or when teachers and tests seem unfair. All such responses can affect success and comfort at school.

Children are fundamentally complex and resilient. There are many adolescents whose difficult family situations do not lead to school problems, and there are countless well-balanced students from well-functioning and poorly functioning families. Of course, a lack of obvious problems does not necessarily mean that teens feel no anger or rage. They may have decided that they will not allow such feelings to interfere with their relationships. Or they simply may not be used to expressing feelings. Sometimes the response to having just one parent at home is to develop a relationship with a teacher, coach, or boss who is the same gender as the absent parent. Probably more than educators are aware of, students whose parenting has been inadequate or inconsistent look to the school for guidance and support.

A teen may resist authority for reasons other than parental absence or abuse. For example, sometimes one or both parents are broadly "anti-system" and have long modeled resistance to authority. A child might be loyal to a family tradition of resistance or troublemaking. Or perhaps there is a reservoir of rage over parents who are highly controlling, have unreasonable expectations, or "overfunction" (that is, do things for their children that the children should or want to do for themselves). All of these situations can be found at any socioeconomic level.

Whatever the reasons for it, or apparent lack of reasons, difficulty with authority can be a lifelong problem. Employment may eventually be affected, as can marriages or partnerships and the next generation of parent-child relationships.

Another aspect of this topic relates to those who are "no problem" at school. Compliant students can have problems with authority in the sense that they always defer to it. Perhaps they never question authority, always do what they are told, do not think for themselves, and are simply unable to respond creatively to situations that demand a flexible response. Currently or in the future, they may be afraid to question anyone, whether it be a demagogue, a cult leader, a corrupt boss, or an abusive partner or spouse. They may expect to be told what to do in any complex situation.

There is also the possibility that a young person's cultural background does not encourage challenging authority or does not promote individualistic thinking either at home or at school. Such cultural attitudes may cause conflict in dominant-culture contexts. For instance, group members might challenge students who clearly put family concerns ahead of their own. Group facilitators should model respect for others' cultural values; they may also invite those from nonmainstream cultures to explain their beliefs, if they are comfortable doing so.

A discussion group can give students a chance to explore their responses to authority in a supportive, rational, safe environment, with an adult whose main function is to listen. "Just talking," without expecting criticism and evaluation, can help them better understand themselves as they relate to others.

Objectives

- Group members discover that there are many ways to respond to authority and many possible reasons for that variety of responses.

- They learn that unquestioning compliance with authority can be as problematic as automatic resistance.

- They consider why they respond to authority as they do and, if there are problems, whether they might consider making some changes.

Suggestions

1. Introduce the topic briefly, but do *not* read the background information to the group. It is simply meant to remind you, as a facilitator, of this topic's complexity—not to encourage interpretation and analysis or to instruct the group. The value here will be in group members talking with each other about authority, not in receiving directives, admonitions, or explanations from you. Teens rarely have such an opportunity to be heard.

Then have the group complete the "Responding to Authority" activity sheet (pages 181–182), which gives them a chance to think about several authority figures in their lives. The activity sheet helps to bring about more specific comments during discussion. Writing down examples helps students be objective and see possible patterns. This is not to say that discussion of group members' feelings about authority should be avoided. It is also important to discuss these, openly and safely, without judgment. Writing can assist in that process.

2. Encourage students to share their written responses and/or comments about the patterns they see. Ask questions like the following to generate discussion after they have all shared. The questions can be directed to the group as a whole, with members making the choice to respond or not. Give them time to respond.

~ Does your list of authority figures include all males? all females? some of each?

~ Are there differences between how you respond to females in authority and how you respond to males in authority? If so, can you describe the differences?

~ Where do you have problems with authority—mostly at school? at home? at work? in the community?

~ Are your problems at school mostly with your classroom teachers, with administrators, or are they also with adults who coach and advise extracurricular activities? Can you give an example of a situation that was not comfortable for you?

~ If you have problems with authority at school, are they with a certain kind of personality?

~ If you have problems with authority at home, and if you have two parents at home, are there differences between how you respond to one parent and how you respond to the other? If so, how would you describe their personalities?

~ If you have problems elsewhere (for example, treatment center, residential facility, police, probation), what kinds of people in authority do you have trouble with?

~ What do you gain by resisting authority? What price do you pay?

~ Have your interactions with authority changed recently? Do you resist authority more? less? Has this affected your stress level? how you get along with others?

~ If you never question authority figures, even though you would like to, how do you explain your hesitancy? Is there any authority you wish you could challenge? (Be aware that compliant group members may find this question odd. Respect their perspectives.)

~ If you have few or no apparent problems with authority, why do think that is?

3. For closure, invite summary statements from several students. Did they gain any insights from this session? Was it helpful to hear from others in the group about dealing with authority? You might close by saying that the subject of dealing with authority is complex. It is good to talk about it and to hear what others feel and think about it. Dispose of the sheets or add them to the group folders.

Responding to Authority

Name: _____

1. List the adult authority figures in your life—people who give you advice, suggestions, or orders. Describe their position (for example, teacher, principal, coach, parent, boss). Then tell how you typically respond to their authority.

   NAME   POSITION   YOUR TYPICAL RESPONSE

   a. _____

   b. _____

   c. _____

   d. _____

   e. _____

2. If you have problems with the authority of any of the people listed above, what usually "sets you off"?

   _____

   _____

   _____

3. Does it appear that you have trouble with only certain types of authority figures? If so, explain.

   _____

   _____

   _____

4. Do you have any "unfinished business" with people whose authority you have trouble accepting? (For example, are you angry about something they did in the past?) If you do not, go on to question #5. If you do, complete this question.

   List the people who fit this category.

   _____

   _____

   _____

   What do you feel when you are confronted by any of them?

   _____

   _____

   _____

   (continued)

Responding to Authority (continued)

What feelings do you have after a confrontation?

_____

_____

_____

What are your options for responding to these people?

_____

_____

_____

Can you think of anything that might change your response to their authority?

_____

_____

_____

5. If you have no obvious problems with anyone you listed in #1, how and where did you learn to respond "okay" to their authority?

_____

_____

_____

6. In which parts of your life do you believe you have been treated fairly? (For example, home, school, friends, neighborhood, work, music groups, sports, church, etc.)

_____

_____

_____

Unfairly?

_____

_____

_____

7. If you do not deal well with authority in general, how does that affect your life?

_____

_____

_____

FOCUS Relationships

Best Advice

Background

When we are growing up, it seems that adults are always giving us advice. Whether we pay attention at the time or ignore everything they say, we may surprise ourselves later by remembering—and even following—some of the advice we have received. Sometimes we do not even know we are following it. Sometimes we make sure we *don't* follow it.

Advice may recommend a course of action, warn against danger, or cause us to reexamine certain behaviors. When we respect the person who is giving the advice, we probably listen and, if the advice seems good, may act on what we hear, knowing that the advice might make a difference in our lives.

This session gives group members a chance to chuckle over often-repeated admonitions or warnings they heard as children or have heard as adolescents, and to reflect on powerful messages that have had a lasting effect on them.

As always, the purpose of this session is to help teens articulate thoughts and feelings, not to "make a point." As they talk—and perhaps laugh—together, they will think about and have feelings about what they share and hear, but they will not have to worry about advice or admonitions from you.

Objectives

- Group members reflect on various suggestions or advice given to them by adults in their lives.

- They consider how the advice has affected their direction, behavior, and attitudes.

Suggestions

1. Begin by asking the group to brainstorm some areas in which people generally receive advice as they are growing up. Responses might include areas from the list on page 184. If not, you might ask if group members have ever been offered advice about these areas. Be prepared for one or a few saying that their parents have only rarely given them advice. You might ask the group what that might reflect about the parents. What positive effects might that style of parenting have on children and teens? negative effects? Which style do the parents of most in the group seem to have? A nonjudgmental view of responses may help low-advice group members feel comfortable in the discussion.

food	health
safety	strangers
hitchhiking	driving
sex	dating
alcohol and other drugs	careers
cleanliness	chores
clothing	personal appearance
hair	fitness
body decoration	texting
internet use	manners
cell phones	social networking

2. Have the group list on paper some specific advice they have received in four or five of the areas mentioned, or have students talk about one area at a time.

3. Ask, "Have you followed the advice you have been given? If so, how has it affected your direction, behavior, and attitudes?" Give everyone a chance to contribute.

4. Ask, "What is the worst piece of advice you have ever been given?" Allow time for discussion. Then ask, "What is the best piece of advice you have ever been given? What made it so valuable to you?" Again, give everyone an opportunity to contribute.

5. Invite the group to share examples of advice given to them when they were very young. They may find humor in some of these simplistic warnings, especially about safety. They may also find humor in warnings they have received about friendships and dating in recent years. When appropriate, and perhaps to maintain order, ask listeners, "What do you think about that?" You might ask those sharing, "How did/do you feel about that advice?"

6. For closure, remind the group that it's good to think about what can affect their direction, behavior, and attitudes. Ask for a volunteer to summarize what was discussed, or invite the group to comment on the most interesting or most thought-provoking advice they heard in the meeting. You might also invite them to make a few statements about how much impact others' advice has on how teens manage their lives.

FOCUS **Relationships**

Who Can We Lean On?

Background

Everyone needs help now and then. There are times when we all need advice, instruction, encouragement, or simply someone to listen. When adults need help, they might call a plumber, mechanic, carpenter, physician, financial adviser, therapist, or faith-based leader. When young people need help—for schoolwork, counseling, instruction in a skill, or advice in life—they may not know who to ask, or they may be reluctant to ask anyone. They may not know that school counselors, if available, are trained to be a nonjudgmental, objective resource, with skills and expertise based on at least a master's degree. School counselors are usually involved in responding to school or individual crises, and veteran counselors have often worked individually and in groups with thousands of students. Nothing shocks them. They are prepared to hear anything, and their complex ethical code guides their actions. Students can talk with them about personal, academic, peer, or family issues. However, they are more likely to ask a peer than an adult for help. Even then, they may feel uncomfortable about needing and asking for something.

Some teens are reluctant to ask for help because they don't want to appear incompetent, vulnerable, or weak. They may also believe they should resolve problems themselves. Others may avoid asking for help because of barriers between themselves and significant adults in their lives. They may feel that no one could possibly understand their situation, empathize, and be able to help.

This session invites students to explore the idea of asking for help when help is needed. It can be beneficial for adolescents to hear others speak openly about confused feelings in this regard. A caring adult and a supportive group of peers can "give permission" to ask for help.

Objectives

• Group members learn that it is normal to need assistance at times.

• They explore how they feel about asking for help in various areas.

Suggestions

1. Introduce the topic by asking students to think of the last time they asked someone for help—at school, at home, with friends, or on the job. Encourage them to share these situations with the group. You might share (briefly) an example or two from your own life; however, if group members are eager and open, let the focus stay completely on them.

2. Ask, "What are some times when it's hard to ask for help?" If group members do not mention a variety of circumstances, introduce some into the discussion, perhaps one at a time, and encourage comments. (Suggestions: For academic problems or direction; for advice about life; for problem-solving; for personal dilemmas; for social situations; for family problems.) Explore with the group why it might be difficult to ask for help in each situation. How do they feel when they ask for help?

3. Ask, "Are there certain adults in your life you would never ask for help?" (For example, parents, siblings, teachers, a certain teacher, counselors, a certain counselor, faith-based leaders, neighbors, or relatives.) Encourage them to explain their answers.

If several group members voice reluctance to talk to counselors, consider inviting a well-liked counselor (from the school or community) to come in and speak with the group. Let the group ask questions about how counselors view their work, how they communicate with teens with personal problems, how challenging or easy it is to work with teen clients, what kinds of training counselors have, and what ethical principles guide them. Even if there are no apparent concerns about counselors, you might invite a counselor to talk about these areas.

4. Remind students that the adult world revolves around help sought and received (see the background information) and that asking for help is normal. Acknowledge, however, that many adults do not know how to ask for help, especially about emotional issues. Make the important point that it is easier for professionals to help people before problems become crises.

5. For closure, ask for volunteers to offer advice about asking for help. Remind the group that people can support each other in many ways. Remind them, too, that everyone needs help of various kinds throughout life, that asking for help is not a sign of weakness, and that asking is always a compliment to the person who is asked.

FOCUS Relationships

Gifts from People Who Matter

Background

Probably most people feel something is missing somewhere in their lives. Children may long for time and attention from busy parents. They may yearn for a sign of appreciation or encouragement—or simply less nagging, drinking, television, or arguing in the home. They may wish for support or kind words from brothers and sisters. Sometimes these wishes are easy to articulate, sometimes not. This session can become a "wish list," honestly spoken and sympathetically received by a supportive group, willing to listen. This topic is certainly appropriate during a gift-giving season.

Objectives

- Students focus on their needs and wants.

- They learn to express their feelings about significant people in their lives and what they need most from them.

Suggestions

1. Introduce the topic in concrete terms by asking the group to tell about the best gift/present they ever received from someone who meant a lot to them. Encourage them to give more than one example.

2. Move into the abstract by asking students to think of meaningful things they have been given by significant people in their lives that cannot be held, touched, or seen. Mention the following ideas if they are not introduced during the discussion.

attention	direction
love	unconditional love
friendship	concern
support	self-confidence
affection	encouragement
understanding	acceptance
role-modeling	a shoulder to cry on
the right words at a difficult time	instruction in a skill or talent
a sense of fun	a place to relax
appreciation for something	

3. Hand out the "My Wish List" activity sheet (page 189). Ask the group to think about what they wish they could receive/have from various family members. Model this activity, mentioning something specific you wish each of your parents would give (or had given) to you. Remember to quickly move the focus back to the group after your sharing.

4. Give the group a few moments to complete the activity sheets. Then encourage students to share their "wish lists."

5. For closure, summarize what you heard from students and what wishes they seem to have in common. Or ask a volunteer to summarize the session. Dispose of the sheets or add them to the group folders.

My Wish List

Name: _____

Write what you would most like to get or have from each family member. This should not be something you can hold, touch, or see.

From my mother: _____

From my father: _____

From my sister: _____

From my brother: _____

From _____ : _____

From _____ : _____

From _____ : _____

From _____ : _____

If you need ideas:

time	a hug
attention	understanding
support	good role-modeling
affirmation	patience
less competitiveness	advice
less jealousy	guidance
less pressure	instruction in something
more caring and concern	information
more personal interest	a compliment
encouragement	better behavior
honesty	listening
less criticism	healthful food
less tension	privacy
a smile	concern

Relationships

Getting Our Needs Met

Background

Many people do not know how to ask for what they need. Perhaps they would rather be givers than receivers, thereby avoiding debt. They may not want to give anyone the satisfaction of helping them, may feel unworthy of assistance, or are afraid of appearing weak. Maybe they do for others what they wish others would do for them. Whatever the explanation, their needs may go unmet, and they might feel sad and discouraged—without knowing why.

Ideally, students should express their classroom needs to teachers. A student might say, "It's hard for me to understand things when I can't see them. I need a summary sheet to look at while you explain things." Teachers can also communicate needs appropriately. If a teacher cannot concentrate because of student behavior, the teacher can say, "I have a hard time concentrating when you do that, and I need to concentrate to teach."

People in relationships should also express their needs—whether those relationships are related to friendships, marriage or partnerships, neighbors, dating, or work. One person might say, "I would like to be asked for ideas about what we could do," or "I wish we would do more fun things," or "I would like you to come to my house and not always be at yours." Even close friends often do not know how to express their wishes and concerns to each other.

Ideally, parents should also express their needs to their children with I-statements like those above: "I want you to come to the table when I call, because when you dawdle, I feel that the time I spent cooking isn't appreciated," or "I need to know how long you will be at practice, since I need to pick you up afterward." And children should express their needs to their parents: "I feel invaded when you go through my papers in my room. I need to feel that my personal space is mine," or "I need to start making more of my own decisions. I feel frustrated when you make decisions for me."

Relationships at home, at school, with friends, and at work are enhanced when people are able to express personal needs clearly and directly. This session will help students learn to do this.

Objectives

- Group members become aware of the value of expressing needs clearly and directly.

- They clarify their own needs.

- They practice asking for what they need.

Suggestions

1. Begin by conveying some of the general ideas in the background information. This time, if you are working with older teens, the paragraphs are appropriate for reading aloud, perhaps with group members taking turns reading the paragraphs. Then ask, "On a scale of 1 to 10, with 1 being 'very poorly' and 10 being 'very well,' how well do you express your needs to other people? Think of your parents, siblings, teachers, friends, employers, or significant other."

2. Hand out the "My Needs" activity sheet (page 192). Tell group members to read down the list quickly and put a check mark by any item that seems true for them. Then encourage them to share their lists. Reassure students that they can choose how many of the items to share, and remind them of the confidentiality guideline.

3. Instruct the group to look back at the items they checked on their lists, circle anything they think they could actually ask for, and underline anything they think they could do something about—even today.

4. When the group seems ready to continue, ask the members to choose one item they circled and put it in the form of a request, as practice. Explain that they should begin their request with "I." Encourage them to be clear, direct, and genuine, and to phrase their request in a way that does not attack or demand. If someone has difficulty composing a request, ask if he or she would like to ask the group for help. If help is desired, the group can give suggestions. Then invite students to read one or two items they underlined. Ask them to explain what they could do to meet those needs.

5. Begin a discussion about the difficulty most people have in addressing needs directly. Ask closed questions like the following to provoke thought (not to be answered out loud):

   ~ Do you ever drop hints about your needs or let your moods communicate them, and then feel angry or sad if no one gets your message?

   ~ Do you sometimes use bad behavior to get the attention you need?

   ~ Does your school performance—"bad" or "good"—help to meet your needs?

   ~ Do you ever do things for other people in the hope that they will do things for you?

   ~ Do you think that asking for something you need is wrong or not nice or too pushy?

   Invite comments about indirect ways people try to communicate needs.

6. Ask, "Is there anyone you know who does a good job of expressing needs?" After some examples, ask, "What could you learn from these people?"

7. Invite the group to imagine themselves as adults—as employees, bosses, parents, spouses/partners. Ask, "How could learning to ask for what you need benefit you in the future?"

8. For closure, ask one or more volunteers to summarize the session. What did they learn about themselves? about others? about asking for what they need? How did it feel to express needs? Dispose of the sheets or add them to the group folders.

My Needs

Name: _____

Check anything from this list that you feel you need. If something you need is not on this list, add it to the end and check it too.

- ☐ someone to say, "I care about you"
- ☐ attention
- ☐ support for a problem I have
- ☐ a hug
- ☐ kind words
- ☐ space
- ☐ privacy at home
- ☐ peace and quiet
- ☐ less (or no) criticism from others
- ☐ more contact with people
- ☐ order
- ☐ direction
- ☐ kind words from my mom or another woman
- ☐ kind words from my dad or another man
- ☐ a better relationship with a stepparent
- ☐ peace with a sibling (or siblings)
- ☐ a good night's sleep
- ☐ a good meal
- ☐ a feeling of success
- ☐ less stress
- ☐ fewer demands on my time/more time to myself
- ☐ fewer "pieces" in my complicated life

- ☐ less confusion and craziness around me
- ☐ less arguing with someone else
- ☐ less arguing at home by others
- ☐ a feeling of hope that things will get better
- ☐ someone to listen
- ☐ a conversation that doesn't get interrupted
- ☐ someone to love
- ☐ someone to love me
- ☐ something to keep me busy
- ☐ teachers who care about me
- ☐ a different teaching style in a teacher
- ☐ teachers who can appreciate that I am going through a bad time right now
- ☐ approval
- ☐ respect from my peers
- ☐ guidance from an adult
- ☐ something to look forward to
- ☐ _____
- ☐ _____
- ☐ _____
- ☐ _____
- ☐ _____

FOCUS Relationships

Small Talk and Social Graces

Background

Social ease comes from experience—and sometimes from courage and conscious effort to learn social skills. Most teens do not readily admit to being uncomfortable socially, but most do worry about what to do or say on occasion—or often. Some parents take the time to teach specific skills. Others do not, and children are left to learn by observation and through trial and error.

Some students might have little faith that conversations could ever feel comfortable and smooth. Teens who have had little opportunity to practice formal behavior may feel uncomfortable whenever they sense that something proper is in order. This session encourages them to discuss such situations, talk openly about what they feel inept at, and practice some skills.

Objectives

- Group members learn and practice important skills for social ease.
- They appreciate the need for social skills in and outside of school.

Suggestions

1. Introduce the topic by exploring with the group what is difficult for them socially. Ask questions like these:

   ~ What social situations are uncomfortable for people your age? (If not mentioned, ask if they have trouble with small talk, introductions, talking with people they don't know, formal situations, being around people from a culture different from their own, or being around someone with a gender identity different from their own.)

   ~ How much trouble do you have starting conversations?

   ~ Where are you more uncomfortable—when socializing in groups or when talking to only one person?

   Ask for examples of social situations where they feel uncomfortable.

2. Invite group members to give suggestions for behavior and general etiquette in the following situations:

> funerals
> weddings
> visiting someone in a hospital
> being introduced to your parents' friends
> being introduced to parents of a friend
> meeting new people your own age
> formal concerts where classical music is played
> music events geared to your age group
> eating at a nice restaurant
> dances
> job interviews
> visiting someone else's place of worship
> eating a meal with a friend's family
> receiving a gift
> staying overnight at a friend's house
> needing to thank a host family for an overnight visit
> meeting your significant other's parents

For each situation, you might ask these questions:

~ If you have ever been in this situation, what have you felt uncomfortable about?

~ What have you learned that has made this type of situation easier for you?

~ What have you been told is appropriate behavior for this?

3. Offer the group a chance to practice various skills. Set up role-playing situations to practice the following:

~ a firm handshake and some etiquette surrounding that action

~ introducing a friend, a parent, a teacher

~ starting a conversation with a stranger

~ starting a conversation with someone on the way out of class

~ asking someone if it's all right to eat lunch with him or her

~ striking up a conversation with a seat partner on a bus, a plane, the subway, at a bus stop, at the swimming pool, at a recreation center, at a party

~ responding to someone who makes a comment about the weather

~ asking questions of someone as a way of showing interest (beginning with "Do you live around here?" or "Are you new here?" or "What do you think of this class?" or "Do you often come here?" and following that idea with interested comments and further questions)

4. For closure, have students pair off. Explain that a good handshake may help them get a job someday. Invite them to shake hands firmly (without pumping the arm), and, while holding the other person's hand solidly, to express appreciation for something (for example, "I really appreciate what you say in our group," "I'm glad you're in our group," or "I've really appreciated getting to know you"). If necessary, model this interaction by shaking someone's hand. Encourage them not to worry about sounding clichéd. Explain that sometimes a plain, simple, direct comment is best. Then have them change partners and wish each other well in life (for example, "I hope you have a good life"), again with a handshake.

Before they leave, ask them how the activity felt. Ask questions like these:

~ How comfortable was this session for you?

~ What does a handshake accomplish?

~ How did it feel to say something plain, simple, and direct?

FOCUS **Relationships**

Gossip

Background

There is usually no shortage of gossip among young people—in school and elsewhere. Gossip is no stranger to many age groups, of course. It has power, and it can bully, hurt, control, backfire, boomerang, become more and more distorted, and cast a negative shadow on both the gossiper and the person who is gossiped about.

Gossip has been called the "female" counterpart to "male" aggression. It is more difficult to know who the aggressor is when gossip is the weapon than when the first strike is shoving or hitting. In recent years, rumor-spreading has been listed as one kind of bullying. Some might argue that gossip is even more cruel than physical bullying. There will be plenty to discuss here.

Objectives

- Group members consider the role gossip plays in adolescent conversation.

- They consider how gossip affects their lives and the lives of others.

- They consider how much they participate in gossip themselves.

Suggestions

1. Ask the group to define *gossip*. Ask them whether it is a positive or negative force in society generally and in their lives. Steer the discussion toward gossip as related to conversation and relationships.

2. Invite discussion about their experiences with gossip. Ask questions like these, perhaps in a polling manner (asking for raised hands), and encourage group members to elaborate when appropriate—discreetly, of course:

   ~ Have you ever been hurt by gossip?

   ~ Have you ever known of someone else being hurt by gossip?

   ~ Have you ever passed along some gossip and then found out it wasn't true? What, if anything, did you do about it?

   ~ Do you think you are a gossip?

   ~ Do your peers think of you as a gossip?

   ~ Do you knowingly add dramatic details to gossip when passing it on?

   ~ How common is gossip?

~ Do you know someone who refuses to gossip, or who seems not to be excited by it?

~ Have you ever told someone that you didn't want to hear his or her gossip?

~ Are you able *not* to pass gossip along when you have heard something interesting?

~ How do you usually respond to an invitation to hear some gossip?

~ How often do you think gossip is actually true?

~ Does your family gossip a lot?

~ Does your group of friends gossip a lot?

~ What do gossips get out of gossiping? (Possibilities: A sense of power, control, a feeling of belonging, a chance to hurt someone.)

~ How would you rank these in importance in your social world:

  • talking about things (possessions, purchases, clothing, houses, cars, hair, etc.)

  • talking about people (who likes whom, friends and acquaintances, movie and music stars, people in the news, etc.)

  • talking about ideas (thoughts about life, politics, meaning, creative ways to do things, insights about self and others, etc.)

~ How would you rank these same items in terms of conversation quality?

Important	With all of the questions, remember that it is important not to pass judgment or to moralize. Just let group members express their feelings, experiences, and opinions, and you will probably be inspired by their conclusions. The most important messages will be in their own comments.

3. For closure, ask someone to summarize the session. Ask the group if the discussion made them more aware of the power of gossip and what it is used for. What feelings did the discussion provoke? Did it raise their awareness about themselves? (Let head nods suffice.)

Relationships

Bullying

Background

Just as when raised awareness of sexual harassment in schools and in the workplace created a cosmic shift in perceptions and policies more than three decades ago, bullying is now solidly on the radar screen in schools and in the workplace. State legislatures have passed pertinent legislation about definition, anti-bullying programs, documentation, and reporting. Court cases against school districts are new territory, requiring lawyers on both sides to become knowledgeable about definitions of bullying, laws and school policies, school climate, school reporting protocols, and school leadership. They also need to become skilled in deposing administrators and peers of bullying targets and preparing young witnesses. Administrators are becoming aware that plaintiffs' legal teams look at what kinds of prevention and intervention were done—and how reports of bullying were responded to. It is another cosmic shift.

Research on bullying became established in the United States only relatively recently, prompted in large part by school shootings, which have implicated bullying. Internationally, bullying has been studied longer. However, findings have varied considerably, perhaps because bullying has often not been defined in surveys, or has been defined narrowly, and researchers have looked at widely varying time frames (for example, during the past week, during the past year, during all elementary and middle school years) and have targeted differing age groups (such as sixth graders, second graders, all school years). Nevertheless, in general, it appears that the vast majority of school-age children are bullied at some time during the school years and that fewer, but still significant numbers, of students bully others. Repeated absences, debilitating anxiety, depression, and even suicide are associated with bullying, and even single incidents may have long-term repercussions. Teasing may actually have more negative effects than physical bullying does, according to researchers. Scholars and books have called attention to bullying among girls (such as social exclusion and rumor-spreading), and, as a result, assumptions about pertinent gender differences have been challenged. Studies have found that bullying occurs fairly universally, regardless of race, ethnicity, population density, or socioeconomic factors.

Schools are responsible for providing a safe environment where learning can occur. Currently, legislation in many states demands that schools have anti-bullying policies and programs in place. When administrators and teachers are all on the same page about what bullying is and what their response should be when they see it, when school counselors are trained to do prevention-oriented and social-skills-building classroom lessons, and when students feel that educators will take reports of bullying seriously, then school climate change is possible. Students can relax rather than fear peers, can feel safe coming to school and opening up their phones, and can focus on learning. Because bullying often occurs out of the sight of adults, increased monitoring of hallways, bus lines, playgrounds, lunchrooms, and restrooms can help lower prevalence. However, cyberbullying has added a dangerous layer to the problem, challenging schools to clarify what is and is not their responsibility off school premises, to provide specific prevention and intervention, and to be alert to the effects of trauma from bullying. Cyberbullying is much more difficult to escape than conventional types of bullying. It doesn't disappear or stay at school. Peers far and near can see the texts and compromising photos. Senders are likely not identified or identifiable.

Bullying appears to peak during school-transition years, when it may be related to anxiety about social status and jockeying for position. Although bullying can occur at any grade level, including kindergarten, prevalence typically peaks during early middle school years. It should be understood that it may actually be dangerous for targets of bullying to "just ignore" or "tell" or "fight back," since students who bully often are larger, have more social support, and can escalate the bullying. Interventions need to be implemented (and enforced) by someone with more power than the person who is bullying. Witnesses to bullying may be part of the broader culture that allows and supports bullying. However, according to clinical professionals, bystanders have legitimate fears about injury if they intervene and can actually be traumatized by witnessing bullying.

All students—those bullied, those doing the bullying, and those silently watching—need to be the focus of prevention programs. While empirical studies have generally not connected bullying to family characteristics (such as parenting style or domestic violence), students who bully in adolescence may continue their aggression as adults in spousal and partner relationships, in parenting, and in the workplace. Evidence has linked school bullying to later involvement in corrections and to depression. Educators and parents should not assume that perpetrators of bullying have low self-esteem. Instead, they may enjoy high social status, may feel allowed to bully, and may enjoy the drama and sense of control associated with bullying.

This session gives group members, whether they bully others, are bullied, or are bystanders, a chance to talk about the issue. Targets of bullying sharing experiences and feelings and students who bully being encouraged to focus on their own feelings and the perspectives of others can contribute to important raised awareness. Groups mixing students who bully and targets of bullying are often more successful than groups organized for just perpetrators of bullying, although groups for just targets can be good for mutual support and social connection.

Objectives

- Group members consider the impact of various kinds of bullying.

- Those who have been bullied feel heard, with feelings validated.

- Those who have bullied gain insight about their behavior and its effects.

- Group members understand the potential role and impact of passive bystanders.

1. Begin by asking the group to define *bullying*. After they have offered their views, tell them that it is usually understood to be hostile, intentionally intimidating behavior by someone with more power. While most researchers and many school policies include *repeated* in their definitions, it is important to recognize that even a single incident of bullying can have a traumatic effect.

2. Ask students to brainstorm different types of bullying. (Possibilities: Both verbal and physical types, such as teasing, name-calling, excluding, spreading rumors, gossiping, knocking books to the floor, damaging or taking possessions, tripping, hitting, threatening, and beating up, as well as online forms of many of these in addition to posting embarrassing photos or videos.) You might nudge students toward considering how bullying differs among genders.

3. Continue by asking open-ended questions, allowing time for spontaneous discussion for each. Be aware that the discussion may need to develop for a while before targets share their experiences. Therefore, begin with general, abstract questions.

   ~ How serious a problem is bullying in our/your school?

   ~ What kinds of bullying are you aware of in our/your school?

   ~ Where does it happen?

   ~ What types of students typically bully others? (Encourage them not to name names.)

   ~ What makes someone vulnerable to bullying? (Possibilities: Size, weight, appearance, low social status, being new, not having a group of friends, being withdrawn, being highly intelligent and/or a high academic achiever, having a learning or physical disability.)

   ~ How might being bullied affect someone? (Possibilities: Low confidence, poor self-image, being ostracized, being shunned.)

   ~ How might bullying others affect someone later in life? (Possibilities: Domestic abuse, being in trouble with the law, bullying others in the workplace, heavy-handed parenting.)

   ~ Do you know anyone personally who has been bullied? (Again, ask students not to name others.)

   ~ What do you know about the person's experience? (If someone believes it was traumatic, say, "That makes sense that it hurt that much.")

   ~ Do you know anyone personally who bullies others? (Ask students not to say specific names.)

   ~ What do you think might make bullying happen?

~ What grade levels in school do you think have the most bullying?

~ If you've been bullied, would you be willing to share what that was like? How did you feel? What did you do to try to stop it (or what are you trying to do to stop it)? How did it affect your feelings about school (or another place) in general?

~ If you've bullied someone, would you be willing to share what that was like? How do you make sense of your bullying? What feelings did you have toward the target?

~ If you've watched or known about bullying and haven't tried to help the person being targeted, would you be willing to share what that was like? What were your feelings? What did you do? Is there something you could realistically have done, if anything—at the time or later—to help? What should adults understand about bystanders?

~ How does it feel to talk about this topic?

4. Move into a problem-solving mode. Ask questions like these:

~ What do you think our/your school should do about bullying? What has been tried?

~ What do you think teachers should do? administrators? What have they tried?

~ What can students do to combat bullying and harassment? Some experts say that bystanders should be seen as "helping" bullying. What do you think about that? What reasons might a bystander have for not getting involved? (Possibility: Potential for permanent injury.)

~ What should parents do if their child is miserable because of being bullied?

~ What could someone who is bullied do to be less vulnerable?

~ What do you think when you hear that some people see bullying as "normal," "okay," "just part of growing up," or "something kids need to take care of themselves"? (If the group rejects those views, ask, "What could help to change this general attitude?")

~ What kind of school rules about bullying would help to make bullying happen less—or not at all?

~ What would you like to tell (or suggest to) a committee making these rules?

~ What do you think the consequences should be for someone who is caught bullying?

5. For closure, thank the group for being open, genuine, thoughtful, respectful, mature (or whatever other descriptors are appropriate). You might offer a summary statement yourself or ask the group to do that. Expect that this discussion will leave some or all quiet and thoughtful.

FOCUS Relationships

Being Interesting

Background

Adolescents are sometimes concerned that they are not interesting, or that someday they will lose a relationship because they are no longer interesting. They may believe they have seen it happen in their lives—perhaps in their families. Even in school, many worry they will not be accepted or become popular because they do not have enough to offer. To enhance their appeal, they buy the right clothes, make sure they can talk about certain things, develop strong likes and dislikes to be shared in conversation, and work hard to become good at something. But they still may not be sure they are interesting. Others, of course, may choose not to worry about how they appear or to compete for that kind of "interesting." Still others may believe they *cannot* compete.

Some may not have to work at being interesting. They just *are*—in the eyes of their peers. For some students, being interesting means being popular. For others, it means that they are seen as colorful, dramatic, mysterious, or complex. Whatever the label means, probably even kindergartners can judge who is interesting—and perhaps therefore appealing.

This topic is pertinent to all teens, for all are developing identity, and all want to be noticed—to some degree, at least. Whether they are the most successful students in school, the most shy, or the ones who are most often in trouble, they probably want to know if they are interesting. If the discussion is light and relaxing, enjoy it. Your group may need that. If your group approaches this topic darkly, stand beside them. If the discussion focuses on popularity, follow their lead, perhaps eventually bringing them back to the connection (or lack of connection) to "interesting." Note that this session is not called "Popularity," since it is meant to encourage looking at the social world without the popularity lens.

Objectives

- Group members feel affirmed as interesting.
- They learn that they may differ in their views about what is interesting.

Suggestions

1. Introduce the topic by asking the group what makes people interesting. They might consider their own age group first, and then adults. List their criteria on the board, if one is available, or on a large sheet of paper.

2. Invite group members to name some interesting peers—and then some interesting adults—and to support their nominations with a statement or two.

3. Ask them if being interesting is a concern for them. Introduce the idea that we are all more interesting than we think we are. There are probably many, many personality traits, experiences, situations, accidents, struggles, traumas, moments, and neighborhood memories that we have not thought about for a long time, but which, if they were known, would make us come to life for someone. However, we also need to remember that just responding to whatever is around us, and showing that we are interested in whomever we are with, is interesting enough to make us good company and pleasant to be around.

4. Ask the students to make a list on paper of five to ten interesting things about themselves—things that few group members, if any, know. (Maybe they have a significant scar, a family history of frequent moves, a musical talent not displayed in school, a position in a religious organization, ten siblings, an eccentric relative, a penny collection, a weird recurring dream, an attic bedroom, a unique part-time job, a strange allergy, a fascination for off-beat movies, a strong *dislike* for video games, a weakness for chocolate, or . . . ?)

   Have each person share his or her list with a partner, who will ask for elaboration on just one item from the list. Re-form the group and have each person tell what he or she learned about his or her interesting partner, reporting on more than one of the five to ten items, or concentrating on the one that was elaborated on.

5. If popularity has not been discussed, ask, "Some people might believe that popularity means that someone is interesting. What do you think about that? Make an argument for and against that belief."

6. For closure, affirm them as interesting individuals. Let them know that history, habits, and quirks of personality do make people interesting. In relationships, sharing the down-to-earth personal side, the quirks, and the stories makes people real and human—and interesting. When people say "Yes!" to who they are and where they have been, in addition to showing interest in those they are with, they are likely to be easy and enjoyable to be around. Ask the group for comments about how it felt to share their interesting details.

FOCUS **Relationships**

With Parents, Guardians, and Other Caregivers

Objectives

- Group members learn that parent-child struggles are common in their age group and are relatively normal.

- They examine their relationship with their parents.

- They learn to articulate some of the complexities in their relationship with their parents.

- They explore the idea that parenting styles differ.

- They gain some understanding of both themselves and their parents.

Important

For discussion purposes, "parents" can refer to biological and/or adoptive parents, stepparents, foster parents, guardians, or other significant caregiving adults. Be aware that, if a parent is no longer living, even if the relationship was brief, that relationship may still be significant here. The same may be true for a former stepparent or foster parent.

Suggestions

1. If group members have not already described their family situation earlier in your group, invite them to briefly describe the family they live with. Some, of course, may be in situations involving blended families, current or past stepparents, absent parents, deceased parents, distant parents, single parents, adoptive parents, gay parents, grandparents, or unknown parents. Remind them at the outset that what was once considered a typical family may no longer be typical. Encourage students to consider all parent relationships as important and worthy of discussion. All such relationships have an impact on a young life.

2. Hand out copies of "Relationships with Parents, Guardians, and Other Caregivers" (pages 207–208) and ask the group to fill out the activity sheet with brief responses, anonymously. Use the activity sheet to generate discussion. Or simply give each member a copy of the questionnaire to use as a reference during the discussion. You might go quickly around the group for brief answers to one question at a time for some of the questions. As always, the value is in raised awareness and experience in expressing concerns. Be aware that the activity may be unsettling for some group members, given their complicated relationship with their parents or loss of a parent. Remind them that they always have the option of passing when it is their turn.

3. Introduce the idea of parenting style. Use the following questions to explore this. Beware of overtly passing judgment on responses, even though biases and values are implicit in several of the questions. The questions for this suggestion and suggestion #4 refer to "parents," but not all group members will have two parents or even one. Those with two might have differing relationships with each parent. Steer the direction accordingly, and invite group members to consider their parents individually when responding to the questions. Depending on the circumstances of group members, you might want to omit some of the questions. Tell the group that they should think of parents, stepparents, guardians, or other main caregivers for these questions.

~ How unified are your parents/guardians? For example, if they both live with you, do they agree on rules about discipline and support and not disagree in front of you and your siblings? Or, if they don't live together, do they agree on how you should be parented?

~ How clear are their guidelines for you?

~ How patient are your parents/guardians? How casual? formal? rule-oriented? consistent?

~ When you do something you shouldn't do or break a family rule, is punishment immediate? harsh? fair? appropriate?

~ How much do your parents/guardians preach or lecture? allow you to learn from your mistakes? give advice?

~ How much independence do they give you? How much do they allow you to make decisions?

~ How protective of you are they?

~ How affectionate are they toward you?

~ How seriously do they take parenting?

~ Which of them leads—in various areas of family life?

~ How do they divide their parenting responsibilities?

4. Ask these questions:

~ Have you been easy for your parents/guardians to raise?

~ Have your parents/guardians been easy to have as parents/guardians? (Acknowledge that some teens may even feel that they have had to "raise their parents"!)

~ What kinds of feelings do you have when you think about, or talk about, your parents/guardians? (They might use words like *grateful, angry, frustrated, happy, sad, lucky, depressed, nostalgic, secure,* or *guilty.* Remind them that it is good to practice communicating about feelings—to enhance relationships and to learn how to identify feelings and behaviors in others accurately.)

~ What are the major "jobs" of parents, in your opinion?

~ Which of these jobs have your parents/guardians done well?

5. Invite the group to consider how their relationships with parents, stepparents, guardians, or other caregivers have contributed to the following:

their personal goals
their view of life
their understanding of what "family" is
their school success
other relationships
their feelings about themselves

6. For closure, summarize—or ask a student to summarize—the most significant ideas that were discussed during this session. The relationship with each parent is significant in forming the self. There is value in discussing these relationships, which are always complex and sometimes troublesome, especially during the teen years. Thank students for their honesty and thoughtfulness and for helping the group to understand better the complexities of relationships with parents. Dispose of the sheets.

Relationships with Parents, Guardians, and Other Caregivers

Use your own judgment about how to answer these questions if you don't live with one or both parents; if you live with a stepparent, but have contact with the parent not living with you; if you live with foster parents or adoptive parents; if a parent is no longer living; if you live with grandparents; or if you live with any other nontraditional family. Feel free to "pass" on some questions or to think about how your parent was when he or she was with you.

1. Describe the relationship you have with your mother.

   _____

2. Describe the relationship you have with your father.

   _____

3. How are these relationships different from the way they were two years ago?

   _____

   Five years ago?

   _____

   Ten years ago?

   _____

4. What specific problems, if any, interfere with your having a good relationship with your parents?

   _____

5. Which parent are you closest to?

   _____

6. Which parent do you think you resemble the most physically?

   _____

   Emotionally?

   _____

   In interests?

   _____

7. Is one or both of your parents absent? ill? no longer living? not around much?

   _____

   If so, how have you coped with that?

   _____

   (continued)

Relationships with Parents, Guardians, and Other Caregivers (continued)

8. How do your parents cope with stress and frustrations?

   _____

9. How do they handle parenting?

   _____

10. How are they coping with your getting older?

    _____

11. How do they respond when you are ill?

    _____

    When you are in trouble?

    _____

12. What do you respect most about your parents?

    _____

13. What have your parents done well in life? (Your answer can relate to any area of life.)

    _____

14. What are the most important things your parents have taught you?

    _____

15. Write five words that come to mind when you think "Dad" or "Father."

    _____

16. Write five words that come to mind when you think "Mom" or "Mother."

    _____

Relationships
With Siblings

Background

This session focus might not be appropriate if your group has a large number of "only" children. However, those students might enjoy hearing about sibling relationships, and you might get them interested in participating with open-ended questions about how they view not having siblings.

Objectives

- Group members gain insight into their relationships with brothers and sisters.

- They gain skills in articulating feelings and concerns about their family.

- They consider how family conflict can help to form personal identity.

Suggestions

1. Introduce the focus, and then ask each group member to do the following:

    ~ Give the names and ages of their siblings and step-siblings (even if this was done in a previous session). If group members are from cultures that refer to cousins or others as brothers and sisters, invite them to include all whom they see as such.

    ~ Briefly describe each sibling, using two or three adjectives.

    ~ Explain what kind of relationship they have with each. (For example, close, not close, competitive, best friend.)

    ~ If a sibling no longer lives at home, has died, or is at home only part of the time, describe what kind of relationship they once had and, if the sibling is still alive, whether it has changed.

    Another option here is to have group members quickly draw a picture of themselves and their siblings, perhaps even just stick figures in a line, and then use the picture while explaining the above.

2. Move the discussion in the direction of conflict with these questions:

    ~ Do you argue a lot with siblings?

    ~ Has there been more, or less, conflict this year (or lately)?

    ~ How close do you feel to each sibling, on a scale of 1 to 10, with 10 being "very close"?

~ How much conflict do you have with each sibling, on a scale of 1 to 10, with 10 being "a lot of conflict"?

~ What kinds of conflicts have you had with your siblings? What are they about?

This sharing offers students opportunities for problem-solving and learning from others' experiences. Group members might mention conflict areas such as these in response to the last question above:

competition	differing interests
jealousy	gender issues
criticism	needing to be different from each other
favoritism	competition for parents' attention
age differences	personal space
personality differences	private space
guilt	bullying

3. Give group members a chance to speak positively about their siblings. Ask the following questions:

~ What do you appreciate about your siblings?

~ How much support and encouragement do you feel from your siblings?

~ Do you worry a lot about a sibling? If so, what are you concerned about?

~ How much do you think sibling relationships change over time? Do you know of siblings in other families whose relationship changed and got better or worse?

4. Offer the idea that children often strive for a separate identity in the family, different from their siblings', and they try to get attention from their parents in various ways. Ask some of the following, selecting questions and adjusting vocabulary according to the developmental level and concerns of your group.

~ What are you known for in your family?

~ Has it been easy or difficult for you to become known for something?

~ Are you someone everyone in the family is always aware of? not very aware of?

~ How do family members usually describe you to others?

~ How have you felt about that description? Are they right? Do you enjoy having what you are known for in the family? If not, what don't you like about it?

~ What kind of attention do you and each of your siblings get in your family? Does it differ from person to person?

~ Do you feel you have had enough attention from your family? too much attention?

~ How do you feel around each of your siblings? (Possibilities: Confident, unconfident, superior, inferior, stronger, weaker, comfortable, uncomfortable, content, irritated.)

~ Do you think that each child in your family feels important to the family?

5. Invite group members with siblings to ask questions of the "only" children about what their life is like without brothers and sisters.

6. For closure, ask for a volunteer to summarize the discussion. Or ask for various group members' impressions. Do most seem to have smooth relationships with siblings, or do most have relationships with a lot of conflict? How did they feel during the discussion? Encourage them to use feeling words—like *comfortable, uncomfortable, sad, happy, uneasy, guilty, pleased, proud, grateful,* or *irritated.*

This may also be a good time to ask students how they are feeling about the group at this stage in its development—especially if this and recent discussions have gone well, and if they have been meeting long enough to develop a good comfort level with each other. Your asking gives them a chance to affirm themselves as a group.

You might also ask them what makes a good group. "What would someone notice if observing your group when you're all doing your best?" Then ask, "On a scale of 1 to 10, with 10 being perfect, how would you rate your group at this point?"

FOCUS Relationships
With Teachers

Background

Teachers are major players in the lives of young people. The teacher-student relationship is often a key relationship in a teen's school experience. A good relationship can motivate the student in the classroom and may support the student in other ways as well. An uncomfortable relationship can likewise negatively affect learning.

With that said, however, most students are probably not aware of how "human" teachers really are. They may not realize that teachers do become concerned when students are ill or are in difficult situations; that teachers are often hesitant to ask personal questions; that teachers sometimes wonder how to express concern adequately or acceptably to students; and that teachers do see *individuals* in their classes each day, but numbers and time constraints often make it difficult to make conversation, express concern, or make one-to-one connections.

In addition, teachers have their own lives, and clear boundaries between school and family help them to give appropriate energy and attention to both parts of their lives. However, part of what makes teaching satisfying and rewarding is having healthy and comfortable teacher-student relationships. Such relationships probably help to sustain coaches and extracurricular advisors during their great time commitment to activities. Nevertheless, it is important that teachers remain *teachers* in student-teacher relationships. They are not peers of students, and they have special ethical responsibilities. Teacher-student relationships always have a power imbalance, for example, and there is a fine line between support/advice and interference/ imposition/manipulation. Teachers who *need* to be close to students—for their own benefit, not the students'—may cross another fine line. And there is a great difference between teachers confiding in students and students confiding in teachers; the adult is always responsible for setting appropriate boundaries. Teachers can be of most help to students when they are *teachers first,* with all the complex dimensions of that position.

Some teachers, of course, are shy, just as some students are. Some teachers are very private people, just as some students are. Some teachers communicate easily with students outside of class, just as some students can with teachers. Each teacher and each student probably has unique wishes about communication with the other.

Objectives	• Group members learn that attitudes about relationships with teachers vary within the group.

Objectives

- Group members learn that attitudes about relationships with teachers vary within the group.

- They articulate their thoughts and feelings concerning relationships with teachers.

- They explore the advantages of having a good relationship with a teacher.

Suggestions

1. If you are a teacher or counselor, introduce the topic by sharing your own thoughts about relationships with students, perhaps considering questions like these: What are your roles and responsibilities (and what are not)? What helps you maintain clear boundaries between yourself and students, and between their lives and yours, even as you become an important teacher/counselor to them? Why are boundaries a concern? Then ask the group questions like these:

   ~ Have you ever had a teacher who was a "teacher-friend"? (Suggest that a teacher-friend can be a special kind of friend and valuable ally—an adult to talk with, to trust, and to seek guidance from. A teacher-friend can be *most* helpful when the emphasis stays on *teacher*, just as parent-friends are best when they remember that they are parents. Whereas peer-friends are equal in sharing confidences, for example, adult-friends of students may be most helpful in being *un*equal and able to offer adult wisdom and support.)

   ~ How was that a unique relationship, different from any other friendship? How was it similar to other friendships?

   ~ Was that friendship different from friendships you have with other adults?

   You might want to mention the idea of professional boundaries. See the background information for ideas.

2. Hand out copies of "Relationships with Teachers" (page 215), and ask the group to fill out the activity sheet with brief responses, anonymously. Use the activity sheets to encourage further discussion. Or make it an oral exercise only, with students using the questionnaire as a reference during the discussion.

3. Ask the group these questions:

   ~ Who are some teachers that most kids appreciate? What do you think helps them to be appreciated?

   ~ What are some possible advantages of having a good, comfortable relationship with a teacher?

   ~ Have you ever known a teacher well enough to trust him or her with personal information?

   ~ Has a teacher ever advised or guided you about a personal situation?

   ~ How important to your learning is liking a teacher?

~ How can students build a good teacher-student relationship?

~ How could a teacher benefit from having a comfortable, communicative relationship with a student? with students in general?

4. Invite the group to problem-solve:

~ Is there a teacher you aren't getting along with this year?

~ What would that class be like for you if you had a better relationship with the teacher? What would the teacher be doing? What would you be doing? How would you be feeling?

~ How could you make the problem bigger? (This question is meant to help the teen figure out what is in his or her control.) smaller? (Possibilities: Ask for help; make eye contact; make small talk; answer questions in class; recognize that teachers need warmth and support, just like anyone else; arrange to speak individually with the teacher.)

~ Do you think parents or counselors should ever intervene to try to improve a relationship between a student and a teacher? (Suggest that it is probably best for the student to try to take care of the situation with the teacher alone, perhaps after guidance from parents or a counselor. If that attempt doesn't help, however, then someone else might be asked to serve as an objective third party in conflict mediation or to advocate directly.)

5. To prepare for closure, ask these questions:

~ What do you need personally from teachers in general?

~ What do you definitely *not* want from teachers?

6. For closure, ask someone to summarize what has been shared and/or learned during this discussion. Compliment the group on their ability to articulate thoughts and feelings. Dispose of the sheets.

Relationships with Teachers

1. What kinds of relationships have you usually had with your teachers?

   _____

2. As you have gotten older, have your relationships with teachers become closer and more comfortable, or more distant and less comfortable?

   _____

3. Name one great teacher you have had: _____. Describe the teacher with two or three words:_____

4. What kind of teacher do you like best? Check one or more:

   ☐ is highly organized   ☐ uses a lot of worksheets
   ☐ is loosely organized   ☐ assigns projects to do at home
   ☐ is very flexible   ☐ shows information on the board and with pictures, etc.
   ☐ has lots of variety   ☐ doesn't talk much with individual students
   ☐ has few rules   ☐ gives information by talking to the whole class
   ☐ has many rules   ☐ teaches by having kids do activities
   ☐ gives clear directions   ☐ uses a lot of technology
   ☐ is warm and friendly   ☐ uses humor

   Do your choices here fit the great teacher you named in #3?   Yes ☐   No ☐

5. Do you like to have teachers know you well personally?   Yes ☐   No ☐

6. What kind of information do you like teachers to know about you?

   _____

   What kind of information do you *not* want teachers to know about you?

   _____

7. If you were having a very difficult time in your personal life, would you want your teachers to be aware of that?   Yes ☐   No ☐

8. How do you know when a teacher likes and enjoys you as a student?

   _____

   Do most teachers seem to like you?   Yes ☐   No ☐

9. How do you let teachers know that you like their teaching?

   _____

Relationships

Masculinity and Femininity

Background

Sexuality involves much more than just having sex, of course. Sexuality is personal. It is not synonymous with sexual orientation, which is interpersonal. Sexuality is how we are distinguished, or distinguish ourselves, as male or female (regardless of sex assigned at birth), nonbinary (not identifying exclusively with either gender), transgender (gender identity not matching gender assigned at birth), or agender (not identifing with any gender). Sexuality is how we behave in response to emotional and physical sensations, how we interact in social relationships, how we notice the responses of others, and how we think of ourselves. People differ in what behaviors they think are appropriate for various gender identities. For example, opinions vary about how to "be masculine" and how to "be feminine"—within and among cultures, families, and groups of friends and peers. Adolescents, already struggling with identity issues, may have reason to be confused about gender expectations, behavior, and sexual feelings. Public awareness of and media attention to complex concerns related to gender identity add to the confusion and entrenchment of opinions and call attention to related civil-rights challenges.

This session introduces a brief series of sessions focusing on gender relations. Regardless of the gender identities represented in your group, suggestion #2 offers a chance for cisgender (sex identified at birth is in agreement with gender identity) males and females to find out how each other thinks about gender and also what group members with other gender identities think about gender. This session is also an opportunity for you to learn about group members' views and concerns. Suggestion #2 usually generates enough interaction to fill a session. Suggestion #3 could be considered as a follow-up session in itself, especially if a film is used. Looking at ads can be an effective second half of an introductory session on gender relations.

Students usually appreciate having a safe place, with an attentive adult listener, to discuss these important matters. As with all other sessions, it is important to listen and not feel compelled to inform or moralize. However, it is appropriate for you to give opinions carefully and sensitively if the group asks for them or seems to be looking for guidance.

Important	You will need to do some advance preparation for suggestion #3 in this session. If you plan to show a video/DVD concerning media messages about gender and sexuality, check with your media center or library for ideas. (See also the Recommended Resource section on page 279.) If you plan to have the group analyze advertisements, make an assignment at the end of the previous session for the students to bring in five ads that prominently feature female or male models (or parts of models).

Objectives

- Group members consider their gender identity.

- They think about cultural attitudes regarding being masculine and being feminine.

- They find comfort in the fact that their peers also have anxieties about sexuality.

Suggestions

1. Invite the group to think of someone they find attractive. Then ask, "What is it about that person that you find especially appealing?"

2. Have group members make lists on the board or on a large sheet of paper of "what makes someone masculine" and "what makes someone feminine." All students should make or contribute to both lists, regardless of gender identity. (If yours is a single-gender group, they should still do the two lists.) Then ask a spokesperson for each group to report.

   This activity usually elicits a wide range of behaviors, from silliness to arguing to quiet thinking, but it probably will also provoke serious thinking. The students undoubtedly will consider physical attributes at the outset, but very quickly they will probably list emotional, expressive, and other behavioral characteristics. At times they may find it difficult to assign specific qualities or characteristics to specific genders. Ask questions like these when they are done:

   ~ Is being gentle, nurturing, artistic, and emotional only "feminine"?

   ~ Is being assertive, strong, athletic, and a leader only "masculine"?

   ~ How much are you a mixture of these traits?

   ~ (If someone insists on clear distinctions) How do you all feel about those distinctions? How much do you need clear distinctions to be comfortable?

   ~ Who tells us that there need to be clear distinctions?

   ~ What are some mysteries you wish you understood about gender?

   Reassure the group that most people are uncomfortable at times about how they feel and act, because they wonder how they fit society's expectations of what they should be and do.

3. Discuss a video/DVD concerning media messages about gender and sexuality. Or show and analyze advertisements the group was asked (at the preceding meeting) to bring to the meeting, focusing on gender roles and stereotypes, sexuality, and subtle messages (see the background information). Ask these questions:

   ~ How much are feminine and masculine bodies used to sell products?

   ~ What impact do messages in advertising have on relationships?

   ~ What do you think about the possibility that the way people are portrayed in ads is related to the way they behave on dates, in marriage, and at work?

   ~ How do media images like these contribute to gender expectations and stereotypes—and even to sexual harassment, abuse, and domestic and other violence? Explain.

4. For closure, ask the group if this was a comfortable topic to discuss. Where else have they discussed sexuality? Assure them that adolescence is a time when gender and sexuality are significant concerns. Thinking a lot about sex and sexuality is quite normal. Gender and sexuality will probably continue to be interesting topics for them.

FOCUS Relationships

Gender Behavior and Sexual Harassment

Background

Many expectations are placed on people based on their gender identity and expression, and these expectations can cause confusion, not only in romantic relationships, but also in other areas of life. Recent rising awareness about sexual harassment in the general culture has highlighted appropriate versus inappropriate behaviors in school, in the workplace, and in other environments and situations. The media continue to "teach" gender roles, significant adults may model gender behaviors that do not fit well in the current world, and shifting understandings of gender and its expression cause many to feel unsure about what is proper and expected. Adolescents must sort out many messages about gender, sexuality, and relationships.

Our sense of who we are as sexual beings reflects cultural attitudes, expectations, and taboos about gender behavior. Our sexuality involves affection, attraction, intimacy, social behavior, and communication styles, among many aspects. It is appropriate to consider sexual and gender behavior in regard to relationships, and this session does that.

Important

If this session takes place in a school or an organizational setting, it is important for you to familiarize yourself in advance with the school's or organization's policies and procedures regarding sexual harassment. For example, if someone in your group describes a specific incident of sexual harassment or assault, you will want to know about mandatory reporting and how to follow up. Your school or organization likely has guidelines specific to these issues. It is best to know them ahead of time.

Objectives

• Students learn about gender differences in communication styles.

• They consider the importance of mutual respect among people of differing gender identities.

• They consider some possible meanings, reasons, and effects of sexual harassment.

Suggestions

1. Introduce the topic with material from the background information and add to it with information from books, newspapers, or magazines related to gender expectations and stereotypes, sexual harassment, relationships, and communication

styles, for example. (See Recommended Resources on page 279.) Acknowledge that what we hear about gender behavior and expectations is often confusing and is not always accurate.

2. Pursue the idea of communication differences related to gender. Ask students if they believe the following stereotypes are true. Invite comments. Several individuals in the behavioral sciences have made statements like these; however, remind students that they do not have to agree with them. Encourage them simply to *consider* the thoughts presented. Obviously, no statement is true for *all* persons of that gender—at all ages.

   ~ Girls are good listeners. They support what others say.

   ~ Boys offer information and opinions, interrupt each other, change topics.

   ~ Girls finish each other's sentences in conversation and stick with topics.

   ~ Boys aren't used to having people agree with them.

   ~ Girls are concerned about keeping friendships going. They smile more than boys do in groups.

   ~ Boys' and men's voices are louder. Girls often feel as if they are not heard when they are in groups and classes with boys.

   Suggest that large and small differences in how people communicate can contribute to communication problems in families, at school, at work, and in romantic relationships. Ask the group how the statements above might be true for adults.

   If yours is a mixed-gender group, ask students if the statements above are true of their group.

3. Explore the idea of sexual harassment by asking these questions:

   ~ What does *sexual harassment* mean? (Check to see if group members can distinguish between sexual harassment and sexual abuse. The latter is usually defined as inappropriate conduct—such as fondling, intercourse, or oral sex—usually with the victim below an age and the perpetrator above an age determined by law in a particular state. It is also possible that sexual abuse can occur within a marriage or other adult relationships, since the key element is physical or psychological coercion. Sexual harassment is behavior that is unwelcome and inappropriate, whether it takes the form of sexual advances, requests for sexual favors, or other behaviors that are sexual in nature. Sexual behavior that is welcome, appropriate, and clearly consensual is not harassment. However, harassment does not have to be physical, dramatic, or threatening. Whether or not it is frequent, and even if it is only semi-uncomfortable, harassment may lead to general, long-term uncomfortableness and anxiety in the environment where it occurs. The harasser is often someone with more power—in the family hierarchy, in the job position, in social stature, or in height and weight.)

~ Can anyone be a target of sexual harassment? Do you think a person's gender makes them more or less likely to experience sexual harassment? If so, how do you think the experience and its effects differ based on gender? (Point out that sexual harassment or sexual abuse does not have to be by someone of another gender. Use the previous descriptors for guidance.)

~ What kinds of sexual comments and behaviors are you uncomfortable with?

~ What are some possible reasons for comments and behaviors like those? (Possibilities: Power and control, displaced anger, adult modeling, ignorance.)

~ Where do we learn how to behave toward people of other genders? (Parents are probably every person's first models for this. Other significant relatives, peers, and the media instruct as well. Emphasize that we can *un*learn those lessons by becoming sensitive to how our behavior affects others and practicing new behavior.)

~ Have you ever felt sexually harassed? Describe the experience, if you are willing to do that. What were your feelings? (Respect and reflect feelings and comments related to this question—for example, "That sounds very uncomfortable," or "I can see how that would be embarrassing," or "I'm glad you recognized that those comments were inappropriate," or "I'm glad you trusted us enough to tell us about this." Be aware that inappropriate actions and touch can happen even in kindergarten by peers.)

Emphasize that negative feelings can be strong, even if the harassment is subtle. People who are harassed often blame themselves; fear taunting or further harassment if they complain; wonder what the behavior means; feel powerless, embarrassed, ashamed, or trapped; and feel less free to be themselves. Point out that harassing behaviors are practiced when young. Now is the time to be aware of them and to change them. The key to social ease and successful relationships is respect, not power and control over someone else.

4. For closure, ask students to comment on the discussion. How did they feel? What new thoughts or understandings did they have? You might also summarize the concerns about sexual harassment you have heard in the group. If a group member revealed an experience that warrants your consulting someone in your institution about legal definitions, impact, age difference, and need for reporting, follow up as soon as possible.

FOCUS Relationships

Sexual Aggression

In recent years, date and acquaintance rape have received more than passing attention as a serious social problem. However, although media attention to this kind of sexual aggression is increasing, it is still not reported often. No one knows how prevalent it is, but surveys and clinical histories indicate that it is not uncommon. Even though victims may blame themselves for being naive, drinking, or not being able to control the situation, rape is never justified. However, adolescents often are not enough aware of what contributes to vulnerability. Those who are not naive may also find themselves unprepared and feeling defenseless in situations with sexually aggressive individuals—even in middle school.

Most sexual attacks during middle school and high school are made by someone the victim knows. Social upbringing often does not prepare a person for sexual aggression, and it often does not provide survival skills. As students begin dating and attending parties, even in middle school, they need to be alert and wise to the social scene. Talking about this topic with young teens can serve as prevention. No matter what the social situation, and no matter what their background, students of all ages and circumstances need to be aware of the problem of date and acquaintance rape. Assess the maturity level of your group carefully when considering whether to use this session, but beware of underestimating the vulnerability of middle school students to sexual aggression.

Keep in mind that boys and men can be victims of sexual aggression as well. Regardless of the gender of the aggressor, the experience can have long-lasting effects.

Important

Before this session, compile a list of school and community resources students can contact for help/counseling. Then pass out this list if, during the discussion, someone mentions having been the victim of date/acquaintance rape or attempted rape, or if someone comes to you afterward and tells you about such an experience.

Whether or not you are a counselor, listen attentively and compassionately. It is probably difficult for the individual to talk about the experience, and it is appropriate to commend the person's courage in speaking of it. Remind the group about confidentiality. Be aware of criteria and protocols for reporting and follow through accordingly.

Objectives

- Group members will become more aware of the prevalence of date/acquaintance rape.

- Through discussing realistic situations, group members will become wiser, more informed, and less vulnerable to date/acquaintance rape—and less likely to perpetrate it.

Suggestions

1. Some group members will feel uncomfortable speaking about this subject, but most will be willing to discuss expectations, vulnerabilities, responsibilities, pressures, and socialization about masculinity and femininity. Introduce date/acquaintance rape as falling under the general category of "when parents worry about their children finding themselves in situations they can't handle." Consider asking these general questions. Encourage group members to be discreet in answering.

   ~ Does anyone have the right to demand sex under any circumstances?

   ~ Have you ever been in a situation where sexual aggression caught you off guard?

   ~ What do you know about the effects of date rape?

   ~ What are some strategies for dealing with sexual aggression?

   ~ What can contribute to date/acquaintance rape? (Possibilities: Alcohol, dress, being alone, intimidation, flirting, manipulation, attitudes—regardless of gender.)

   ~ What can someone do to be less vulnerable to it?

   ~ We usually think of girls and women as victims here. But can homosexual, heterosexual, and transgender boys and men be victims of sexual aggression?

2. Brainstorm and discuss the differences among consensual (based on expressed mutual consent), manipulated, coerced, and forced sex. Ask the group which ones are illegal (psychologically coerced or physically forced). Make lists on the board, if one is available, or on a large sheet of paper. Group members may suggest the following differences, or you might provide a handout, selecting descriptors and perhaps adjusting vocabulary for your group:

   ~ Consensual sex probably involves smiles, closeness, affection, shared pleasure, comfortableness, and verbal and nonverbal communication.

   ~ Manipulated sex could involve alcohol or other drugs, one person's planning and expectations, or playing to the other's vulnerabilities.

   ~ Coerced sex probably involves power and strength, guilt, threats, claiming that sex is "owed" for something, and discomfort, and may also involve alcohol or other drugs.

   ~ Forced sex probably involves fear, fighting, unwanted physical touching, aggression, threats, submission to survive (not consensual), and possibly temporary inability to move.

3. Emphasize that individuals can reduce their vulnerability. Have the group make a list of recommendations. You might suggest the following if they are not mentioned:

~ Think carefully about the limits you want to set on sexual behavior prior to going out. Have your phone handy. Ideally a parent or guardian should know where you are.

~ Express feelings honestly and don't be afraid to communicate assertively and with certainty when you are uncomfortable.

~ Pay attention to what you wear (even though dress should never excuse a rapist) and make sure that your verbal (what you say) and nonverbal (facial and other physical expressions and behaviors) messages agree—and that they match your intent.

~ Don't leave friends alone in situations where they are vulnerable (and don't put yourself into such a situation). If you unexpectedly find yourself alone and vulnerable, make a call.

~ Don't give in to pressure to have sexual intercourse or oral sex or give in to return a favor.

4. Create some scenarios for or with the group to discuss and problem-solve, or hand out copies of "Problem Scenarios" (pages 225–226). Explore with the group what makes the person vulnerable in each situation. Scenarios I and J involve males, one as the aggressor and one as a potential victim. Your group may want to discuss more situations where males feel uncomfortable about sexual activity or perceive that sex is expected.

For Scenario A, encourage the group to address the young woman's wish to talk when she learns that the young man's parents are gone for the weekend. For Scenario B, pay attention to the vulnerability of the sister. Scenario F is about a bisexual male and might be especially thought-provoking. Scenario G was written with a female in mind, but if someone mentions that the victim could be male, explore that possibility. The scenarios, some of which describe situations on college campuses, are included here because of the particular vulnerability of students who enter college unaccustomed to sexual aggression and, possibly, to drinking. Even if yours is a middle school group, make use of the scenarios that include older individuals, since your group members will be older very soon.

5. For closure, tell the group what you have heard them say, in general, or have one or two of them summarize what has been discussed. Compliment them for handling the discussion well or for articulating difficult matters, if appropriate. Stress that if they are ever raped or are otherwise sexually assaulted, they should seek help immediately, make a report, be examined, and be counseled. Counseling will be important, since feelings about self-worth, sexuality, and relationships likely will be affected. Many victims do not report an attack because they blame themselves for losing control of the situation. Remind the group that loss of control *never* justifies one person forcing sex on another. In addition, warn them about making false accusations, since more than just the accused can be harmed.

Problem Scenarios

A. You are a high school junior girl, and have been going out with someone from another school casually for a few weeks. You do not feel committed to the relationship and have strong reservations about having sex with him. You enjoy talking with him. In fact, he is the first person you have dated who is interesting to talk with. You look forward to the conversations. After a movie and pizza, which he paid for, he asks if you would like to see where he lives with his parents. You arrive at his home, and then he tells you that his parents are gone for the weekend.

B. You are an eighth grader. Your older sister agrees to drive you to a community dance in a nearby town. You are wearing tight, revealing clothing. A cute twenty-year-old dances with you, and you enjoy flirting and dancing together for most of the night. You would like to go out again. Your dance partner asks to take you home. You see that your sister is also quite occupied with someone. You leave with the cute twenty-year-old.

C. You are at a party with many of your friends. There is alcohol, and everyone is drinking. Some are dancing, some are disappearing, and you are beginning to feel a bit drunk. You are dancing with someone you've been casually involved with for a week or two.

D. You are an attractive college freshman and are attending a dance sponsored by the school. It is your first college dance. You are not naive about sexual behavior, but you are uneasy about what you have heard are the sexual expectations of this particular dance. You are getting a lot of attention from a senior.

E. You have never considered yourself to be a physically attractive woman. In fact, you are quite self-conscious. Your strengths are, you feel, your intellect and your ability to read others well, to be nice to everyone, and not to be confrontational and demanding. You were surprised when you were invited to join a sorority of the "beautiful ones." One night, your sorority has a party. A good-looking, fairly smooth guy asks you to dance. You are flattered when he dances with you for the next four dances, even though you wonder if maybe someone has dared him to, and he seems overly complimentary. He radiates confidence and sexuality. The dance is nearly over, and he's asking to take you to his friend's apartment, where some of his friends "probably are."

F. You are a male ninth grader who is bisexual, but not "out." Three older male athletes regularly tease you in the hallways with homophobic slurs, but otherwise the school feels safe. One afternoon they corral you and force you into a storage area near a locker room, where a girl their age is waiting. The athletes leave, but can be heard patrolling outside of the door. The girl moves toward you and says, "They want me to put you on the right path."

(continued)

G. You were raped by an acquaintance three nights ago after a party. You are uneasy about telling even your best friend, since you feel that you shouldn't have let yourself get into that situation, and you know that the acquaintance would be believed more than you would be. You are very upset, feel violated and depressed, are shaky, and haven't slept much since then.

H. You are a commuter college student and need to make a phone call, but your cell phone battery is dead. You know several people in a coed dormitory and decide to stop to call there. In the lobby, you see someone you've met in a class, and you tell your classmate about your need to call. He invites you to use the phone in his room.

I. You have not dated much. You're a conscientious, fairly quiet guy who doesn't feel comfortable at parties and is shy around girls. An aggressive, sexually experienced girl approaches you at the first party you've attended all year. She seems to have taken on the responsibility of instructing you in sexual behavior. You and she are now in the back of her friend's pickup truck. You feel quite uncomfortable about the way things are going, but you are aroused and feel unable to leave the situation. You are very concerned about what she might think of you—no matter what you might say right now.

J. You are a sexually experienced young man. A beautiful woman your age has accepted an invitation to come to your apartment for a drink after a party. You know that she is not inexperienced sexually, because you know others who have dated her. She looks hot and has been flirting with you quite obviously. The two of you have been kissing on the sofa, but she has said she wants to go home now, and when you persist with more physical aggression, she begins to cry.

K. You are a high school student in a relationship with a classmate. You are quite sure you have never behaved improperly in the relationship. Your classmate was very upset when you said last night that you wanted to break up. Today you heard your ex is accusing you of rape and may even press charges.

FOCUS Relationships

....

Patterns of Violence and Abuse

Background

Violence among teen couples is not uncommon. Therefore, the topic of relationship violence certainly deserves more attention than just one session. It can be approached with statistical information (available on the internet), in the context of our changing society, as a response to violence in the media, as connected to adult modeling of violence, or as a power and control issue, among many possible approaches. This session will focus on just one aspect of violence—abusive relationships.

The purpose of this session is to help students understand that abusive relationships occur at all levels of society, in all age groups, and continue from one generation to the next. All young people learn how to treat a partner, and what to expect from a partner, by observing the adults in their lives. People may stay in abusive situations because they learned young to accept abuse. Unfortunately, many in such relationships, including teens, do not feel they can do anything to help themselves. They fear what the abuser might do if they leave, or they are afraid of being alone. They believe they have no choice but to stay.

Raised awareness through discussion may encourage a young abuser to seek help or to take personal stock and stop an early abusive habit, or encourage abused individuals to seek help. Unless changes are made, the abuse will continue. Adolescents can benefit from knowing that adults in abusive relationships can pursue crisis centers, leaving the relationship, or individual or couple counseling to take stock of the relationship in general and examine abusive patterns. Of prime importance for teens is awareness that marriage does not cure an abusive dating relationship.

Important

This session encourages an honest look at abusive relationships that may help to prevent them or give teens courage to leave them. Although you should be prepared that group members may share experiences with past or current abuse, eliciting that kind of information is not the intent here. There can be great value in this session without any personal revelations. However, some students in abusive situations may seek you out individually. Be aware of laws regarding mandatory reporting before addressing this issue, inform the group at the outset about limits of confidentiality in that regard, and be clear about the purpose of your group. If sensitive information is shared, discreetly or indiscreetly, remind the group about the rules of confidentiality.

You might plan to feature a speaker from a domestic violence shelter/center or from a mental health agency. If so, you will need to make these arrangements in advance, and you will need to discuss how to make the presentation relevant and appropriate for your age group. If you are a counselor, find out what your community offers in counseling resources, expertise related to relationship abuse, and protective services. You should have an up-to-date list available for anyone who asks about resources. If you are in a school, but are not a counselor, channel requests to the school counselor.

Objectives

- Group members learn that abuse can occur in relationships at all levels of society and in all age groups.

- They learn that patterns of abuse can become firmly established in a relationship, that stopping them requires courage and conscious effort, and that leaving the relationship may be the best option.

Suggestions

1. If you have arranged for a speaker to visit your group, open the session by inviting the speaker to present information about abusive relationships (including with teens) and helpful suggestions for avoiding or stopping them. The focus could be on patterns that become established early in relationships, even for adolescents, or on factors that contribute to violent and abusive behavior and to vulnerability to abuse.

2. In addition to, or in place of, hearing the speaker's presentation, group members can respond to the following statements. You might type the statements on separate pieces of paper and have group members read them in turn. Ask them whether the statements are believable.

   ~ Abuse means dominance, power, control, and victimization.

   ~ Abuse can happen at all levels of society, even among people with wealth and status, and at all ages, including between and among young children.

   ~ Abuse can be physical, verbal, emotional, and/or sexual. The abused person can be any gender. Females are more likely to abuse verbally than physically, but are certainly capable of physical abuse. Verbal and emotional abuse may actually be harder to stop than physical abuse.

   ~ Victims of abuse may believe they are responsible for others' behavior and accept blame for the abuse.

   ~ People who are abused may believe they don't deserve respect.

   ~ People who are abused often fear "rocking the boat."

   ~ People who are abused often do not believe they have options.

   ~ Both abusers and their victims may be afraid of their emotions and try to numb them with alcohol or other drugs.

~ People who are abused may fear their abusers so much that they are afraid to request or force changes.

~ People who are abused believe *they* are the ones who need to be better. Abusers sense that.

~ Abusers and their victims both may fear rejection. This fear may increase the danger if a victim leaves the relationship. An abuser who is rejected may become even more violent.

~ People who are abused might keep choosing abusers for partners because they have confused love with abuse.

~ People are often attracted to the *pattern* they grew up with. If their experiences contributed to positive self-esteem, and if they experienced and witnessed healthy relationships, they will probably be attracted healthily. The same is true for unhealthful modeling. We learn by observation how couples are "supposed to" behave.

~ People who were abused in the past may become abused *or* abusive. Suffering abuse early in life can be seen as proof of low worth and can make one vulnerable to further abuse in life or lead to abusing in order to "play out" or "undo" what was experienced as a child.

~ Victimization and abusive behaviors are learned. Both can be changed with effort and assistance.

~ The emptiness of abusive relationships leaves people vulnerable to addictions, because the emptiness wants to be filled by something. Alcohol and other drugs may be used to fill the emptiness. Self-injury (such as cutting or burning) and eating disorders (including overeating) may be connected to present or past abuse.

~ Help is available. Counseling and group work can help victims and abusers heal and make positive changes.

3. Ask the group how they would know if they were in an abusive relationship. (Possibilities: Being hit, shoved, or slapped; being constantly or frequently criticized; feeling controlled; being physically or psychologically coerced to have sex or to behave in other ways that go against personal values.)

Brainstorm options for avoiding and stopping abuse. Emphasize that everyone in the group is worthy of respect and kindness in relationships. Nothing they do *makes* anyone treat them badly. Inform them that groups to help abusive partners are common and that individual or group counseling can help to change patterns. This information is important for all future relationships.

4. For closure, summarize, thank any invited speaker, and commend the group for their attentiveness and comments. Emphasize again that they do not deserve abuse in any situation, including dating relationships, and that abusive behavior is *never* okay.

FOCUS Relationships

Living Online

Background

The internet can help people meet and communicate. Distant relatives and school and community friends can communicate often. Shy teens and those who live in remote areas can connect with peers who share their interests. Ideally, such relationships contribute to development.

However, schools increasingly are teaching about digital citizenship because of serious concerns about students' safety online. News media give attention to, for example, the addictive power of online activity and video games, revelations of social-media data-sharing, the reality that people cannot know for sure who their contacts are, and the availability of pornography and violent content, such as live shootings and videos of police brutality and egregious bullying.

Middle and high school counselors tell me that their major concern about students is social media. The younger the students, the more they are developmentally underprepared for the freedoms involved with social media use. They may be enticed, because they feel known, to post more and more personal information and compromising photos of themselves, with little sense of how public these postings may become or of the implications for future job and college applications and relationships. Regardless of whether contact is in real time or whether an online group is intended to bring together like-minded people, sharing personal information online involves some level of risk.

Parents, teachers, and students are all probably somewhat naive about the dangers of fake, untraceable profiles; how predators can present themselves as teens; how predators can learn about adolescents' daily routines, appearance, relatives, and friends to create a complex understanding of a target; how texting groups can spawn insincere invitations and be audiences for peer-bashing. Even the most concerned parents cannot regulate access. But kids want protection. Police are overwhelmed, likely to deal only with emergencies. School counselors also feel overwhelmed by students in crisis because of online aggression, including bullying, stalking, harassment, seduction, threats, and other content intended to disturb and frighten.

This discussion can raise group members' awareness of their vulnerability. Perhaps they have not considered how public their posted information is and what the dangers are. Like many high-risk behaviors, online networking may seem like something students can handle and that others, not they themselves, are at risk. Risk might

230 | Relationships

even seem exciting. The realities that digital communication is not secure, that online friends might replace friends in school or community, and that huge amounts of time can be absorbed online are probably also worth talking about.

Now discussed at conferences, addiction of children and teens to internet porn also deserves mention here. Unlike in the past, pornography today is accessible, affordable, anonymous, and, for some, acceptable. All students can become addicted to it—preoccupied, compulsive, despairing, shame-filled, and needing increasingly higher doses and deviance. Unfortunately, they may be first exposed to pornography at sleepovers, with a profound biochemical rush. First experiences may seem harmless, but sex is distorted and viewers learn to "do sex" through porn, which often involves domination and depersonalization. Porn can have drug-like effects: euphoric recall, which can interfere with concentration at school; private, preparatory rituals at home; and less focus on relationships and activities. Therefore, porn can affect students' development. According to clinical professionals, addiction to porn may be more difficult to treat than even the most addictive drugs.

Objectives

- Group members become more aware of dangers associated with "living online."
- They reflect on their own attitudes about the internet and their online behaviors.

Suggestions

1. Begin by asking the group about the communication technology they use. Then ask what other communication technology they are acquainted with or aware of. Group members might also tell how much they use each form of communication and the various purposes of their use. Keep in mind that these questions may not lend themselves to go-arounds if there are considerable economic differences among group members. Respect any hesitation to contribute to the discussion.

   Group members may differ greatly regarding technology they are aware of and technology they have. Assumedly, those with less knowledge and access will become more aware and more conversant by listening. If someone talks excessively, dominating the discussion, ask the others for opinions—perhaps about technology in general, about how their peers differ in being able to afford electronic tools or in having interest in them, about their degree of ease or discomfort with online learning at home or at school, about the amount of available assistance for technology at school, or about hurdles and challenges related to electronic tools.

2. Mention that print and other media and community and school programs continue to raise awareness of dangers associated with social media and vulnerabilities of young users. Ask the group about the risks they are aware of and about negative (frightening situations, cyber-aggression) and positive (developing friendships through shared interests) experiences they or their peers have had. Ask also about other online dangers they are aware of. Ask if they think risks and dangers online differ according to age. Ask how safe and secure group members usually feel online. Ask about "electronic achievements" they have had. Be nonjudgmental and receptive, and let them teach you about their world. You may discover that they are quite aware of the dangers. Respect any hesitation to share.

3. Depending on the developmental level of your group, at this point, you might consider offering some information from the background, including about internet pornography. Ask for students' reactions to what you have explained.

4. For closure, ask group members to volunteer responses to the following:

   ~ What advice would you give a younger person about being online?

   ~ What advice would you give parents about keeping their young children safe online?

   ~ What advice would you give parents about keeping a middle schooler safe online?

   ~ How might teachers, principals, and counselors provide guidance to help people your age stay safe online?

   Express hope that students will be vigilant, careful, and wise when networking online.

FOCUS
Family

FOCUS Family

....

General Background

The family is usually our first environment. That environment teaches us about life, instills values, provides a context for learning social skills, and provides a base for exploring the outside world.

Families differ, of course. Some are great nurturers, and some are destructive. Some are full of overt conflict, and others rarely raise voices or tension levels. Some adapt well when new situations arise, and some do not. Some families are emotionally close, and some are emotionally distant from each other. Some families talk easily and well, and some have difficulty sustaining conversations—or are simply not inclined to talk. Some have experienced great trauma, and some very little. Some must worry about providing basic needs, such as food, clothing, and shelter, and some never have to worry about those essentials. And there are families all along the continuum in each of these areas.

No matter what a family is like, it strongly influences a child's personal development. Family patterns influence whether a child trusts others, expresses anger (and expresses it without hurting others), lives optimistically or pessimistically, has empathy, is concerned about global issues, and is successful at school. Whether any child becomes an emotionally healthy person depends to a large extent on how well the family nurtures that child.

Adolescents are in the process of figuring out who they are within the family unit and how they can become appropriately and increasingly independent with age. That process affects the way family members interact with each other. Sometimes relationships are strained even before a child enters adolescence. Sometimes there is little tension even during adolescence. It can be assumed, however, that the expected gradual separation process, as the child grows into adulthood, will involve some stress and strain for those involved.

Group discussion can help adolescents deal with family stress. Although this section contains just two sessions, others throughout the book discuss topics that are related to family and to the process of growing up and separating from family. Students usually enjoy the two sessions in this section, since the activities are informative and thought- provoking but not invasive. Group members are usually highly interested in what their peers have to say here and are amazed at how different families can be. The activities are structured so that they do not suggest "better" or "worse" values. Be sure not to pass judgment as a facilitator—even with your nonverbal behavior.

Important

Family, for purposes of discussion, includes anyone who lives (or lived) together and may include grandparents, aunts and uncles, cousins, married older siblings, friends, and even pets. It may also include people in more than one household in cases of divorce and remarriage, especially when a child's time is regularly divided between them. *Extended family* usually refers to whatever generations of the family are still living, whether or not they live near each other. *Nuclear family* usually refers to parent(s) and children; the adults may be biological parents, stepparents, adopted parents, same-sex partners, foster parents, surrogate parents, or grandparents.

Depending on their cultural heritage, family traditions, and family situation, group members may have different beliefs about what a family is and what *family* means. It is important to be sensitive to, and accepting of, all group members' situations and perceptions of family. Some may even speak of close friends as family and may not want to speak at all of blood relatives they feel cut off from. A discussion group is a good place to increase appreciation for diversity. Emphasize that various types and beliefs about families are simply different, not better or worse. Certainly avoid stereotyping or judging single-parent families as "less," and do not refer to families affected by divorce as "broken." In both categories, there are certainly competent, high-functioning, nurturing parents who manage well, even in difficult circumstances.

General Objectives

- Group members take a closer look at their families.
- They think about their place in the family context.

Family

Family Values

Background

In the recent past, some politicians, faith-based organizations, and other institutions and groups routinely referred to "family values." Depending on the context, family values seemed to refer to the value of the family in general, traditional family structure, high moral standards, or what is right and good. Separate values usually were not specified, and still might not be.

This session looks at family values without moral overtones, and instead simply as how and to what extent they are reflected in how a family interacts socially and how it feels about work, play, change, diversity, religion, and the news, to name just a few areas that reflect values. It may be both helpful and interesting for the adolescents in your group to think about their family's values in these areas and to see how the family priorities expressed in the group differ.

Objectives

- Group members consider what is important to their families.

- They think about how much their own personal values are like or unlike those of their families.

- They learn that attitudes and values vary within their group.

Suggestions

1. Introduce the topic and ask the students what they think of when they hear the word *values*. They will probably have a variety of associations and/or definitions.

2. Hand out copies of the "Family Values" activity sheet (page 238) and ask students to complete the activity. Use the statements to spark discussion. Group members might tell everyone their numbers, going around the group (perhaps with students each offering a comment about this number) for one statement before moving on to the next.

3. As an alternative, use "Family Values" to do a continuum activity (which involves no writing and no photocopying). Have group members line up along one wall of a room (or form an angle along two sides). Tell them that they have just formed a "continuum." Designate one end of the continuum as 10, "my family would agree strongly," and the other end as 0, "my family wouldn't agree at all." Explain that you are going to read aloud a series of statements about family values. After you read each statement, individuals should physically move to the point on the

continuum that best represents where they feel their family belongs. Depending on the developmental level of your group, time available, and expectations regarding discussion, you may want to choose only some of the statements for the activity.

For each statement, ask only two or three students to explain why they placed themselves where they did. If time is short, do this only for selected statements. (NOTE: This activity needs to move along quickly, and it is best not to spend too long considering individual statements.) Expect that there may be more than one way to interpret each statement. Some of the statements may generate discussion.

4. For closure, ask one or a few group members to name some common values in their group. Or ask what thoughts and feelings the discussion or continuum activity evoked. Remind the group that recognizing and talking about values is one of many ways we learn about ourselves. Understanding that families differ from each other in values helps to raise awareness of how a family uniquely influences personal values. It also challenges any assumption that other families and our peers have the same values as we do. If paper was used, dispose of the sheets or add them to the group folders.

Family Values

Read each of the following statements. For each, ask yourself, "Would my family agree or disagree with this?" Rate the statements from 0 to 10, with 0 meaning "They wouldn't agree at all" and 10 meaning "They would agree strongly."

____ Being social is important—being around people, having friends.

____ Work is good—it feels good, and it offers more benefits than just money.

____ It is important to know what is going on in the news.

____ Parents, not others, are responsible for guiding their children about what to believe and how to act.

____ Parents should communicate their beliefs to their children clearly, strongly, and often.

____ Everyone needs similar amounts of work and play.

____ Having fun at home with your family is better than entertainment outside the home.

____ It matters what people think of us.

____ It's good to be creative. Unusual creations are great!

____ The arts are important—music, dance, painting, drawing, theater, etc.

____ Taking risks is good—socially, personally, on the job, financially, and in play. It's best *not* to play it safe and sure.

____ Being physically fit is important.

____ Family privacy is important. What is said and done within the family should not be talked about outside of the family.

____ A family should solve its own problems and not ask others for help.

____ It's a father's responsibility to decide how to solve family problems.

____ Eating healthfully is important.

____ Athletic ability is important.

____ Paying attention to sports on television is important.

____ Being associated with a faith community is important (church, synagogue, or mosque participation, for example).

____ It's best to put the past behind you—and not talk about it.

____ Change is good. We change things often.

____ The more experiences a person has in life, the better. We go after new experiences.

____ Being respectful of others' lifestyles and beliefs is important.

____ Achievement is important—in school, at work, or in the community.

____ Getting a good education is important.

Family

Family Roles

Objectives

- Students learn that family members play various roles in the family.

- They think about how personal needs are met and not met in the family.

- They recognize that family members may not like the roles they have.

- They recognize that role assignments might be altered—with effort.

Suggestions

1. Introduce the topic and ask the group to consider these statements:

   ~ Members of any family play various roles in that family.

   ~ You undoubtedly have some roles in your family.

   ~ There are probably advantages and disadvantages for you in playing those roles.

2. Hand out copies of "Family Roles" (page 241) and ask the group to fill out the questionnaire with brief responses. Tell them that there is no correct or incorrect way to interpret the words and phrases. However, if your group can think abstractly, encourage them *not* to list an animal under "pet," but rather to consider that a person might fulfill that role. The terms in quotation marks are roles any family member can take on and should not be interpreted literally ("adult" might in fact be a child and vice versa). This activity sheet is usually very popular, regardless of group composition. It provides a safe, individualized way to be known to others. Group members usually pay close attention to each other as they share their roles.

   In a typical school group setting, with limited time, I recommend that students *not* note all family members' roles, but rather only their own (perhaps with just a check), since *their* family roles will be of greatest interest to the group. An effective way to have members report is to have each read all roles that are *theirs*—as a list. For example, "I'm the responsible one, easy to raise, peacemaker . . ." All group members should have an opportunity to share their roles in this way. Perhaps ask the group if they would like more information on a role just mentioned by someone.

   Another option is to have everyone, in turn, read down one column of responses, then have everyone do the same with the second column, and then the third column. Stop after all have completed one column and ask if they heard anything surprising about anyone in the group, given that person's usual behavior in the group. People often are not the same at home as they are in other settings, including school.

You might choose to tally the number of times each role is mentioned. Afterward discuss what roles the majority of group members have.

3. If your group has good abstract-thinking ability, ask if they have ever wondered, even though they might *despise* how a family member behaves, if they might simply *let* that person take care of an emotion or a behavior for the family. For example, one person might "do" all of the anger in the family, or all of the sadness, responsibility, seriousness, emotionalism, rebellion, or risk-taking. Explore this issue further by asking the following questions:

   ~ What would happen if all members of your family were equally serious—if everyone shared that characteristic, not at an extreme level, but at a low or moderate level? What if all were equally angry? equally sad? equally responsible? equally a worrier and anxious?

   ~ How would that affect the person who currently "does" all (or most) of the anger (or other emotion or characteristic) in your family? (Maybe that person could then relax a bit, knowing that *everyone* could express justifiable anger, or that *everyone* could be lighthearted sometimes, or that *everyone* could feel sad about a sad situation, or that not just one had to be "responsible.")

   ~ How would it affect various individuals in the family if emotions were expressed equally by all family members? (How might topics of conversation change? Would anyone lose his or her reputation or image within the family?)

   ~ Can only one person in a family be smart? hot-tempered? happy? sensitive? worried? depressed? What do you wish your family recognized in you (for example, that you are smart, creative, sensitive, athletic, musical, worried, sad)?

   ~ What do you think happens when we mentally label our family members according to the roles we think they play? (Possibilities: Members are not seen as complex individuals. They live up to their images. They feel they cannot be or do otherwise. They believe they cannot or do not have the characteristic that someone else is noted for.)

4. Ask, "Would any of you like to change a role you play in your family?" Follow up with these questions:

   ~ What would you have to do to make the change?

   ~ Who would be affected?

   ~ If you changed, what else would likely change?

   ~ What could be a first step in making that important change?

5. For closure, ask someone to summarize the discussion, or ask volunteers to tell what they learned through the discussion, thought about in a new way, or felt. Thank them for their thoughtful contributions. Dispose of the sheets, add them to the group folders, or invite students to take a blank activity sheet home to work through with their families. Family members could each fill out a separate sheet and then review—and disagree with—some of the labels given to them or to others. The activity can help each to feel heard about roles, expectations, and wishes.

Family Roles

Name _____

Which family member(s) do you associate with the following roles?

leader	teacher of skills	"adult"
_____	_____	_____
planner	"child"	sensitive
_____	_____	_____
responsible	easy to raise	easily upset
_____	_____	_____
gets the most attention	difficult to raise	calm
_____	_____	_____
gets the least attention	social	hot-tempered
_____	_____	_____
playful	peacemaker	joker
_____	_____	_____
happy	sentimental about the past	sad
_____	_____	_____
emotional	instruction-giver	disciplinarian
_____	_____	_____
business manager	worrier	map-reader
_____	_____	_____
caretaker	angry	has many new ideas
_____	_____	_____
rule-maker	not taken seriously	"pet"
_____	_____	_____
"wise one"	"smart one"	perfectionist
_____	_____	_____

Use these spaces to write in other roles that apply to your family:

_____   _____   _____

_____   _____   _____

Now go back and circle any role assignment that bothers you. You may circle more than one.

FOCUS
The Future

FOCUS The Future

....

General Background

Students often hear that school is preparation for life. They probably have heard all through school that they should do well—so they'll have success at the next stage, which, they hear, is more important. So elementary school is just preparation for middle school, which in turn becomes just preparation for high school, which is just preparation for a trade school or for college or university, which is just preparation for another next step, which is . . . ? Their parents might also perpetually speak in terms of "when we get this done, we can relax and really *live*."

Looking at each successive stage as preparation for something yet to come means that no stage is seen as real life, including the life that is anticipated. Each stage, in fact, *is* life—to be lived *in the present.* The "dessert" may not be there when the preliminary stages are finished. The savory tastes of the main course may be missed, too, if attention is only on what is yet to come.

Then there are those who spend too little time being concerned about the future. They live only in the present. They may be impulsive and spontaneous in the extreme, unpracticed in delayed gratification, procrastinating with important preparation for the future, closing doors with unwise choices, resisting advice, and perhaps seeing little value in school and other responsibilities.

How can teens find middle ground? How can they prepare for the future without becoming anxiety-ridden and joyless? How can they relax and enjoy the present without letting it blot out concern for what's coming? This final section offers sessions to help teens focus appropriately on the future. It's good to talk about it with a comfortable group of peers. Some middle school students have difficulty visualizing the future, but some may already focus excessively on it. By now, you probably know your group well enough to know which of the following sessions would be appropriate and helpful to them.

General Objectives

- Group members look realistically into the future, while understanding the importance of living in the present.

- They look at themselves as moving along a continuum of development.

- They contemplate direction and change.

The Future

....

What Is Maturity?

Objectives
....
- Students learn that maturity is a nebulous concept that means different things to different people.

- They apply the term to both adolescent and adult behavior.

- They appreciate the ways they feel mature and realize that they're *in the process* of maturing.

- They have fun discussing a term that's often used to point out what they are *not*.

Suggestions
....
1. Ask the group to define *maturity*, orally or in writing. Then ask them to explain what they think various age groups (teens, parents, employers, teachers, the elderly) mean when using the term.

2. Then pursue these ideas:

   ~ When do you feel mature now?

   ~ When do you not feel mature now?

   ~ How will you know when you're mature?

3. Ask the group if others often comment about their being or not being mature. You might ask, "How has that affected you?"

4. Invite them to consider the following (you might be a bit playful with the words as you ask the questions, since *mature* and *immature* are both simply terms that reflect individuals' perceptions):

   ~ What is immature behavior?

   ~ Can adults be immature? If so, give some examples of immature adult behavior.

   ~ What is the upside of being mature in behavior? of being immature?

   ~ What is the downside of being mature in behavior? of being immature?

   ~ When adults say a teen is "mature," what do you think they mean?

5. Move the discussion to the topic of early and late maturers. Ask the following:

   ~ What is meant by the phrases *late maturing* and *early maturing* when someone refers to physical growth?

   ~ Do you think you're ahead, behind, or right on schedule in the process of maturing?

   ~ If teens mature early physically, how might that affect them socially? emotionally? academically? during adolescence? as an adult? (Ask these separately, allowing responses for each.)

   ~ If teens mature late physically, how might that affect them socially? emotionally? academically? during adolescence? as an adult?

   ~ If you've matured early physically, or seem to be maturing relatively late, how has that been for you? (Convey to students that there is a "normal *range*" of development within every life stage, such as adolescence, but large differences are not unusual.)

6. For closure, thank and compliment the group members for their insights and comments, and either summarize the session yourself or ask a student to do that.

FOCUS The Future

Finding Satisfaction in Life

Background

During middle school and high school, especially for young people who don't feel satisfied with their current situations, it can be helpful to step back, take the focus off themselves, and consider the future in broad terms. In an era where success seems to be linked more and more with material wealth and possessions, it is important for teens to plant their feet solidly on the ground, take a deep breath, and contemplate what might bring them satisfaction in adulthood. Such thought may even help them meet developmental challenges in the present, such as forging identity, finding direction, establishing mature relationships, and achieving separate-but-connected relationships with their families.

Objectives

- Group members will ponder what helps adults feel satisfied with their lives.

- They consider their tendency to be optimistic or pessimistic about the future.

- They look to the future while contemplating the present.

- They imagine the future realistically in terms of lifestyle.

Suggestions

1. Introduce the topic by asking the following questions:

   ~ What do you think helps adults feel satisfied with their lives?

   ~ What might help a retired person feel satisfied with life?

   ~ What might help someone who is thirty years old feel a sense of satisfaction?

   ~ Which adults do you know who seem satisfied with their lives? What do you think helps them feel satisfied? How do you think they were when they were your age?

   ~ Which adults do you know who seem to enjoy their work? What do you think helps them to enjoy their work?

   ~ What seems to be the most important thing in life, based on the adults you know:

a satisfying job?	health?
a satisfying relationship?	an impressive career?
children?	social status?
money?	living near extended family?

   (Ask group members to rank the above eight items, on paper, from most to least important in helping people feel satisfied as adults.)

~ How much do you think your choices and decisions as a teen affect your later life satisfaction?

~ Are you optimistic or pessimistic about finding satisfaction in adulthood? Explain.

~ What can you do now, at your age, that will help you to find satisfaction in life later, as an adult?

~ How satisfied are you with your life right now—in the present? (If not satisfied) What do you think could help you to feel more satisfied with your life right now?

2. Provoke thought about how various life events or circumstances affect a person's view of life. Assure group members that you're interested in their individual views and that you expect their responses to differ. Ask questions like these:

~ How might pain and struggle affect someone's view of life?

~ In your opinion, do struggles in life have any value? Give reasons for your answer.

~ Is it possible to have no struggles during an entire lifespan? not enough? too many?

~ Do you know any adults who struggled as kids (for example, in their families, with poverty, individual or family health problems, parental death, divorce, frequent moves, loneliness) but who seem to feel satisfied with their lives now?

~ How do struggles teach us about ourselves? about people? about life?

~ What do you think about the idea that struggles help people develop compassion?

~ What do you think about the idea that struggles help people develop wisdom?

~ How important is feeling connected to others?

3. Direct their attention to the future by asking these questions:

~ What kind of life will you lead?

~ Do you think you will marry or develop a serious partnership early in life? later in life? not at all?

~ Do you think you will have children? If so, when?

~ What kinds of interests will you have?

~ What will you do to relax?

~ Do you think you will prefer to relax at home or go out when there is free time?

~ How physically fit will you be?

4. For closure, ask how it felt to discuss this topic with the group. For example, was it inspiring, discouraging, frustrating, energizing, or something else? What did they feel as various group members offered thoughts and opinions? Was the discussion thought-provoking? Let nods suffice.

FOCUS The Future

Attitudes About Work

Background

Some teens, especially those in the lower middle school grades, may feel that any discussion of career, college, or other special training does not apply to them for a variety of reasons. However, all adolescents can benefit from discussion about employment in general. This session provides an opportunity to discuss the world of work, attitudes toward work, gender roles and work, and the meaning of work.

Even those who foresee only low-paying jobs for themselves in the future will benefit from this discussion. This session can also encourage realistic thinking about managing life alone, especially regarding child-rearing, given the statistical likelihood that many teens will eventually experience divorce and/or single parenthood. If you choose to omit two upcoming sessions, "Thinking About Careers" and "Expectations, Wishes, and Dream Images," you might incorporate into this session some of the ideas about personality, uniquenesses, skills, and personal needs in regard to work. The hope is that ultimately *all* group members will find a good fit, and personal satisfaction, in the workplace.

Objectives

- Group members assess their attitudes about work.

- They learn that what is said about work by family members, the media, and others affects their attitude about work.

- They consider how gender expectations affect job and career.

- They realize that there are many ways to view work.

- They realize that work has personal value in itself.

Suggestions

1. Ask the group to define *work*. Expect their definitions to vary. Then ask these questions:

    ~ Does work have to involve pay?

    ~ Does it have to take place outside the home?

    ~ What is your view of work that people do in a home office, such as for home businesses? Are there differences between that work and work that is done in a place of business elsewhere?

~ Should our attitude toward household work, such as cooking, cleaning, and washing clothes, be different from the attitude toward work done outside the home?

~ Does gender matter in the world of work? when it comes to leadership positions? What do you think about working parents? parents who stay home with their children?

~ Can money-earning work be enjoyable? Who do you know who obviously enjoys, and has fun, doing money-earning work?

~ Can other work be enjoyable—even household chores? If so, can you think of some examples?

~ How important is work in feeling satisfied about life?

~ How do the media portray work? positively? negatively? rewarding? important? Can you think of examples from television programs, movies, magazines, or newspapers?

~ What is your attitude about the work that volunteers do in providing services to others? Do you see this as work? (You might mention that the United States has a somewhat unique and long tradition of volunteerism, which many community institutions depend on.)

~ Do you think it is work if someone pursues a personal interest or project and invests many, many hours in it, with no thought of pay? Can you think of an example?

~ Have you ever known anyone who worked a rather grim "day job," but devoted leisure time to acting, singing, playing in a band, artwork, or some other satisfying expression of talents and interests, such as auto mechanics, furniture building, or raising animals?

~ Have you ever known anyone who did difficult, heavy labor for many, many years and never seemed negative about it?

2. Ask the group to tell how they feel about work in general. Encourage them to elaborate, challenge each other, and communicate honestly. After they've expressed views, ask the following:

~ How much do you think a person's attitude affects satisfaction in work?

~ How much do you think adults' feelings about work affect their families?

~ Do you think that attitudes about work are "habits"? If so, can you give examples of negative-attitude habits? positive-attitude habits? (Encourage students to think of people they know, but not name names.)

~ How can people improve their attitudes about work? (Possibilities: Use positive self-talk; not resist doing necessary work; be rested, alert, and pleasant to coworkers; enjoy the social aspect of work.)

~ What can work do for a person? (Possibilities: Provide wages, occupy time, provide social contact, contribute to society, provide a sense of pride for doing something well.)

3. Hand out copies of "The World of Work" activity sheet (pages 252–253) and ask students to complete the questionnaire with brief responses, anonymously. Explain that they are to complete the list of significant adults (which may include anyone who has had an influence on their life), identify each person's workplace and position, and make a brief statement about the person's attitude toward work. Then invite them to select a few individuals on their lists and explain the impact these adults have had on students' own attitudes toward work. Group members may choose what to share and what not to share. If group members have had mostly negative models regarding work satisfaction, ask them to brainstorm ways they could overcome that influence. Then use the questionnaire as a springboard for discussion. Ask these questions:

~ How much will work be a part of your adult life?

~ How many hours per day will you probably spend in paid work in or outside of the home? What kinds of jobs would require longer-than-typical work hours? Under what circumstances might you work fewer than typical hours?

~ How do you think you can help yourself to have satisfaction in your work?

~ What kinds of things can keep someone from feeling satisfied with a job? (The upcoming session "Thinking About Careers" emphasizes paying attention to personal needs in finding a career or job path. You may want to assure the group that this area will be addressed then.)

4. For closure, ask one or a few students to summarize what has been discussed. Did the discussion cause them to think about work in a new way? If so, how? What do they think is the most important benefit of working? Do group members have differing opinions about what is most important? Dispose of the sheets or file them in student folders.

The World of Work

Significant Adult	Workplace and Position	Attitude Toward Work
1. Mother		
2. Father		
3. Grandmother		
4. Grandmother		
5. Grandfather		
6. Grandfather		
7. Teacher		
8. Aunt		
9. Uncle		
10. Neighbor		
11. Neighbor		
12. Older sibling		
13. Other relative		
14. Other relative		

(continued)

The World of Work (continued)

Have most of the significant adults in your life been positive or negative about their work?

_____

Have most of them found satisfaction in their work? Who, especially?

_____

Have most of the adult women in your life been positive or negative about their work? Who, especially?

_____

Have most of the adult men in your life been positive or negative about their work? Who, especially?

_____

For those who have felt good about their work, what do you think helped them to feel satisfied?

_____

_____

_____

For those who have not felt good about their work, what do you think especially affected them?

_____

_____

_____

FOCUS The Future

....

When and If I'm a Parent

Background

Some teens spend a lot of time being angry at their parents, chafing under their restraints, and longing for independence. Yet, most are likely to remain dependent on them for shelter, food, clothing, and financial support for quite a while. That tug-and-pull can produce conflict, which can even become dangerous. During this sometimes stressful period, it is the parents'/guardians' job to provide support and to set limits on behavior. These are important responsibilities, and adults' competence and consistency in meeting their challenges have great impact. However, even when parents perform their tasks wisely, there is potential for conflict, and conflict might not stop when children leave home. Even at midlife, adult children are sometimes still "doing battle" with their parents, silently or overtly.

This session gives students a chance to talk about parent-adolescent issues. Even if some believe they will not have children or marry—or if they haven't yet given serious consideration to these ideas—they can still be involved in a discussion of parenting as if they will become parents someday, since the discussion will inevitably deal with how they themselves have been parented. What do group members hope they'll never do as parents—and will always do? They can share important feelings about their present life as they talk about parenting.

If yours is an older group and there are members who already are parents, their opinions and feelings can be especially valuable in the discussion, which can be helpful to them as well. They are undoubtedly already aware of some of the difficulties and challenges of parenting.

Objectives

- Group members learn to articulate feelings about how they have been parented.

- They look ahead to the future while assessing their own past experiences.

- They think about their personality styles, beliefs, and values as they imagine themselves as parents.

Suggestions

1. Begin by having the group define *parenting*. Then proceed with broad questions like these:

   ~ What is the "job," or responsibility, of a parent?

   ~ When does parenting begin? When does it end?

2. Generate discussion with some of the following questions (*parenting* refers to the roles of any primary caregiver):

   ~ What's difficult about parenting?

   ~ What's important in parenting very young children?

   ~ What are some typical conflicts between parents and children?

   ~ What conflicts are probably related to figuring out how to be separate from, yet connected to, parents? (Possibilities: Conflicts about privacy, curfews, clothes, friends, choices, direction, achievement, appearance.)

   ~ What makes parenting a teen particularly difficult? (Possibility: The sense of having less control as the teen moves more and more into a world outside of the family and establishes a separate identity—including within the family.)

   ~ What kinds of fears and anxieties do parents probably have about their children?

   ~ How much independence is appropriate for an adolescent?

   ~ What are the challenges of stepparenting?

   ~ What are some challenges for parents when two families blend?

   ~ What's the most important positive quality in a parent? (There are many possible answers, of course.)

3. Encourage the group to look realistically into the future by asking these questions:

   ~ What will you be like as an adult? Give three to five adjectives that you think might fit you someday. (If students have difficulty here, suggest some of the following as starters.)

restless	critical
settled	stable
moving often	unstable
content	wise
tense	impulsive
in a lot of conflicts with others	consistent
serene	inconsistent
calm	spending as much time as possible with my children
"hyper"	spending little time with my children
patient	lazy
impatient	hard-working
long-suffering	workaholic
accepting of people's differences	balanced in both work and play

4. Continue the discussion by asking the following (again, *parent* refers to any primary caregiver):

~ What have you learned from your parent(s) about parenting?

~ How will you want to be like your parent(s) in parenting style?

~ How will you want to be different from your parent(s) in parenting style?

~ In your opinion, when is a good time for a couple to begin having children?

~ Will you stop your career when children are born or ask for maternity/paternity leave if it is available? How long would you like to be home with the children?

Mention that people's own parenting behaviors often reflect ways their parents behaved with them, *especially when under stress*. Parents are models, and, even if adolescents are convinced that they will never behave like their parents, they might someday find themselves sounding like their parents or "behaving badly" when they're stressed. Assure the group that they can change those behaviors through insight and effort. They have choices. If they understand themselves and stay calm, even in difficult circumstances, they are more likely to choose wisely. Even the work they are doing now—learning to listen and respond in a discussion group—can help them to change well-established family patterns and parent differently someday. Many communities offer parenting workshops to help parents become more effective as parents.

5. For closure, ask the group what they are thinking or feeling, now that the discussion of future parenting is finished. Tell them that they do not have to be perfect parents, just caring and responsible parents—if they choose to be parents. They will likely have many/several years to think about and prepare for parenting.

FOCUS The Future
....

Thinking About Careers

Background

Although middle school may seem too early to be talking about career choices, current trends in school counseling and in education in general are toward beginning—even in elementary grades—to give attention to the interpersonal skills and attitudes that enhance life in the workplace. Young children can also steadily develop awareness of general career categories so that by eighth grade, perhaps, they can participate in a discussion about school grades/scores, postsecondary education, realistic future salaries, lifestyle, and general money management. Developmentally, most eighth graders can grasp the connections between school and work. However, even earlier adolescents can benefit from activities that help them envision themselves in a particular category of careers and connect schoolwork to adult work.

For many students, choices made during early adolescence lead toward or away from certain career choices. Even with more and more proactive enticements to prepare for STEM fields, too many girls choose courses that move them away from these fields. Boys might shun the arts or ignore interests in the humanities, foreclosing early on career possibilities because parents or teachers direct them toward jobs deemed more worthy, appropriate, practical, and lucrative. For both college-bound and non-college-bound teens, this session can be valuable for personal assessment. Researchers have discovered that middle school is where decisions are made about what is possible, including a college education, and courses are selected or not selected accordingly. Adolescents then continue to pass through decision "gates," later having difficulty backing up and remaking decisions. Thus, it is important and timely to discuss possibilities and provide career information during middle school, when class choices are usually first available.

Some teens have many and varied abilities and options, and some have limited ability and options. Across a continuum of ability and socioeconomic circumstances, however, more than just interests and abilities should be considered during career guidance. For example, just because a student is good in math, engineering may not be a good fit. Great talent in the arts might not translate into a career choice for a student who is also pragmatic and deeply concerned with financial security. Some students may receive conflicting advice from significant adults in their lives, while other students may receive no advice at all.

Career exploration can be complex and exciting. Might interests be combined in a career path? Could a single, seemingly narrow college major or trade open the door to a multitude of career paths? What about areas of great talent and interest? Could these become avocations instead of vocations? This session provides an opportunity for teens to consider personality, personal needs, dreams, and even values as related to career decisions. Sorting through these areas can be helpful in moving toward a clearer vision of the future. I have used this session with teens across a wide range of ability, achievement, and risk factors.

Important

An option that can work well for a discussion group is to arrange to have three or four adults from the community visit the group and speak about finding satisfying careers. Try to find a diverse range of middle-aged people who have made thoughtful and purposeful career *changes* in order to find a "better fit." If your group includes students at risk for poor outcomes, perhaps even high-ability underachievers, locate speakers who once were "square pegs in round holes" or who had extremely difficult home situations but who became successful as adults. The panelists can represent the reality that people do not necessarily know, when young, what they will find satisfying in the future. Consider the needs and interests of your group, and invite panelists who represent various occupations, with a wide variety of educational requirements. Prepare a list of questions ahead of time for the group to use when interviewing the visitors. For ideas, see suggestion #3.

Another option is to contact a local corporation and invite a panel of employees in various positions—perhaps an executive, a manager, a human resources head, and someone who has been promoted steadily from "working on the line." Conduct an interview with the panel, asking about their aspirations as teens, their education, what qualities are important in workers, and what school classes helped them to succeed in the workplace.

Objectives

- Group members sort out personality factors, personal needs, lifestyle dreams, and a multitude of thoughts about careers.

- They learn that it is important to pay attention to personality and personal needs for the sake of life satisfaction as adults.

- They learn that there is probably no perfect career choice for them and that there are probably several possibilities worthy of consideration.

- They learn that change is part of life and growth, and that education and adulthood might include changes in direction.

Suggestions

1. Hand out copies of "Choosing a Career" (pages 262–263) and ask the group to complete the activity sheet. Comment that it is important to pay attention to needs and personality when considering "fit" in a career. Personal characteristics are emphasized on the activity sheet.

2. Invite them to share their responses by reading their lists. (They might instead indicate by a show of hands who has chosen various responses for questions #2 and #3.) Depending on time available, discussion of the sheet might be enough for one session. If so, store the sheets for a second session on this topic. If not, continue with suggestion #3.

3. Ask questions like these:

~ How many of you found that your responses for #2 and #3 match the careers you listed in #1?

~ Does your lifestyle description for #6 match anything on your list for #1?

~ How much education is needed for the careers you have listed in #1?

~ Are the careers you listed likely to involve a salary or an hourly wage? What do you know about the differences? Do you think the careers you listed differ regarding time at work, education needed, extra financial benefits available, responsibilities, etc.?

~ Which of these words about financial management are you familiar with: *mortgage, loan, budget, investment*? (It is important not to assume that adolescents are familiar with these terms. Explain what they refer to, if needed. Understanding these words may help them to make sense of media messages about money management and consider their own and adult financial responsibilities.)

~ What are some ways that people can protect their money? (This question may be especially important for immigrant children from countries where banks are not believed to be trustworthy. But many other young people are also unaware of the function of banks.)

Emphasize that it is important to pay attention to needs and personality when considering a career.

4. Explore group members' attitudes about needing to find a career direction right now. Ask the following questions:

~ How important do you think it is to know what you want to do with your life before you leave high school?

~ At what age do you think most people figure out what they want to do for work as adults?

~ What advice have your parents and teachers given you about finding a career?

~ How much are you worrying about finding a career for yourself?

Encourage students to continue to explore career options as they learn about their abilities and discover interests, but to relax about needing to find *the* direction while still in middle school or high school. For those planning to attend college, let them know that they can begin with an "undecided" major and can usually delay choosing a major for a year or more—and even then they can change their minds. For students who expect to pursue other education options or to enter the workforce immediately after graduation, assure them that there is still time to consider direction carefully, including checking to see what vocational, technical, or trade institutions are available. Remind all students that it is not unusual to change careers or pursue new directions *within* a particular career as an adult.

5. If you have invited career-changers from the community to visit your group (see "Important" after the background information), group members might ask these questions:

   ~ How did you get to the career you have today? Was it a straight path?

   ~ Which positions have been a good match for you, and which have not?

   ~ What risks did you face in making career changes?

   ~ What advice would you give to young people about career decisions and job possibilities?

   ~ What educational or life experiences were most valuable for finding your career?

   ~ Who or what influenced you regarding career choices along the way?

   ~ How important to you is work satisfaction?

   ~ Have your jobs allowed adequate time for family and a life outside your career?

   ~ What do you like best about your work? least?

   ~ What are some challenges in your work?

   ~ What have you learned about yourself through your work experiences?

   Again, it is important to communicate that all jobs have positive and negative aspects, and that a person does not have to remain locked into one career for forty-plus years. That might relieve some group members' anxiety about finding the "perfect niche." In fact, job changes are increasingly common in response to changes in technology, markets, and tastes.

6. To introduce a new dimension, ask this question:

   ~ Which do you think is more important—finding a satisfactory career or finding a satisfactory relationship? Why?

   Suggest to the group that maybe they should make finding a satisfying career a higher priority than finding a satisfying relationship, given the impact of job dissatisfaction on relationships. (This may not be a popular thought.) However, it is also possible that a relationship could come through the career, since people in a particular work setting probably have some personal characteristics and interests in common. Satisfaction in the world of work may reflect feeling in control of one's life. Satisfaction in the workplace probably contributes to general happiness. Making good academic choices, even in middle school, improves the chances of having options and career satisfaction later. Making poor choices might close doors later. It is wise to keep the doors open by making sure important classes are taken and doing one's best work.

7. Encourage students to set up their own brief career-shadowing experience, or do that as a group activity. You might devote a session to arranging a one-day (or half-day) experience for each individual who is interested in a professional career. Each student could focus on one career, decide on a community location for the experience, and, with you, make arrangements (see "Important" below). They could then spend some time before the shadowing experience researching the career.

Important

For individual career-shadowing, it is best to have an adult make the call, in order to assure the professional that the experience will be relatively brief, that it will be supervised and prepared for, that only one teen will be observing, and that the teen will be learning about a typical half or full day at work—including, perhaps, the sore feet, the fifty phone calls, the research, the long hours, the interruptions, and the stress (in other words, beyond the obvious). The person being shadowed need not put on a show. Explain that the teen would like to do a fifteen-minute interview sometime during the day about career preparation, career path, and career satisfaction. This length of experience is best for older adolescents, since it can demand stamina and a long attention span, and since professionals can probably talk more comfortably about the realities of the workday with an older teen. It is good to remember that a busy professional's day might be somewhat constrained by having someone "at the elbow" and that a service is being done. Emphasize to students that they be on time, dress appropriately, be attentive, and thank their mentor. It is also important that both you and the group member send a written thank-you after the experience.

For careers that do not require a college education, but which typically require some postsecondary training, one possibility is to arrange a series of field trips, taking a small group to worksites perhaps not familiar to adolescents. (For example, an auto-body shop, a heating-and-cooling business, a landscaping firm, or a trades institution that offers various training programs.)

8. For closure, have group members create a one-line bit of career advice for themselves. Remind them that it is wise to keep their options open and to gain broad-based education and experience, while at the same time paying attention to themselves and to pertinent career information. The self-advice could be "I need to keep my options open and get a good, broad education to prepare me for whatever I might decide." Dispose of the sheets or add them to the group folders—or encourage members to take these particular activity sheets home with them, for possible reference in the future or to share with parents/guardians.

Choosing a Career

Name _____

1. List any and all career possibilities that you have considered in the past year:

_____

_____

_____

2. Check any of the following that you would prefer to have in your future work.

- ☐ being around people
- ☐ writing
- ☐ working with my hands
- ☐ helping people
- ☐ researching, finding out things
- ☐ feeling a sense of contributing to the world
- ☐ working outdoors, not indoors
- ☐ putting things in order
- ☐ working with and around machines
- ☐ doing creative, nonconforming activities
- ☐ having rules and regulations
- ☐ working with scientific ideas

- ☐ performing in front of people
- ☐ dealing with "fine print" details
- ☐ teaching others new things
- ☐ selling things or ideas
- ☐ working with data, numbers
- ☐ figuring out how things work
- ☐ meeting new people
- ☐ "getting my hands dirty"
- ☐ making beautiful things, or making things beautiful
- ☐ constructing, building things

3. Check the two to five personal *needs* that will probably be important to you in a career:

- ☐ independence, making my own decisions
- ☐ to finish, not to have many unfinished projects
- ☐ order
- ☐ a sense of play
- ☐ achievement, rewards
- ☐ being the center of attention
- ☐ travel

- ☐ helping/guiding others
- ☐ to feel "done" every day when leaving work
- ☐ predictability, knowing what to expect
- ☐ belonging to a group
- ☐ guidance from others
- ☐ advancement, going up the career ladder

(continued)

Choosing a Career (continued)

- ☐ contact with people
- ☐ flexible schedule
- ☐ maternity/paternity leave
- ☐ a quiet, calm environment
- ☐ variety every day
- ☐ adequate time to be a parent
- ☐ living close to my extended family
- ☐ deadlines to work toward

- ☐ adventure and excitement
- ☐ a city setting
- ☐ a rural setting
- ☐ teamwork, working in a group
- ☐ solitude
- ☐ many things happening at once
- ☐ being in charge

4. How firm is your career direction right now?

_____

5. Are you listening mostly to yourself or to others as you consider career possibilities?

_____

6. What kind of lifestyle would you like to have as an adult? (Consider income level, things owned, recreation, location, type of home, etc.)

_____

_____

_____

_____

_____

The Future

Meaningful Work

Many students may graduate from high school after little or no thoughtful adult input about planning for the future. Perhaps their parents and relatives are ill-equipped to provide guidance, for a variety of reasons. Their school counselor, probably with a typically too-large student load, may have been able to arrange only a brief annual check-in with the student, and even a meeting during the senior year might have come at a time when the student couldn't, or wouldn't, think about the future. Even though some older teens may have received little or no vocational guidance in the past, it is not too late to focus on the work world and assess their needs and options. If you're a school counselor, the suggestions for this session may be helpful for doing career planning with individuals or with groups.

This session is intended for non-college-bound older teens. It appears late in this series, and in this book, but it could certainly be used earlier in the life of a group, along with "Thinking About Careers" and/or "Attitudes About Work," for taking stock of the self and of work options in planning for the future.

This session is probably most appropriate for students in grade eight and older, since course selection is then increasingly a concern. Thinking about the future may make upcoming schoolwork more meaningful.

Even if you are not in a school setting, this would be a good time to invite a school counselor or someone from a vocational-technical school to make a presentation, answer questions about those schools, and discuss other options for students who are not planning to go to college. Prior to inviting a speaker, take time during a preceding session to ask students what they feel frustrated about in terms of planning for the future, what they would like to know more about, what they have already done, and what others have told them. You might even write down their specific questions and concerns and give them to the speaker in advance. Encourage the speaker to talk about various assessments that might be given (or that are already in the students' school files) to assist them in finding direction and to help them find a good match in employment. Perhaps it is possible to pull out various assessment results for the group to look at during the session, with options noted for each individual. Financial aid can be discussed, and those who have already made plans for job training or immediate employment might share what they have learned about the process of establishing a direction and finding financial and other assistance. Middle school students who assume that their family cannot afford such training can learn that financial aid can make it possible.

If you plan to use suggestion #1, and if you did not previously use the "Thinking About Careers" session, adapt (if necessary) the "Choosing a Career" handout (pages 262–263) to fit your group, including appropriate items, in preparation for this session.

Objectives
- Group members learn about non-college options.
- They think about their strengths and limitations and consider possibilities for meaningful work.

Suggestions
1. Find out what kinds of work experience group members have already had. Ask these questions:

   ~ What kinds of part-time jobs have you had—including very short-term jobs, such as helping a neighbor fix something, babysitting, or doing a regular household chore?

   ~ What kinds of duties did you enjoy the most in each part-time job?

   ~ What did you enjoy the least in each one?

2. Hand out copies of "Choosing a Career" (pages 262–263) (adapt if necessary; see "Important" on page 264) and ask the group to fill out the activity sheet with brief responses. Invite each individual to read down the entire sheet, with the group listening for potential fit among the reader's dreams, personality, and personal needs.

   Respect individual situations and goals, and offer to find out additional information for them or with them, if that would help. Tell group members about resources they can take advantage of in the counseling office, the school media center, the local library, or elsewhere in the community. Arrange to introduce them to counselors or librarians, if that would be helpful and if it is possible.

3. If you didn't already use the "Thinking About Careers" session, you might incorporate suggestion #5 on career-shadowing here (see page 260).

4. For closure, ask one, a few, or all to comment on what they learned. In the event that some say they are thinking about dropping out of school, remind them that a diploma will improve their chances of finding solid employment, as will the knowledge gained later in school. Encourage them to talk to you individually or to some other specific person (not just "to someone") about ways to overcome whatever obstacles seem to be standing in the way of their staying in school. Make appointments to talk more with the students yourself, or help them to arrange to talk with others, if possible.

The Future

Continuing Education

Background

Many students with enough ability to succeed in college (college here means education in a college or university) do not know much about that world. Some have no college-educated family members to learn from. Some, because of their family's low socioeconomic level, assume that college is not an option. Some, even when their families are highly educated, are poorly informed about college particulars but do not ask basic questions because they do not want to appear "stupid." They wonder what certain terminology means, such as the following:

major, minor	work study	five-year program
credit hour	liberal arts	fraternity, sorority
advisor	orientation	commuter

core course (or whatever an institution calls its required courses)

quiet residence halls (or whatever term is applied to housing for serious students)

presidents, deans, directors

full professors, associate professors, assistant professors, adjunct faculty, instructors, teaching assistants

university, colleges, departments, programs (Explain that *college*, *department*, and *program* refer to different entities from context to context. A large university may have a "College of Pharmacy" within it, for instance. Also explain that *college* and *university* can both refer to four-year institutions, and, even though universities are more likely than colleges to have graduate—master's level and doctoral—programs, that distinction has become more and more blurred.)

They wonder about other aspects of college life as well:

where students study	where students can get academic help
how roommates are selected	how students find their way around
where medical help is available	what constitutes success in college
if a student can change majors	what the level of competition is
how accessible professors are	what a community college is
how to get financial aid	

what typical personal and academic adjustment problems are

what the differences are between public and private colleges

what the differences are between large and small colleges

what the differences are between colleges in big cities and in small towns

how teaching, testing, and studying styles differ from high school

what classes are important as preparation for college

whether a person needs to have career direction before going to college

This session acknowledges that college is only one of several options for high school graduates. Society needs people with skills for repairing, creating, maintaining, and designing things, as well as skills related to caring for and providing services to people. A college education is not needed in many of these areas. However, even for students who will not be attending them, information about colleges and universities can broaden their understanding of the academic world. Any knowledge about college-level education can help people communicate *about* education and also interact comfortably in their future careers with college-educated individuals. This session focuses largely on the college experience and is most valuable for students for whom college is, or should be, an option. The discussion can also be crucial for teens whose capabilities are not, but should be, on teachers' or school counselors' radar screens. In addition, middle school students who plan to attend college might not be aware of all of their options during high school, such as enrolling in local or online college courses while in high school, attending college-preparatory schools, or participating in summer programs for college-bound students. (If you choose to use this session with a younger group, research these options before the session.)

Students who have the ability to do college work, but feel they do not have enough money to go to college, should be encouraged to find out about financial aid—and to check out a variety of institutions, including community colleges. Many institutions, including respected small colleges, are concerned about maintaining enrollment levels, and some readily develop workable financial packages, especially for those with high ability. A number of young adults delay college or spread it out over several years, so that they can work and attend classes. School counselors can steer students toward local and other funding and help them ask colleges about scholarships. This session can encourage students, even those in middle school, not to give up on the idea of higher education.

For students whose parents' dream is to have them accepted by a prestigious institution, there might be more interest in the process of getting into college than in preparing for the social and emotional dimensions of college life, which often are the keys to surviving the first year. Sometimes even students with high intellectual ability, adequate financing, and good high school records are not successful during that critical period.

This session can help to raise awareness of, and prepare students for, the inevitable adjustments of college. It can also help to relieve anxiety in those who are concerned about not having a major in mind yet. And it can make the vocabulary of college and university life familiar.

Important
This session requires advance preparation. It should be scheduled for a time when concerns about college, high school course selection, or college applications are being expressed. Just prior to the Thanksgiving holiday break is an ideal time to schedule this session, especially for seniors who are thinking about applications. In addition, first-year college students will probably arrive home for break before your school or institution dismisses and will be available to visit your group.

Therefore, you might invite a panel of four to six college students to be interviewed by you and your group. Try to have a variety—from large and small colleges and from a variety of socioeconomic, family, and high-school-success situations. You might also include someone attending a local community college.

Sometime before the session, ask your group to write down questions they have about college, anonymously—about schedules, campus residence halls, orientation, courses, academic terminology, private versus public institutions, costs, and financial aid. With older high school students, you might preface the invitation to write questions with "What concerns, fears, and anticipations do you have when you think of going to college in the next year or two? What questions do you have?" Collect the questions and have them ready for the panel.

If you choose not to invite a panel of college students, you might address these concerns yourself. Find out, first, what group members know about various aspects of college, how they see themselves as potential college students, and what kind of educational expectations others have of them, and then fill in the gaps either with your own knowledge and experience or with information from people with recent or current college experience.

Objectives
- Teens become familiar with college terminology.
- They consider challenges that college students face and imagine themselves as college students.
- They learn that financial aid might make college possible for those without great financial resources.
- They view college as an option.

Suggestions
1. If you have a panel, interview the college students, using the questions your group prepared earlier, some of the ideas mentioned in the background information, and new questions from your group. You might also choose to pursue some of the following directions. (If you do not have a panel, generate discussion and provide information in response to the students' questions and directions listed here.)

~ experiences with homesickness, illness, loneliness, finding friends

~ adjustments to fewer and new kinds of tests, less teacher feedback, heavy reading assignments, mid-term pressures, a new level of competition, extent of preparation needed for exams, rapid pace of courses, note-taking

~ adjustment to roommates

~ social life, comfort level, relaxing, finding people to eat with at the outset, getting along in a residence hall

~ size of institution (as related to a sense of identity), finding friends, variety of cultures, access to professors, getting academic help, distance between classes

~ food, weight gain, illnesses, fatigue, sleeping in noisy residence halls or apartments

~ self-discipline and adjustments to less or more structure in life

~ time management: balancing jobs, social life, studying

~ money: how much is enough, budgeting, miscellaneous expenses, books

~ personal adjustments to other cultures and lifestyles

~ taking advantage of speakers, programs, campus events, campus groups

~ which high school courses give good preparation

~ grades

~ financial-aid processes

~ deciding on a major

~ if the institution is a good fit for them

~ personal growth and maturity (when, and in what ways)

~ personal changes, in order to adjust

~ which colleges they looked at and how they managed to select one

2. For closure, ask group members what was most helpful about this session. What feelings do they have when they think of college?

FOCUS The Future

Expectations, Wishes, and Dream Images

Background

As children grow, they watch and listen to the adults around them. If significant adults pay attention to them, they hear themselves described, hear assessments about their potential, and listen as others dream their futures for them. Even at a young age, they probably imagine themselves in the work world. As they get older, these images may change. Of the messages coming from significant adults in their lives, some may be encouraging them in particular directions. Sometimes the messages conflict with the images they have of themselves, and sometimes that conflict produces stress. Family members may not even realize they are communicating various expectations (including high, low, or perceived lack of) or that their expectations contribute to stress. Parents and other adults might welcome the chance to clarify what they do and do not expect of the student.

This session provides a chance for teens to sort through the messages they hear, whether or not they are in conflict about them. It might be a rare opportunity for them to pay attention to, and find support for, independent thoughts and dreams. This discussion is probably most appropriate for older adolescents, but even for older middle school children the focus can be important for thinking ahead and examining what they are hearing from others. Be aware, however, that many adolescents may have had little guidance from the adults in their lives, including parents and teachers. If you notice that someone seems "stuck" with the activity sheet, you might say, "It's okay. Maybe you'll get some ideas when we discuss this." Other group members may later be able to offer supportive comments, including about strengths they have noticed. There will probably be many ideas about the future, and everyone is likely to find something that is thought-provoking.

Objectives

- Group members look realistically into the future.

- They consider the impact of parents' and others' projections on their vision of the future.

- They affirm positive and helpful input from significant adults.

- They assess the potential for conflict with significant adults about career direction.

- They learn that it is important to discuss their own expectations with family and to express feelings about those and others' expectations.

Suggestions

1. Hand out copies of "Expectations" (page 272) and ask students to fill out the activity sheet with brief responses. Use the questionnaire to spark discussion. You may want to have each student read down the entire sheet, with the group listening for themes, potential areas of conflict, and points of agreement. Follow their comments with questions or comments of your own, perhaps like these:

   ~ What kinds of big choices does a person make in life that others might object to?

   ~ How much do you usually agree with the adults who advise you about future lifestyle? future education? future location?

   ~ If there is conflict, how does it affect your relationship with parents, teachers, or other significant adults?

   ~ If there seems to be no conflict between your vision for yourself and others' visions for you, can you explain that?

   ~ How much do you pay attention to your own wishes and needs in making decisions and finding direction?

   ~ Who has the highest expectations for you—you, your parent(s), another relative, teachers, or friends?

   ~ How important is it to match ability level with educational level, job level, spouse/partner, fellow workers? (Avoid providing an "answer" yourself.)

   ~ What are some careers that require a college education or technical training?

   ~ What do you know about college or about the technical training that is available in your town/city/area?

2. Focus on paying attention to dreams. Ask these questions:

   ~ Do you have an interest that you passionately hope to pursue?

   ~ If you are able to pursue that interest, what would you like to do with it? How much of your life would you spend on it?

   ~ What would be an ideal, fantasy, perfect life for you?

   ~ How much should a person pay attention to such dreams?

   ~ What kinds of hobbies or leisure activities do you hope to have in the future?

   ~ How involved do you expect to be in a church, in a community organization, in adult sports, with extended family, etc.?

   Whatever direction the discussion takes, consider it productive if group members seem honest about their personal wishes and self-assessment. Validate their feelings (for example, "I can sense your strong feelings for that," or "That would obviously mean a lot to you"). That will help more than analyzing the content of their comments.

3. For closure, ask students about thoughts and feelings they had while filling out the questionnaire and during the discussion. Dispose of the sheets or add them to the group folders.

Expectations

Name _____

1. How high (scale of 1 to 10, with 10 being "high, definitely expected") are the expectations that adults in your life have for you regarding schoolwork? _____ Being involved in school activities? _____ Having an after-school job? _____ Having a romantic relationship? _____ Graduating from high school? _____ Pursuing more education after high school? _____

2. What were some of your earliest images of yourself as an adult? How did you picture yourself? What kind of work did you see yourself doing? Where did you imagine yourself living? If you'd like to, draw a small picture of one of those images on the back of this sheet.

   _____

3. What do you think your mother (or another significant woman in your life) imagines you doing and imagines that you'll be like in ten or fifteen years?

   _____

4. What do you think your father (or another significant man in your life) imagines you doing and imagines that you'll be like in ten or fifteen years?

   _____

5. What do you see yourself doing in ten or fifteen years, and what do you think you'll be like then?

   _____

6. Who expects the most from you (in your family, among your relatives, among your teachers, among your friends)?

   _____

7. How much would your family, relatives, friends, and teachers agree with each other about what they expect of you? Check one:

   ☐ A lot   ☐ Not much at all   ☐ Some

8. Who is giving you ideas and advice about your future these days? What are they saying?

   _____

9. Have peers and adults in your life generally been supportive of you when they talk about your future?

   _____

10. Are your wishes and dreams for yourself generally the same as the wishes and dreams others have for you?

    _____

11. What level of education will you need to pursue your goals?

    _____

FOCUS The Future

Wishing Then, Wishing Now

Background

As your group nears the end of a series, especially at the end of a school year, members may bring up serious matters for the first time. Some may have waited a long time to feel safe enough to ask for advice about a personal situation or to check out group reaction to a personal concern. Others may still not feel comfortable enough to mention something in the group, but will arrange to speak with you individually. In order not to close the door on such needs, while still preparing the group for closure, it is wise to let the year wind down with increasingly relaxing and comfortable topics. This one is meant to be light. It encourages group members to "cap" ongoing concerns, prepare to end their group experience, and look ahead.

Objectives

- Group members assess both past and present by making wish lists.

- They express sincere personal wishes.

Suggestions

1. One or two meetings prior to ending a series, remind the group that the discussions are nearly at the end. It is important to state that directly. Mention that again during the second-to-last meeting, which might be this one.

   Explain that this session is meant to help to draw the experience to a close. Then encourage them to think back over some of their personal discussion "themes." Ask these questions:

   ~ What problems and concerns do you remember hearing about in the group?

   ~ What thoughts kept coming up for you, whether you mentioned them or not?

   ~ Which concerns and problems have stayed the same for you during the entire time the group has met? Which are no longer a problem?

   ~ What concerns and problems will likely continue to be in your thoughts in the future?

   ~ How would you describe your group, now that you know everyone better?

   ~ Based on your group, what are some concerns that seem to be quite common for people your age?

2. Ask students to think of endings to the following sentence stems, and then go around the group, with each member finishing both stems. Explain that "I used to wish for . . ." can refer to any time in life.

~ "I used to wish for . . ."

~ "Now I wish for . . ."

Students can list many wishes for each sentence stem. After hearing from everyone, encourage the group to relax and to add as many more "used to wish/now I wish" combinations as they want to, offering them whenever they come to mind.

3. Address the differences between "young" and "older" wishes. What has changed (if anything)?

4. Invite students to share other current wishes for their own lives, their families, or their friends. They might later share wishes for their community, nation, or the world. They might also make wishes for various members of the group, based on concerns heard during the life of the group.

5. For closure, affirm their wishes as good wishes, and convey that you hope their wishes will come true. If the next meeting will be the last one, remind them of that, and follow the guidelines for ending a series in "Session Closure and Series Ending" (page 15). Be aware that any change in format (including the addition of food or music) changes group dynamics and may even contribute to discomfort at a time already stressed by the ending. Everyone must interact in a new way. Therefore, you may not want to mention options. Sometimes maintaining the same format, but with an "endings" activity (with a little food, perhaps), is most smooth. A closing ritual of some kind helps to bring closure to a rare experience like being in a group, but that can be as simple as having a discussion about endings and filling out an evaluation form. In fact, this session, about wishes, is very appropriate for a final session, especially if suggestion #4 includes wishes for each other.

FOCUS **Final Session**

An Informal Assessment

Background
As a possibility for concluding a series of sessions, one last questionnaire is offered here. It should be fairly easy for the group to complete, and they'll enjoy hearing one another's creative, sincere, and thoughtful comments. This can be a good, upbeat way to end a short or long series of group discussions. The sentence stems on the questionnaire look back or look ahead. Some of them might generate discussion. The questionnaire can also be used as a light break at any time during a series of sessions.

For additional thoughts and suggestions on bringing your group to a close, see "Endings" on pages 17–18.

Objectives
- Group members feel a sense of closure to their discussion experience.
- They interact with one another in a positive way.

Suggestions
1. Hand out copies of "An Informal Assessment" (page 277) and ask students to write brief endings to the sentence stems. Invite them to be sincere, serious, clever, critical, sentimental, or all of these, but they should, as always, give their genuine feelings. Remind them that you have respected their ability to share thoughts and feelings, and you assume they'll want to do that here too. They can be as open as is comfortable for them. Tell them that the assessment is meant to help them look to the past and look forward.

2. Invite group members to read down their lists. If a particular item provokes discussion, pursue it. Keep in mind, however, that all group members should have a chance to share their lists during the session. At the end, you might have the group read the italicized lines at the bottom in unison.

3. If this is the final group meeting, encourage members to share, orally or in writing, what they've gained through the group experience. Written summaries can be valuable personal feedback for a leader, since they give group members a chance to express private thoughts. This is one time where it's appropriate for students to identify themselves by name, since this is personal communication to you as facilitator. Assure them that you'll keep their remarks confidential. As an alternative to this suggestion, see suggestion #5.

In addition, if it might be helpful and necessary for building support for discussion groups in your community or school setting, invite group members to add a sentence for administrators or brochures, expressing the value of the experience for them. Assure them that these statements will remain anonymous.

4. Encourage the group to talk about ending the experience. This is perhaps the most important suggestion in this session, since endings are difficult for many people. Talking about feelings at this point is an important part of the group process. Ask these questions:

~ How does it feel to know that this is our final meeting?

~ What have endings been like for you in the past? Can you recall an example or two?

~ What have you done to deal with endings in the past?

5. As an alternative to suggestion #3, hand out copies of the "Discussion Group Evaluation" (page 278). Have group members fill out the evaluation during this session. Emphasize that you want their responses and opinions. Point out that they should not sign this form; it's meant to be anonymous.

6. For closure, tell the group you're glad they committed themselves to the discussion group, took it seriously, became a group, or whatever else is appropriate. Thank them for their special contributions to the group. Wish them well.

Use your own judgment about collecting and destroying the "An Informal Assessment" handouts. Group members might like to keep them as souvenirs and to look back at them sometime in the future.

If you have been storing the activity sheets in group members' individual folders, you might bring the folders to this final session. Invite the teens to look at their sheets, consider whether their responses reflect personal growth, and then (if you've brought a shredder), invite them to shred their sheets or assure them that you will shred the sheets yourself. If some want to take their sheets home, I am strongly against allowing that. First, the sheets are private communication. Some written comments might be misunderstood or taken personally by someone else. Sheets also might inadvertently be dropped or scattered at school, again without context for anyone who picks them up. Likewise, at home, no one heard the context, directions, and discussion for each sheet. The sheets were saved in the folders for the purpose of members being able to use them to reflect on the group experience.

An Informal Assessment

Finish as many of the sentences as you can or wish to.

1. As I leave this group, I'm glad that _____ , but I regret that I didn't _____ .

2. Someone in the group I'm glad I know better is _____ .

3. I remember the day we talked about _____ .

4. Something I learned in the group is _____ .

5. In the group, I discovered that I _____ .

6. I learned that others in the group _____ .

7. I also learned that _____ .

8. I was surprised that _____ .

9. I probably changed in this way during the group: _____ .

10. During this whole year, I've probably changed in this way: _____ .

11. When I think of our group in the future, I'll remember that it was _____ .

12. I'll probably never _____ and will probably always _____ .

13. Something I'm working on doing better now is _____ .

14. I will know I'm grown up when I _____ .

15. Some advice I'm going to follow is _____ .

16. I wish I knew more about _____ .

17. I wish everybody would understand that I _____ .

18. My parents will probably be happy if I _____ .

19. I hope I never have to _____ .

20. Someday I'll _____ .

21. I'm glad I was part of this group because _____ .

I know I don't have to be perfect.
I understand that I'm not a "finished product."
I am not done learning. Life will continue to teach me.
I will continue to develop.

Discussion Group Evaluation

What did you think of the discussion group experience? Your feedback is important! Your responses will help future groups. Please complete and return this evaluation form. Do not put your name on the sheet. Thank you.

1. Circle the number that best describes how you would rate each of the following.

1 = excellent
2 = good
3 = average
4 = fair
5 = poor

1 2 3 4 5   Being in a group.

1 2 3 4 5   The leader's ability to guide the group.

1 2 3 4 5   The group leader's warmth and concern.

1 2 3 4 5   The leader's respect for every member of the group.

1 2 3 4 5   The value of the group for people like me.

1 2 3 4 5   The value of the group for me personally.

1 2 3 4 5   The comfort and trust we had for sharing feelings.

1 2 3 4 5   The comfort and safety I felt in the group personally.

1 2 3 4 5   The respect I felt for the other members of my group.

1 2 3 4 5   Other members' respect toward me.

2. What I will probably remember most about the group is _____

_____

_____

_____

3. I would / wouldn't recommend this group to a friend because _____

_____

4. Additional comments: _____

_____

_____

Recommended Resources

Helplines

Boys Town National Hotline
800-448-3000
A 24-hour crisis line where both male and female teens can talk with professional counselors about any issue, including depression, suicide, and identity struggles.

LGBT National Hotline
888-843-4564
A confidential helpline for LGBT teens, open Monday through Friday from 3 p.m. to 11 p.m. and Saturday from 11 a.m. to 4 p.m. (CST). Staffed by trained peer counselors.

National Association of Anorexia Nervosa and Associated Disorders
630-577-1330
A helpline for anyone struggling with an eating disorder. Open for calls Monday through Friday from 9 a.m. to 5 p.m. (CST).

National Child Abuse Hotline
800-4-A-CHILD (800-422-4453)
A hotline for anyone suspecting that a child is being abused.

National Domestic Violence Hotline
800-799-SAFE (800-799-7233)
A 24-hour hotline that provides support, assistance, counseling, and other services for anyone facing domestic violence.

National Helpline—Substance Abuse and Mental Health Services Administration
800-662-HELP (800-662-4357)
Offers confidential help related to substance abuse and addiction.

National Suicide Prevention Lifeline
800-273-TALK (800-273-8255)
This is a confidential source of help 24 hours a day.

Abuse, Assault, and Harassment

Child Welfare Information Gateway
Children's Bureau / ACYF
330 C Street SW
Washington, DC 20201
800-394-3366
www.childwelfare.gov
Sponsored by the U.S. Department of Health & Human Services, this organization promotes the safety and well-being of children and families. The website provides extensive information about abuse through its electronic publications, online databases, and links to outside sources.

Rape, Abuse & Incest National Network (RAINN)
1220 L Street NW, Suite 505
Washington, DC 20036
800-656-HOPE (800-656-4673)
www.rainn.org
The largest anti-sexual-assault organization in the country, RAINN provides extensive information about sexual abuse to the public. In addition, the organization sponsors a national hotline that connects callers to rape and abuse crisis centers in their area.

Students Against Violence Everywhere
322 Chapanoke Road, Suite 110
Raleigh, NC 27603
866-343-SAVE (866-343-7283)
www.nationalsave.org
A student-initiated program that promotes nonviolence within schools and communities. It also provides education about the effects and consequences of violence.

For Teens

TeensHealth
www.teenshealth.org
This website addresses many of the questions teens have about their mental and physical health. Includes information about rape, bullying, abuse, and where to go for help.

In Love and In Danger: A Teen's Guide to Breaking Free of Abusive Relationships by Barrie Levy (Emeryville, CA: Seal Press, 2006). Describes the experiences of teens in violent or abusive dating relationships and offers advice on how to create relationships that are violence-free.

It Happened to Me: A Teen's Guide to Overcoming Sexual Abuse by William Lee Carter, Ed.D. (Oakland, CA: New Harbinger Publications, 2002). Written by a psychologist who works with sexually abused teens, this book helps young adults reflect on what happened and begin to develop healthy relationships.

Alcohol and Drug Abuse

Al-Anon/Alateen
1600 Corporate Landing Parkway
Virginia Beach, VA 23454
888-4AL-ANON (888-425-2666)
www.al-anon.org
The mission of Al-Anon is to help families and friends of alcoholics recover from the effects of living with a substance abuser. Alateen, sponsored by Al-Anon, is a recovery program specifically for young people.

Club Drugs
www.drugabuse.gov/drugs-abuse/club-drugs
An informative web resource about drugs prevalent in the young-adult party scene.

National Institute on Drug Abuse (NIDA)
6001 Executive Boulevard, Room 5213
Bethesda, MD 20892
301-443-1124
www.drugabuse.gov
NIDA is one of the world's leading organizations supporting research on drug abuse and addiction. The website contains a wealth of information in the form of articles, statistics, and research for parents, teachers, teens, and kids. Includes curriculum guides, education materials, and classroom tools for educators.

For Teens

NIDA for Teens
www.teens.drugabuse.gov
Created by the National Institute on Drug Abuse, this website contains facts, stories, and activities about the science of drug abuse. Includes blogs, interactives, and videos that address a wide range of teen questions about drugs.

Anger Management

American Psychological Association: Anger
750 First Street NE
Washington, DC 20002
800-374-2721
www.apa.org/topics/anger
A part of the APA website, this section defines anger, offers anger management strategies, and gives advice about when specialized help is needed.

Healthy Anger: How to Help Children and Teens Manage Their Anger by Bernard Golden (New York: Oxford University Press, 2006). This book helps adults identify the causes of child and teen anger and offers practical strategies that adults can use to help their teens with anger management.

For Teens

TeensHealth: How Can I Deal With My Anger?
kidshealth.org/en/teens/deal_with_anger
A part of the TeensHealth website, this section on anger provides numerous anger management tips for teens and advice about when to seek more help.

Cool It! Teen Tips to Keep Hot Tempers from Boiling Over by Michael Hershorn (Far Hills, NJ: New Horizon Press, 2003). With this guide, teens explore the causes of their anger and look for healthy, nonviolent ways to express their feelings.

Mad: How to Deal with Your Anger and Get Respect by James J. Crist (Minneapolis: Free Spirit Publishing, 2008). This eBook offers teens a range of tools and tips to use in understanding and managing anger.

Picture Books for Group Critiquing

Alexander and the Terrible, Horrible, No Good, Very Bad Day by Judith Viorst

The Berenstain Bears and the Blame Game by Stan and Jan Berenstain

The Berenstain Bears Get in a Fight by Stan and Jan Berenstain

Don't Pop Your Cork on Mondays! The Children's Anti-Stress Book by Adolph Moser

Don't Rant and Rave on Wednesdays! The Children's Anger-Control Book by Adolph Moser

I Was So Mad by Norma Simon

Mad Isn't Bad: A Child's Book About Anger by Michaelene Mundy

That Makes Me Mad! by Steven Kroll

The Very Angry Day That Amy Didn't Have by Lawrence E. Shapiro

When I Feel Angry by Cornelia Maude Spelman

When Sophie Gets Angry—Really, Really Angry . . . by Molly Bang

Bullying

Odd Girl Out: The Hidden Culture of Aggression in Girls by Rachel Simmons (New York: Harcourt, 2011). With data from 300 girls in thirty schools, this book debunks the stereotype that girls are the kinder gender. It closely examines acts of aggression and cruelty among girls and covers the topics of gossiping, ganging up, note-passing, the silent treatment, and more.

Please Stop Laughing at Me: One Woman's Inspirational Story by Jodee Blanco (Avon, MA: Adams Media Corporation, 2010). An autobiographical work about one woman's experience as a victim of bullying. The author describes the verbal and physical abuse she endured as a teen and reflects on how the bullying affected her as a young person and as an adult.

They Call Me Chicken: A Story of Courage by John D. Caporale (Philadelphia: Xlibris Corporation, 2005). Advice for kids about how to maintain self-esteem when dealing with bullying or name-calling. Although this book was written for young children, it can be used with middle school students as a discussion catalyst.

Careers

Best Jobs for the 21st Century by Michael Farr and Laurence Shatkin (Indianapolis: JIST Works, 2012). Contains over 500 job titles and descriptions. Includes numerous "best job" lists based on age, salary requirements, level of education, personality type, and more.

For Teens

Mapping Your Future
www.mappingyourfuture.org
A public service project of the financial aid industry, this website gives information to students and parents about college, careers, and financial planning.

Where Do I Go from Here? Getting a Life After High School by Esther Drill, Heather McDonald, and Rebecca Odes (New York: Penguin, 2004). In teen-friendly language, this book discusses the many options available to teens after high school and helps teens decide which path is right for them.

Counseling Services

American Counseling Association (ACA)
6101 Stevenson Avenue, Suite 600
Alexandria, VA 22304
www.counseling.org
800-347-6647
The ACA is a not-for-profit professional and educational organization dedicated to the growth and enhancement of the counseling profession.

National Board for Certified Counselors (NBCC)
www.nbcc.org
NBCC's website can be accessed to find counseling resources in your area.

Creativity/Fun

American Coaster Enthusiasts (ACE)
P.O. Box 540261
Grand Prairie, TX 75054
469-278-6223
www.aceonline.org
Founded in 1978, ACE is the largest club of amusement ride enthusiasts in the world. The website contains an extensive database of coasters, a newsletter, and information about coaster events in your area.

USA Cycling
210 USA Cycling Point, Suite 100
Colorado Springs, CO 80919
719-434-4200
www.usacycling.org
The official cycling organization of the United States, USA Cycling selects and trains cyclists to represent the United States in competition. The website contains information about races, training, cycling rules and regulations, and a list of cycling clubs in every state.

WebMuseum, Paris
www.ibiblio.org/wm
A place for teens and adults to learn about and view famous art before they explore art venues in their areas.

Hiking and Backpacking: A Trailside Guide by Karen Berger (New York: W.W. Norton & Company, 2003). This handy book is loaded with tips, photos, tutorials, and equipment guides for use on the hiking trail.

For Teens

Teen Knitting Club: Chill Out and Knit by Jennifer Wenger, Carol Abrams, and Maureen Lasher (New York: Artisan, 2004). This book, highlighting an increasingly trendy hobby for teens, gives all of the information they need to start their own knitting club. Includes knitting basics for beginners.

Depression and Suicide

National Institute of Mental Health (NIMH)
6001 Executive Boulevard
Bethesda, MD 20892
866-615-6464
www.nimh.nih.gov
NIMH is the leading federal agency for the research of mental and behavioral disorders. The website contains a wealth of information on mental health topics, including depression, and provides a substantive collection of articles, resources, and research.

SAVE—Suicide Awareness Voices of Education
8120 Penn Avenue South, Suite 470
Bloomington, MN 55431
952-946-7998
www.save.org
An organization dedicated to educating the public about suicide prevention and depression.

Overcoming Teen Depression: A Guide for Parents by Miriam Kaufman (Buffalo, NY: Firefly Books, 2001). This book discusses the warning signs and treatment methods for depression in teens. It contains case studies and a thorough analysis of current research. Though written to parents, it offers good background information for a group facilitator to use prior to group discussion.

For Teens

Everything You Need to Know About Depression by Eleanor H. Ayer (New York: Rosen Publishing, 2001). Written for teens, this book explains the science of depression, the causes of depression, and the pros and cons of various treatment methods.

The Power to Prevent Suicide: A Guide for Teens Helping Teens by Richard E. Nelson and Judith C. Galas (Minneapolis: Free Spirit Publishing, 2006). With updated facts, statistics, and resources, this eBook gives teens the information they need to recognize the warning signs of suicide in peers. Includes advice on how to reach out and when and where to go for help.

When Nothing Matters Anymore: A Survival Guide for Depressed Teens by Bev Cobain (Minneapolis: Free Spirit Publishing, 2007). A book for teens on how to recognize depression, get help, and stay well.

Divorce/Family Change

Divorce Net
www.divorcenet.com
Provides a great deal of information about the legal aspects of divorce. Includes a resource page for every U.S. state.

For Teens

Families Change: Teen Guide to Separation and Divorce
www.familieschange.ca/en/teens
Developed by the British Columbia Ministry of Attorney General, this website is a guide for any teen facing parental separation and divorce. Discusses family change, emotions, and legal issues and provides a list of resources and frequently asked questions.

TeensHealth: Dealing With Divorce
kidshealth.org/en/teens/divorce.html
A place for teens coping with divorce and separation. The website contains tips for how to deal with it, what to do when families split up, and life after divorce.

Eating Disorders

Academy for Eating Disorders
11130 Sunrise Valley Drive, Suite 350
Reston, VA 20191
703-234-4079
www.aedweb.org
A professional organization that promotes excellence in the research, treatment, and prevention of eating disorders. The website contains facts, articles, resources, and links for professionals and the general public.

National Eating Disorders Association
1500 Broadway, Suite 1101
New York, NY 10036
800-931-2237
www.nationaleatingdisorders.org
This organization provides information on various eating disorders and treatment options and offers referrals to doctors, counselors, and clinics.

For Teens

Over It: A Teen's Guide to Getting Beyond Obsessions with Food and Weight by Carol Emery Normandi and Laurelee Roark (Novato, CA: New World Library, 2001). Examines the social and cultural factors that foster weight obsession in girls and lists the kinds of behaviors that lead to eating disorders. Contains activities and quotations from teens.

Grief/Loss

Centering Corporation
6406 Maple Street
Omaha, NE 68104
866-218-0101
www.centering.org
A nonprofit organization that provides guidance, education, and resources for the bereaved.

Lifetimes: A Beautiful Way to Explain Death to Children by Bryan Mellonie and Robert Ingpen (Toronto: Bantam Books, 1983). Although this book about the cycles of life is appropriate for very young children, it also serves as a catalyst for discussion with adolescents and teens.

On Death and Dying by Elisabeth Kübler-Ross (New York: Scribner, 2014). The classic, quintessential text on dying, death, and grief, this book gives insight into how imminent death affects patients and the family, friends, and professionals who care for them.

For Teens

Healing Your Grieving Heart for Teens by Alan D. Wolfelt (Fort Collins, CO: Companion Press, 2001). Offers 100 suggestions for dealing with grief.

How It Feels When a Parent Dies by Jill Krementz (New York: Knopf, 1981). In this one-of-a-kind classic, eighteen teens share their personal stories of losing a parent.

When a Friend Dies: A Book for Teens About Grieving and Healing by Marilyn E. Gootman (Minneapolis: Free Spirit Publishing, 2019). With compassion and sensitivity, this book answers the tough questions teens have about grieving the loss of a loved one.

Group Work

Research on Group Work

"High-Ability Students' Perspectives on an Affective Curriculum in a Diverse, University-Based Summer Residential Enrichment Program" by Enyi Jen, Marcia Gentry, and Sidney M. Moon. *Gifted Child Quarterly* 61, no. 4 (2017): 328–342.

"The Peterson Proactive Developmental Attention (PPDA) Model: A Framework for Nurturing the Rest of the Whole Gifted Child" by Jean Sunde Peterson and Enyi Jen. *Journal for the Education of the Gifted* 41, no. 2 (2018): 111–135.

"Small-Group Affective Curriculum for Gifted Students: A Longitudinal Study of Teacher-Facilitators" by Jean Sunde Peterson and Michelle R. Lorimer. *Roeper Review* 34, no. 3 (2012): 158–169.

"Student Response to a Small-Group Affective Curriculum in a School for Gifted Children" by Jean Sunde Peterson and Michelle R. Lorimer. *Gifted Child Quarterly* 55, no. 3 (2011): 167–180.

Identity

In the Mix
330 E 70th Street, Suite 5L
New York, NY 10021
800-597-9448
www.pbs.org/inthemix
A PBS series that discusses relevant teen issues including labeling, stereotyping, and cliques. Educators may purchase episodes online or by phone.

In the Mix: Cliques—Behind the Labels (DVD, 30 minutes). Teens discuss the complex social systems in their schools and the problems of labeling.

In the Mix: What's Normal? Overcoming Obstacles and Stereotypes (DVD, 30 minutes). Teens talk about what it means to be "normal" and share personal stories about dealing with stereotypes.

For Teens

The Courage to Be Yourself: True Stories by Teens About Cliques, Conflicts, and Overcoming Peer Pressure edited by Al Desetta (Minneapolis: Free Spirit Publishing, 2005). True stories from real teens about breaking stereotypes, standing up for themselves, and learning who they really are.

Internet Safety

Federal Bureau of Investigation: Cyber Crime
J. Edgar Hoover Building
935 Pennsylvania Avenue NW
Washington, DC 20535
www.fbi.gov/investigate/cyber
The FBI actively investigates cyber crime in the United States. The cyber crime section of their website contains facts, resources, and news articles about online crime, as well as advice about internet safety.

Internet Crime Complaint Center
www.ic3.gov
Created by the FBI, the National White Collar Crime Center, and the Bureau of Justice Assistance, this online center develops and refers complaints related to cyber crime. Individuals can visit this website to quickly report suspicious online activity.

For Teens

ConnectSafely
www.connectsafely.org
This website contains information for teens about internet safety. Covers blogging, emailing, chat rooms, bullying, instant messaging, privacy, and more.

Mentors/Role Models

Boys & Girls Clubs of America
National Headquarters
1275 Peachtree Street NE
Atlanta, GA 30309
404-487-5700
www.bgca.org
With locations all over the country, this organization works to foster the development of productive, responsible young people through interaction with and support from caring adults.

Who Mentored You?
Harvard Mentoring Project
Center for Health Communication
Harvard School of Public Health
677 Huntington Avenue
Boston, MA 02115
617-495-1000
sites.sph.harvard.edu/wmy
A collection of personal stories and insights by prominent public figures about the importance of their mentors.

For Teens

My Hero: Extraordinary People on the Heroes Who Inspire Them edited by the My Hero Project (New York: Free Press, 2005). A collection of first-hand essays by well-known public figures about the people who influenced their lives for the better.

Relationships

The Fourth R
Centre for School Mental Health
Western University, Faculty of Education
1137 Western Road, Room 1154
London, ON, Canada N6G 1G7
519-858-5154
www.youthrelationships.org
A consortium of researchers dedicated to promoting healthy adolescent relationships by helping educators develop the fourth R (relationships) in their school environments.

LifeStories. A board game that encourages people to share stories about themselves to build interpersonal competence. Available through the Talicor Company at 800-433-4263 or at www.talicor.com.

Beyond the Big Talk: A Parent's Guide to Raising Sexually Healthy Teens by Debra W. Haffner (New York: Newmarket Press, 2008). Helpful tips and practical strategies for adults on how to talk to young people about love, relationships, and sex.

For Teens

Cool Communication: From Conflict to Cooperation for Parents and Kids by Andrea Frank Henkart and Journey Henkart (New York: Perigee Books, 2002). Advice for adults and young people on how to bridge the parent-teen communication gap.

Real Friends vs. the Other Kind: Book 2, Middle School Confidential by Annie Fox, M.Ed. (Electric Eggplant, 2018). This book offers advice for making friends, resolving disputes, and dealing with other common concerns—like gossip, exclusion, cyberbullying, crushes, peer pressure, and being there for friends who need help.

Self-Image

Media Education Foundation
60 Masonic Street
Northampton, MA 01060
800-897-0089
www.mediaed.org
The nation's leading producer of educational videos that encourage young people to critically analyze the messages and images presented by the media.

Killing Us Softly 4: Advertising's Image of Women created by Jean Kilbourne and directed by Sut Jhally (DVD, Media Education Foundation, 2010). This 46-minute video uses over 160 advertisements and television commercials to analyze the images of women in the media. Available through the Media Education Foundation at 800-897-0089.

For Teens

Focus on Body Image: How You Feel About How You Look by Maurene J. Hinds (Berkeley Heights, NJ: Enslow, 2002). Contains personal stories from girls and guys about their experiences related to body image.

Self-Mutilation

"**Adolescents Who Self-Injure: Implications and Strategies for School Counselors**" by Victoria E. White Kress, Donna M. Gibson, and Cynthia A. Reynolds (*Professional School Counseling*, February 2004, Vol 7: 195–201). Strategies for school counselors on how to manage students who self-injure. Covers intervention, education, advocacy, and prevention.

"**A Functional Approach to the Assessment of Self-Mutilative Behavior**" by Matthew K. Nock and Mitchell J. Prinstein (*Journal of Consulting and Clinical Psychology*, October 2004, Vol 72 (5): 885–890). This article analyzes self-mutilating behavior in teens, using data from 108 adolescent psychiatric in-patients.

Sex and Sexuality

American Association of Sexuality Educators, Counselors, and Therapists
35 East Wacker Drive, Suite 850
Chicago, IL 60601
202-449-1099
www.aasect.org
A nonprofit organization devoted to promoting healthy sexual behavior and an understanding of human sexuality. The website contains articles, links, and referrals to professionals all over the country.

PFLAG
1828 L Street NW, Suite 660
Washington, DC 20036
202-467-8180
www.pflag.org
A national nonprofit organization for parents, families, and friends of lesbian, gay, bisexual, and transgender individuals. PFLAG's mission is to promote the health and well-being of GLBT persons through support, education, and advocacy.

Planned Parenthood Federation of America, Inc.
434 West 33rd Street
New York, NY 10001
800-230-PLAN (800-230-7526)
www.plannedparenthood.org
Planned Parenthood is the world's oldest family planning organization and is dedicated to promoting sexual health and sexual education. The website contains extensive resources and fact sheets, as well as a section for teens.

The Sex Lives of Teenagers: Revealing the Secret World of Adolescent Boys and Girls by Lynn Ponton (New York: Dutton, 2000). This book explores the topic of sex from the teen perspective with a goal of helping adults and teens better communicate about dating and sexuality.

For Teens

Planned Parenthood Info for Teens
www.plannedparenthood.org/learn/teens
An award-winning website section for teens created by Planned Parenthood. Contains stories, quizzes, advice, and an "ask the experts" section. The site is available in English and Spanish.

Stress

American Psychological Association
750 First Street NE
Washington, DC 20002
800-374-2721
www.apa.org
A scientific and professional organization that represents psychology in the United States. The website contains the latest information and research on various topics in psychology, including stress.

For Teens

MindYourMind
www.mindyourmind.ca
Created for and by teens, this website provides information and resources to help young people manage their stress. Contains real stress stories, tools for handling pressure, and tips for healthy stress relief.

Index

. . . .

Page numbers in **bold** indicate reproducible activity sheets; page numbers with n indicate a note.

To access this book's digital content and download the reproducible forms, visit **freespirit.com/gst-forms**. Use the password **2connect**.

About the Author

Jean Sunde Peterson, Ph.D., professor emerita at Purdue University, was a classroom teacher for many years, was involved concurrently in teacher education, was a state Teacher of the Year, and developed summer foreign language day camps for children prior to her doctoral work in counseling and development at the University of Iowa. At Purdue, she directed school counselor preparation and focused most of her research on the social and emotional development of high-ability youth, with seminal articles focused on bullying, trauma, sexual orientation, and developmental aspects of academic underachievement. Her workshops, conference keynotes, and national and international presentations have addressed counseling concerns, underachievement, negative life events, development-oriented group work with children and adolescents, and listening and responding skills for teachers and parents. A licensed mental health counselor with several years as an adjunct counselor in substance-abuse treatment centers, she continues to be involved clinically with children and adolescents and their families. In her second career, she has authored twelve books and more than 100 invited chapters and journal articles. She has received ten national awards related to her scholarship and twelve awards at Purdue for teaching, research, and service. She lives in Indiana.

Other Great Resources from Free Spirit

Boost Emotional Intelligence in Students
30 Flexible Research-Based Activities to Build EQ Skills (Grades 5–9)
by Maurice J. Elias, Ph.D., and Steven E. Tobias, Psy.D.
For teachers and counselors, grades 5–9.
192 pp.; PB; 8½" x 11"; includes digital content.

The Essential Guide to Talking with Gifted Teens
Ready-to-Use Discussions About Identity, Stress, Relationships, and More
by Jean Sunde Peterson, Ph.D.
For grades 6–12.
288 pp.; PB; 8½" x 11"; includes digital content.

Interested in purchasing multiple quantities and receiving volume discounts? Contact edsales@freespirit.com or call 1.800.735.7323 and ask for Education Sales.

Many Free Spirit authors are available for speaking engagements, workshops, and keynotes. Contact speakers@freespirit.com or call 1.800.735.7323.

For pricing information, to place an order, or to request a free catalog, contact:

Free Spirit Publishing Inc.
6325 Sandburg Road, Suite 100 • Minneapolis, MN 55427-3674
toll-free 800.735.7323 • local 612.338.2068 • fax 612.337.5050
help4kids@freespirit.com • www.freespirit.com